ST. MARY'S CITY, MARYLAND 20685

The Making of the Modern World

Also by Alan Macfarlane

THE CULTURE OF CAPITALISM

THE FAMILY LIFE OF RALPH JOSSELIN

A GUIDE TO ENGLISH HISTORICAL RECORDS

THE JUSTICE AND THE MARE'S ALE: Law and Disorder in
Seventeenth–Century England (*with Sarah Harrison*)

MARRIAGE AND LOVE IN ENGLAND, 1300–1840

THE ORIGINS OF ENGLISH INDIVIDUALISM: The Family, Property and Social
Transition

RECONSTRUCTING HISTORICAL COMMUNITIES (*with Sarah Harrison and
Charles Jardine*)

RESOURCES AND POPULATION: A Study of the Gurungs of Central Nepal

THE RIDDLE OF THE MODERN WORLD: Of Liberty, Wealth and Equality

THE SAVAGE WARS OF PEACE: England, Japan and the Malthusian Trap

WITCHCRAFT IN TUDOR AND STUART ENGLAND

The Making of the Modern World

Visions from the West and East

Alan Macfarlane

© Alan Macfarlane 2002

All rights reserved. No reproduction, copy or transmission of this publication may be made without written permission.

No paragraph of this publication may be reproduced, copied or transmitted save with written permission or in accordance with the provisions of the Copyright, Designs and Patents Act 1988, or under the terms of any licence permitting limited copying issued by the Copyright Licensing Agency, 90 Tottenham Court Road, London W1T 4LP.

Any person who does any unauthorised act in relation to this publication may be liable to criminal prosecution and civil claims for damages.

The author has asserted his right to be identified as the author of this work in accordance with the Copyright, Designs and Patents Act 1988.

First published 2002 by
PALGRAVE
Houndmills, Basingstoke, Hampshire RG21 6XS and
175 Fifth Avenue, New York, N.Y. 10010
Companies and representatives throughout the world

PALGRAVE is the new global academic imprint of
St. Martin's Press LLC Scholarly and Reference Division and
Palgrave Publishers Ltd (formerly Macmillan Press Ltd).

ISBN 0–333–96446–2

This book is printed on paper suitable for recycling and made from fully managed and sustained forest sources.

A catalogue record for this book is available from the British Library.

Library of Congress Cataloging–in–Publication Data
Macfarlane, Alan.
    The making of the modern world : visions from the West
    and East / Alan Macfarlane.
        p. cm.
    Includes bibliographical references and index.
    ISBN 0–333–96446–2
        1. East and West. 2. Civilization, Modern—1950– 3. Philosophy,
    Modern—20th century. 4. Maitland, Frederic William, 1850–1906–
    –Views on civilization. 5. Maitland, Frederic William, 1850–1906–
    –Political and social views. 6. Historians—Great Britain—Biography.
    7. Fukuzawa, Yukichi, 1835–1901—Views on civilization. 8. Fukuzawa,
    Yukichi, 1835–1901—Political and social views. 9. Philosophers–
    –Japan—Biography. I. Title.

CB251 .M27 2001
909.82'5—dc21
                                                                    2001054582

10   9   8   7   6   5   4   3   2   1
11   10   09   08   07   06   05   04   03   02

Printed and bound in Great Britain by
Antony Rowe Ltd, Chippenham, Wiltshire

To the memory of
Sir Robert Rhodes James
1933–1999

Contents

Acknowledgements

I would like to thank a number of people who have helped. In relation to F.W. Maitland the Maitland Society of Downing College, Cambridge, invited me to give a Bicentenary Celebration lecture on Maitland. Among those who attended and offered comments I am particularly grateful to Professor John Baker, whose work on English law has long inspired me.

My interest in Fukuzawa was first roused by Professor Toshiko Nakamura, who has also given me extensive advice on how to interpret his life and work, and read and commented on my writings. Our collaboration over ten years was originally made possible through a British Council Visiting Professorship and later by a Japanese Ministry of Education grant. Dr Carmen Blacker read my chapters on Fukuzawa twice and has given me much support and advice. The University of Tokyo, and particularly Professor Takeo Funabiki, provided a sabbatical term during which, among other things, I rewrote sections of the text. The Fukuzawa Centre at Keio University, and particularly Dr Shunsaku Nishikawa of Keio University, were always helpful and Dr Nishikawa kindly read a draft of my chapters on Fukuzawa. I was honoured to be invited to give a lecture on Fukuzawa in the 'Speech Hall' which Fukuzawa inaugurated at Keio University. This was facilitated by David Dugan and Carlo Massarella of Windfall Films who shared my enthusiasm for Fukuzawa and made it possible for me to be shown round the club he founded (the Kojunsha) by the Secretary, Mr Reijiro Hattori, and round the Ogata Koan school which Fukuzawa attended in Osaka, as part of the filming for 'The Day the World Took Off' (C4, June 2000) which contained a section on Fukuzawa.

The Research Centre at King's College, Cambridge, funded three seminars which were connected to the themes of this book. The participants in the seminars helped me clarify a number of ideas. Marilyn Strathern and later Stephen Hugh-Jones shielded me from administrative pressures and provided wise leadership. The University of Cambridge provided many facilities and much support in the writing of the book. Lily Blakely, once again, helped me to bring the final chapter to life.

Cherry Bryant, John Davey, Iris Macfarlane, Ruth Toulson, John

Heath and Andrew Morgan have all read drafts of the book and made many helpful suggestions for improvements. Markus Schlecker read the chapter on Trusts and made helpful comments. Cecilia Scurrah Ehrhart helped with checking the footnotes. Penny Lang typed and retyped parts of the text, helped check the notes and aided in many other ways. An anonymous reader for Palgrave made a number of perceptive comments which led me to reshape the book.

In particular I would like to thank two people. Gerry Martin for many stimulating ideas and conversations, for reading numerous drafts of the whole book and discussing it with me at length, and for moral and financial support through the Renaissance Trust. In many ways this is a collaborative work with him. Also, once again, I thank Hilda Martin for her friendship, encouragement and support. Sarah Harrison has, as always, given enormous help in every possible way, including several constructive readings of the text which helped to shorten it by a quarter. This book is likewise a collaborative work with her, and in particular the fruit of many years of discussion of how the English legal system worked and the detailed study of the English parish of Earls Colne, Essex.

Finally, I would like to explain the dedication. Robert Rhodes James, my mother's younger brother, shared my childhood, went before me to the same boarding school (Lupton House, Sedbergh), the same College and University (Worcester, Oxford) to read the same subject (history). He was constantly kind and encouraging to his younger 'brother' and a source of inspiration. Without his courage and example I should certainly never have written this book and I dedicate it to his memory in affection and admiration.

Note on References

Normally, much of the materials in a monograph would be one's own. This book, however, is a work in which I try to let Maitland and Fukuzawa talk to us in their own words. Consequently, it contains many quotations from their work. This has an effect on the style of the book, but I hope that the authenticity of the many thoughts of the chosen authors will enrich the argument.

Spelling has not been modernized. American spelling (e.g. labor for labour) has usually been changed to the English variant. Italics in quotations are in the original, unless otherwise indicated. Variant spellings in quotations have not been corrected. Round brackets in quotations are those of the original author; my interpolations are in square brackets.

The footnote references give an abbreviated title and page number. The usual form is author, short title, volume number, if there is one (in upper-case Roman numerals), page number(s). The full title of the work referred to is given in the bibliography at the end of the book, where there is also a list of common abbreviations used in the footnotes. Works by Maitland and Fukuzawa are listed at the front of the book in the section on 'Abbreviated Titles'.

List of Abbreviated Titles of the Two Major Authors

F.W. Maitland (1850–1906)

Pleas of the Crown: Pleas of the Crown for the County of Gloucester, 1884

History: History of English Law before the Time of Edward I, with Sir F. Pollock, originally published in 1895, 2nd edn., Cambridge, 1923; preface by S.F.C. Milsom to the reprint of 2nd edn., Cambridge, 1968

Township: Township and Borough, Cambridge, 1898

Roman Canon Law: Roman Canon Law in the Church of England. Six Essays, 1898

Political: Political Theories of the Middle Ages, by Otto Gierke, tr. and introduction by F.W. Maitland, Cambridge, 1900

Equity: Equity also The Forms of Action at Common Law; Two Courses of Lectures, Cambridge, 1909

Collected Papers: The Collected Papers of Frederic William Maitland, ed. H.A.L. Fisher, Cambridge, 1911, 3 volumes

Constitutional: The Constitutional History of England, Cambridge, 1919

Domesday: Domesday Book and Beyond, Cambridge, 1924

Selected Essays: Selected Historical Essays, ed. Helen Cam, Boston, 1962

Letters: The Letters of F.W. Maitland, ed. C.H.S. Fifoot, Cambridge, 1965

Letters, ii: The Letters of Frederic William Maitland, vol. II, ed. for Selden Society by P.N.R. Zutshi, 1995

Forms of Action: The Forms of Action at Common Law, eds. A.H. Chaytor and W.J. Whittaker, Cambridge, 1968

Yukichi Fukuzawa (1835–1901)

'Kyūhanjō': *Kyūhanjō* [Early Life], tr. Carmen Blacker, *Monumenta Nipponica*, IX, no. 1/2, Tokyo, 1953

Civilization: An Outline of a Theory of Civilization, tr. David A. Dilworth and G. Cameron Hurst, Tokyo, 1973

Learning: An Encouragement of Learning, tr. David A. Dilworth and Umeyo Hirano, Tokyo, 1969

Autobiography: The Autobiography of Yukichi Fukuzawa, tr. Eiichi Kiyooka, New York, 1972

Speeches: The Speeches of Fukuzawa, tr. and ed. Wayne H. Oxford, Tokyo, 1973

Women: Fukuzawa Yukichi on Japanese Women, ed. Eiichi Kiyooka, Tokyo, 1988

Collected Works: The Collected Works of Fukuzawa, tr. Eiichi Kiyooka, Tokyo, 1980

Part I

F.W. Maitland: The Nature and Origins of the Modern World

Preface to a Study of F.W. Maitland

In order to understand this account of the work of F.W. Maitland it is essential to understand how I came to focus on his ideas. In the *Origins of English Individualism; the Family, Property and Social Transition* (1978) I tried to explore the origins of our modern world. There were, however, several unresolved issues left by the book. One concerned the precise dating and sources of modern individualism. I was unable to explore in any depth where this individualism had come from and why England developed in a way that made it so different from most of continental Europe. Another omission concerned the wider context of power relations, particularly the relations between politics and economics within feudalism. A further area concerned the question of how people as individualistic as those I uncovered achieved so much. In my reaction against certain theories concerning the nature of medieval peasantry, I went to the other extreme and largely reduced the English to Robinson Crusoe-like figures. This was perhaps a healthy corrective at the time, but clearly it is difficult to explain the power and influence of modern civilizations if we do not understand what holds them together as much as what splits them into tiny fragments.

The first part of this book revolves round the thought of the man whom I have found most helpful in rethinking the past and who was the most important single source of inspiration for my earlier book. In studying the work of Maitland I will try to explore some of the difficulties mentioned above and in doing so extend a series of later attempts to move beyond my work on English individualism.[1] In the way in which I have treated him, I have seen Maitland as the man who finally solved the problem of combining individualism and associations in a new way.

This is, therefore, a polemical work and so it should not be read as if it were a highly objective and critical study. As will be clear, I admire Maitland greatly. Inevitably, though, I have found the Maitland I sought, fitting his ideas into my own arguments and experience, though hopefully without distorting his work too much. Inevitably, also, my glosses and paraphrases or summaries of his ideas will sometimes go beyond what he would have said or oversimplify his message. Constantly, I use phrases or words which have a slightly different sense from those which he used over a hundred years ago. The reader needs to be warned of all this, but I hope that I have quoted enough of Maitland to make it possible to check most of my interpretations against his texts.

I am fascinated by Maitland because he seems to have been struggling throughout his life with something more than merely technical, legal and historical problems. I believe he was facing the wider problem of how to combine liberty, equality and fraternity. Through his work, I would argue, he solved more satisfactorily than anyone else, the problem of the dichotomy between group (status-based) and individualistic (contractual) civilizations which has faced many great thinkers. Having solved the problem, Maitland was able to sketch out the powerful mixture of rigidity and flexibility which lies behind much of the achievements of those living in modern societies.

This interpretation of Maitland is different from those of almost all those who have previously written about him. Instead of treating him mainly as a great historian or legal historian (both of which are incontestable), I have tried to set him implicitly and at times explicitly alongside three of the greatest political philosophers: Montesquieu, Adam Smith and Tocqueville. For I believe that if we consider his early interests in philosophy, and look behind his writings, we can claim that he is of the same rank and shares the same interests as these great thinkers. Like Tocqueville who used 'America' as a pretext to write about 'democracy' and 'modernity', so I believe Maitland was ultimately using the history of English law as a way of trying to solve the problems of the origins and nature of the modern world.

1

F.W. Maitland and the Making of the Modern World

In his attempt to win a Trinity College Fellowship, Maitland submitted a dissertation entitled 'A Historical Sketch of Liberty and Equality as Ideals of English Political Philosophy from the Time of Hobbes to the Time of Coleridge'. He published it at his own expense when he was 25.[1] In this long and scholarly piece, he summarized and analysed much of the greatest thought on 'liberty' in the 200 years before his own work, including the work of Hobbes, Locke, Hume, Adam Smith, Rousseau, Kant, Coleridge, Mill and others. The central theme is the way in which the individual is embedded in wider groupings. Having sketched out the philosophical problems in this early work, I believe that his later life's work on English historical records allowed him to re-examine how the modern liberty had emerged. He examined the relations of the state and the citizen from the feudal period onwards, the relations of community and individual from Anglo-Saxon origins, and of the family and the individual.

Maitland tried to show that from very early on there had been a peculiar liberty of the individual in England, particularly in relation to property and power. In opposition to most of his contemporaries, including Sir Henry Maine, he disliked the idea of movement of all societies from Community to Association. He saw a basic liberty and individualism in England from Anglo-Saxon times onwards. Thus freedom and liberty of action, he argued, is indeed a key feature of the curious English structure which, in his day, was spreading all over the world. Yet if the individual is not embedded in the wider group in the usual ways, what about the second great unifying force, hierarchy?

Basically Maitland takes up Tocqueville's central theme, namely the nature and implications of equality and inequality. What he shows is that the nature of English law and social structure is such, and has always been such, that there are few, if any, inherited differences based on birth. All differences, whether of social rank, of parental power or of gender, are the result of contract, or as modern sociologists might say, of achievement rather than ascription. Thus he presents a picture of a competitive and fluid social structure as far back as the records take us. All this, he is aware, is very unusual and very important.

Yet, having spent much of his life analyzing in detail how the development of liberty and equality had worked, and having shown that most of the famous theories of the movement from status to contract were seriously oversimplified descriptions of what had happened, Maitland was faced in his last years with a serious difficulty. If, as Tocqueville realized, people are not held together by birth status (in a community, social rank or family), what will make them cohere? How can they act together to effect things and to protect themselves against the state? This was also the problem for Montesquieu and Adam Smith, but none of the three thinkers was able to devise a solution. Yet I believe that Maitland did find an answer in his arguments, up to now practically ignored, concerning corporations and Trusts.[2]

Another problem he addresses concerns the reasons why England became different from most of its continental neighbours. Here he amplifies, expands and documents the insights of Tocqueville and his predecessors, namely that being an island was the crucial fact. Islandhood had many consequences, some of which Maitland explores in relation to the tension within the balance of power, as with the unusual form of feudalism and the development of the parliamentary system. One manifestation that particularly interests him is the divergent development of law, English common law and equity, as opposed to the restoration of Roman law over the continent. Another major feature which intrigues him is the way in which there can be a 'changing same', that is to say both continuities and change at the same time. His delicate account of change with continuity, avoiding most of the usual pitfalls, provides the possibility of a non-evolutionary and non-revolutionary approach to history.

So, by the time of his untimely death at the age of 56, Maitland had made a lightning sketch of what the essence of English (and hence American) civilization was and how it could balance liberty, equality and fraternity. What is curious is that his findings and vision, though preserved among technical legal historians, have become almost forgotten among wider historians and the general public. I myself do not remember ever encountering him in six years of historical training at Oxford University between 1960 and 1966. This amnesia is a good example of what is not usually considered by those who discuss paradigm shifts, namely the way in which earlier knowledge of a high quality is quietly forgotten.[3]

*

If it is indeed the case that Maitland was part of a long Enlightenment tradition and asking the large questions concerning the nature and origins of liberty, equality and fraternity which concerned them, we need to know more about his ancestors before we assess his contribution. I wrote this account of Maitland originally as the last section of a longer work considering the ideas of three of these thinkers, Montesquieu, Adam Smith and Tocqueville. The account of those three became a book in its own right, but it makes sense to summarize some of the ideas of these three and their cumulative findings in order to see the background to Maitland's quest and my treatment of him.[4]

What these three thinkers did, on the basis of intuition and limited archival research, was to outline a strong hypothesis as to how the change from the *ancien régime* world might have occurred. In so far as the sources were available, their search took them back to the history of the Roman Empire. A study of Roman civilization showed clearly that it had abandoned its democratic ideals and moved into the usual hierarchical and absolutist trap. They believed that the roots of modern liberty and equality must lie elsewhere. Montesquieu famously found them in the 'German woods' where the wandering tribes who overran the Roman Empire returned western Europe to its democratic origins. They were warlike, individualistic, egalitarian. With a surprisingly developed money-consciousness and judicial system, they set up small, balanced kingdoms throughout the old Roman lands.

They suggested that by the twelfth century western Europe was uniformly 'feudal', that is to say the basis of society was an 'artificial' feudal contract, an act of will, an agreement to concede certain economic and political rights. There were no strong birth-based differences. The centre was not too strong, kinship was secondary to politics, and religion was significant but not too powerful. In other words, European states had achieved that unlikely balance between institutional forces, between centre and periphery, between the ambitions of rulers, priests and people, so that none became supremely dominant.

It was during this period of balanced tension that there was rapid technological, artistic and intellectual growth. This was the era of the extension of horse and plough agriculture, the spread of water and wind power, the reception of Greek, Indian and Chinese science by way of Islam, the founding of universities, and the growth of towns and trade.

Although structurally very similar to the rest, England was the extreme example of a propitious balance of forces. In England, largely because it was an island, the Crown became unusually powerful and a centralized, but not too centralized, monarchy emerged under the later Anglo-Saxon kings. The genius of the Normans and Angevins consolidated and homogenized this structure so that by the thirteenth century England was a wealthy, powerful, well-governed land, with a rapidly growing technology, trade links, strong armies and booming towns. It was basically, like the rest of Europe, a Germanic kingdom with an engrafting of a more developed centralized feudalism.

This phase of 'feudal' civilization, the five or so centuries between the eighth and thirteenth centuries, provided the possible gateway to a kind of civilization never before envisaged in the world. A large, diverse, agrarian civilization was broken into small, competing quasi-states, unified under Christianity, yet preserving their differences. The system was based on contractual ties and not birth differences, on achievement rather than ascription. There was an antagonism yet balance between the growing power of the Church and the state, but neither was dominant and they had not yet formed a close alliance. Most of whatever power kinship had once held had been destroyed. Commerce and towns were encouraged, as was technological innovation in the saving of labour in the difficult and population-scarce environment. Thought and recovered knowledge were relatively free of the jealousies of a powerful clergy.

However, they argued that the next 500 years saw the balance destroyed throughout much of continental Europe. The normal tendencies and traps of agrarian structures, the temptations and tools which growing knowledge and wealth provide, worked their usual consequences through time. The threat of war, the threat of 'heresy' (the Crusades, Albigensianism), the desire to predate on the wealth-creators, all these were forces which tipped the balance.

The institutional mechanisms for the emergence of the absolutist state and Church are well known. The Catholic Inquisition, the reception of an authoritarian and centralizing Roman law, the emergence of caste-like birth privileges for the 'nobility', the destruction of the 'liberties' of all intermediary bodies such as trade guilds and town governments, the rising size of standing armies and the central bureaucracy, all these were catalogued by our informants. In essence, European civilization moved away from a 'feudal' one based on the flexibility of 'contract', to an *ancien régime* one based on 'status'. The tensions and separations of spheres were lost. A centripetal force seemed to be at work – everything gravitated upwards and towards the centre.

However, there were exceptions, both at the national or local level – the rise of free cities in northern Italy and Germany being good examples. But they were soon crushed and the tendency continued. By the eighteenth century, the usual barriers – war, famine, disease, an increasingly impoverished peasantry, a parasitic nobility, a conservative clergy, an arbitrary and despotic law, a large and enervating bureaucracy and the heavy taxes to sustain it, increasing predation on merchants and producers, all were widespread.

By the late seventeenth century there were only two apparent exceptions to this. One was the richest (per capita) country in the world, namely Holland, the other was England. Holland exemplified the advantages of a balance between competing forces. It had discovered that a liberal course – separating and balancing, encouraging political and religious liberty, decentralizing power, avoiding extreme stratification, all encouraged a rapid growth of wealth so that a tiny country with such a virtuous structure could defeat the greatest empire in the West. Yet Holland, for various reasons, was unable to develop beyond this high-level commercial economy.

*

These three writers believed that England was the exception that somehow solved the riddle. In 1200 England was a centralized and reasonably well-governed example of the western European pattern. From this we might have expected that, combined with its rapid technological and productive development, it would have been moved by the normal tendencies evident over Europe towards a precocious form of the trap – heavily absolutist, stratified and caught in the grip of an intolerant inquisitorial religion. Yet by the time that Montesquieu visited England in 1739 he believed it hardly resembled the rest of Europe.

What had happened in those 500 years to make the trajectories so different, and why had it happened? In essence the easiest way to explain the difference is negatively. The three great tendencies that had swept most of Europe had not occurred. Political absolutism and centralization, with a ruler above the law and no countervailing forces, had not become established. There had been times when the tendency asserted itself, famously under John, Henry VIII, Charles I and James II. But, in each attempt at monarchical aggrandisement, it had failed and a short period of absolutist rule had led to a reaction; Magna Carta, the rise of the Elizabethan parliament and sale of Crown lands, the beheading of the king and the Whig Restoration. As most European states saw the vestiges of democracy swept away, the power of the Commons grew until by Montesquieu's time the contrast was overwhelming.

The trappings and mechanisms of absolutism which had arisen over much of the Continent failed to develop. There was no large central bureaucracy, but rather the devolution of power through a complex of often voluntary and honorary power holders such as constables and the justices of the peace. There was relatively easy taxation, an arrangement jealously guarded by the Commons. There was no standing army and few hired mercenaries. The legal system bequeathed by the Germanic invaders, the English customary law, was retained and no formal reception of inquisitorial and despotic late Roman law occurred. All these are both signs and associated features of the absence of the normal tendency for power to corrupt. Amazingly the country grew steadily wealthier, yet the wealth was spread, property was secure, people had rights and the king remained below the law. It was a miracle, often at risk, but it happened.

Second, the tendency for the ecclesiastical power to increase and to enter into a pact with the lay authorities never occurred. There remained a deep conflict between state and Church. Neither was strong enough to subdue the other. From Becket to the dissolution of the monasteries, the Crown kept the Church in check. Both conspired to ward off the sweeping resurgence of clerical power in the fourteenth-century rise of the Inquisition or the sixteenth-century Counter-Reformation on the continent of Europe. Instead of coalescing into a fervent and conservative force, England saw the rise of pre-

Reformation independent sects such as the Lollards, then the Reformation itself which placed the individual at the heart of his religion and reduced the mediation of the theocracy, and finally the growth of sectarianism and a balanced toleration whereby religion became a private matter. The final separation of religion and politics, rather than their coalescing, had been achieved, and religion also withdrew from economic life – or left such a life to the private conscience.

The third great absence was the tendency towards internal social predation, taking the normal form of increasingly rigid, caste-like barriers between birth-given orders. As Tocqueville in particular brilliantly argued, it looked as if the normal division into a high nobility, inferior bourgeoisie and crushed peasantry did not occur. A hitherto unprecedented social structure emerged, which was based on wealth and achieved status rather than blood. It was still very inegalitarian *de facto*, but the possibility of movement within it was great. Furthermore, the bulk of the population were placed at the middle level rather than there being a few immensely privileged, and a great mass of illiterate agrarian producers. The peculiar rank of the English gentleman, the exceptional status of 'yeoman', the high position of merchants and craftsmen, the prosperity of country dwellers, all these were signs of something unusual, a proto-class rather than proto-caste or estate system. Such a wide spread of wealth, power and liberty obviously both reflected and affected the possibilities of political absolutism. It was only matched, in a slightly different form, in Holland.

The question still remains, though, why, starting from a fairly similar origin in Anglo-Saxon civilization, England had gone against the normal tendencies. Here our informants developed two interlinked theories. One, developed by Montesquieu and expanded by Smith, concerned the hidden effects of material wealth and in particular trade and consumerism. In its crudest form, the theory was that, all else being equal, if a country could move into a long period of material growth, the tendency of the Lords and the Church to gain power would be deflected by greed. The Lords would prefer consumer goods rather than retainers, and hence lose their military bargaining power. Likewise the Church, through greed, would lose the love of the people as it assembled treasures upon earth and end up like the monastic orders, stripped of almost all influence. The difficulty, of course, was to sustain growth at such a level and for long enough that this conversion of the powerful to the preferability of modified predation, or even dabbling in production, could be achieved. Often it happened for short periods and in limited areas, as in the environs of a city such as Florence or Siena. But such a haven was soon exposed to marauders from outside and would revert to the usual predatory dominance of Lords and priests.

Thus this theory was linked to the one unique feature of England, that it was a large enough island, just far enough away from a sophisticated continent. It was large enough to defend itself and to generate a great deal of internal diversity and trade. It was far enough away to make it difficult to attack or even threaten as long as it was defended by a good fleet. Yet it was not too far away, 20 miles rather than the 100 miles which made Japan so much more isolated. Its major weakness was that it was contiguous with other, more warlike, peoples to the north, namely the Highland Scots. Fortunately for it, there were few Highlanders and they usually only constituted a raiding nuisance. Nevertheless, the unification of the Crown in 1603 eased the threat of land-based invasion, and the events of 1715 and 1745 showed how relaxed the English had become about their land defences.

The advantages of not having large warlike land neighbours were immense. Basically it decreased the temptations to, and possibilities of, predation. Most obviously, a country like England never suffered the kind of levelling catastrophe afflicted by the Mongols, thus avoided a dismantling of its infrastructure. The devastating effects of being fought over by warring armies, which brought northern Italy and southern Germany toppling from their heights, never occurred. The Norman invasion, the Wars of the Roses and English Civil War were as nothing compared to the normal experience of continental countries.

Second, the balance of ruler and ruled was altered. A people could not be held to ransom by the threat of foreign invaders, whose continued hostility gave rulers a weapon with which to extract taxation and obedience from their people. They did not have to suffer from that most powerful tool of political absolutism, a standing army whose presence in England in the 1640s might well have ushered in a continental-style absolutism. An unarmed populace can stand up to an unarmed ruler – or rather one who provides defence only through a strong navy.

A third consequence is on the temptation to external expansion. Such predation, which the English engaged in with some zeal in France and Scotland during the twelfth to fourteenth centuries, had a different nature from that which attracted the Hapsburgs or Louis

XIV or had been a major factor in the destruction of the Roman democracy. In the case of Scotland the target was finite and the aim to eliminate a particular threat. In the case of France, the dynastic claims encouraged adventure, were clearly a luxury not a necessity. If the king wanted to adventure in that way, just as when he wanted to gain merit in the Crusades, he would have to pay for it – by acceding to the desires of the Lords and Commons. Instead of such wars leading to the increase of royal power, as taxation was raised and the people threatened, it was often the warlike adventurer-kings who conceded most to the people. Every concession tipped the balance and though temporary reprieves of a financial kind could be achieved – for instance, by the confiscation of monastic lands – a ruler wishing to be adventurous or loved, like Elizabeth, was too firmly circumscribed to be able to do anything other than sell off the family silver (the demesne lands) and put her successors further at the mercy of a powerful third estate. At a certain point, probably after about 1650, the process was more or less irreversible. Each new gain in production now fed into increased production, rather than internal predation.

The other hypothesis to account for England's peculiar history overlaps, but adds depth to, this account. There were certain initial differences in England before the Norman invasion. Then for a century after the Norman invasion this already different island world came close to the rest of north-west European models of feudalism, except that there was no 'dissolution of the state'. A powerful monarchy maintained its control of the legal system, but delegated power downwards through the feudal links. Thus England reached a balance of centralization and decentralization.

From a basic similarity by about 1200, 'Europe' increasingly gravitated towards other forms, with the reception of Roman law and the growth of a blood nobility and a widespread peasantry. England, after incorporating some of the organizational features of Roman law, rejected almost all the substantive content of the revived late Roman legal system. This meant that England's economic, social and political structure became more and more at variance with much of the continent. Montesquieu and Tocqueville guessed that England largely avoided the apparently inevitable tendency to 'caste' and 'political centralization'.

This unusual situation could not have happened if England had not been protected by the sea. It was possible to be a small replica of England, for a while, without a sea boundary, as in the Italian city-states or Holland, but to sustain such a balance over hundreds of years as a land-bounded nation was probably impossible. There was nothing inevitable about the process. Many islands have existed without any dramatic developments. It was only England's good fortune to be close, but not too close, to a dynamic continent which enabled it to achieve anything. That something which has changed the world happened, was remarkable, unpredictable, and the result of a unique combination of forces.

For what happened was that at a certain point the feedback loop had altered. That strange alchemy whereby military strength was fuelled by high-level production, rather than feeding off it, had begun. The rich became the powerful, rather than the powerful becoming the rich. Extra production led to increased power and England was able to suck in the wealth of inventions and goods of not only Europe, but increasingly of America and Asia, to fuel its attempt to escape for the first time from the agrarian trap. It had, from another viewpoint, become the most powerful predator.

This, then, was the riddle and the hypothesis. Something strange had developed in western Europe and by the time of Tocqueville's death had clearly also been transferred to America. It consisted of a particular set of relationships to which we give general terms such as 'liberty', 'equality', 'wealth', and so on. Its roots were very deep, going back to Rome and earlier. All three of the great analysts guessed that it had developed in its essence in England. Yet they were unable to take the historical part of their surmises further for lack of a systematic survey of the historical records. It was only in the generation after Tocqueville's death that the rise of professional historiography in Europe would make it possible to confirm or refute their suggestions. These chapters on Maitland, then, are a brief overview of the man I believe to be the greatest of their successors.

As is clear from his Trinity dissertation, Maitland was well aware of their work. His questions at a deeper level were shaped by their obsessions, also mediated to him through the work of J.S. Mill. He was also influenced by nearer contemporaries, those in the generation above him. One of the most notable of these was Sir Henry Maine, like Maitland a world-level thinker who combined legal history and wider anthropological and philosophical concerns. It is worth briefly outlining some of Maine's ideas in order to understand better the wide context within which Maitland's ideas emerged.

2
The Legacy of Sir Henry Maine

Sir Henry Maine (1822–1888) was a distinguished lawyer, academic and civil servant of mid-Victorian England, holding chairs in Civil Law at Cambridge and Oxford, the legal member of the Council of India for seven years from 1862 and Master of Trinity Hall in Cambridge from 1877.[1] It is for his prolific writings and their influence on modern anthropology, of which, along with Tylor and Morgan, he is one of the founding fathers, that we best know him. His books included *Ancient Law* (1861), *Village Communities in the East and West* (1871), *Lectures on the Early History of Institutions* (1875) and *Dissertations on Early Law and Custom* (1883). He was a polymath, writing about

> ancient customs, modern politics, scientific theories, the development of languages, statute law, poetry, philosophy, literature, whether women are more conservative than men, the extent to which law changes society and society changes law, Roman agriculture, Greek civilisation, the caste systems of India, the failings of Bentham, the achievements of Bentham, the consequences of imposing British law on societies governed by custom, the merits of American social values and many, many other matters.[2]

Maine was only one of many thinkers, including Herbert Spencer, Karl Marx, Friedrich Engels, Edward Tylor and Lewis Morgan, who were trying to fit the huge influx of comparative data from the expanding European empires into a pattern of world history. Yet it is worth considering him in detail since, as a lawyer and Cambridge predecessor, he had a particular influence on Maitland. In some ways, Maitland's work can be seen as a wrestling with the ghost of Maine, though this is usually concealed. Very often Maitland either ignored Maine, implicitly criticized him or, very occasionally, made disparaging remarks about the quality of his scholarship.[3] Yet a consideration of Maine's writings helps to place Maitland's work within the context of mid-Victorian social thought and to provide some comparative perspectives on topics which would preoccupy him.

Maine's central aim was to explain how modern civilization had emerged in certain 'progressive' societies. His most important generalization was that concerning the movement from societies based on status (kinship, tribe) to societies based on contract (the state). One part of this theory is shown in his treatment of individual rights. His wide sweep allowed him to see 'by what insensible gradations the relation of man to man substituted itself for the relation of the individual to his family, and of families to each other'; 'Ancient Law . . . knows next to nothing of Individuals. It is concerned not with individuals but with Families, not with single human beings, but groups.'[4] If we take all these points together, and then look at nineteenth-century England, Maine argued, echoing his other famous formulation, the

> movement of the progressive societies has been uniform in one
> respect. Through all its course it has been distinguished by the
> gradual dissolution of family dependency, and the growth of in-
> dividual obligation in its place. The Individual is steadily substituted
> for the Family, as the unit of which civil laws take account.[5]

This contrast between group-based and individual-based society is part of that movement from status to contract which Maine thought was the greatest of all changes. 'Starting, as from one terminus of history, from a condition of society in which all the relations of Persons are summed up in the relations of Family, we seem to have steadily moved towards a phase of social order in which all these relations arise from the free agreement of Individuals.'[6] Thus, the relations of parent to child, master to slave, male to female, based on birth and ascribed status, melt before the negotiated relations of free individuals. It is in this sense that 'we may say that the movement of the progressive societies has hitherto been a movement *from Status to Contract.*'[7] Thus, 'the society of our day is mainly distinguished from that of preceding generations by the largeness of the sphere which is occupied in it by Contract . . . old law fixed a man's social position irreversibly at his birth, modern law allows him to create it for himself by convention.'[8]

Maine believed that the earliest societies had been based on large corporate groups of kin, organized through the male line, what was then known as the 'patriarchal theory'. 'Corporations *never die*, and accordingly primitive law considers the entities with which it deals, i.e. the patriarchal or family groups, as perpetual and inextinguishable.'[9] Yet Maine's theory of patriarchal origins left him unable to solve his larger puzzle. His problem was how to explain the origins of modern civilization in the 'progressive' societies. This consisted in the movement from status, or kinship-based, societies, to modern contractual society. The essential bridge was the destruction of kinship in the feudal period. But he never solved the problem of where the magic ingredients of feudalism came from. We will return to this when considering his ideas of property. But it is worth noting here that by assuming the uniformity of the agnatic, kinship-dominated stage, he seemed to leave no room for the seeds of contract. The idea of alienability, or of primogeniture, seemed to spring from a clear sky. Thus, for instance, he says that there is no concept of primogeniture or its associated ideas in Roman law, in Hindu law or in ancient German law. All children were co-owners with their family. Suddenly it emerges.[10]

Maine did recognize that there was something odd about Anglo-Saxon kinship, writing that in the important area of joint property, 'the general usage of the old Germanic peoples – it is remarkable that the Anglo-Saxon customs seem to have been an exception – forbade alienations without the consent of the male children.'[11] Nevertheless, in general, he tended to assume its basically agnatic quality. He never solved this central puzzle. As we shall see in the next chapters, it was solved by Maitland, who provides the key to understanding how Maine's world came about and thus gives us clues to solve our problem concerning the origins of modernity. Maitland was able to show that there were elements in the kinship system of the Germanic peoples which already suggested an alternative to joint property and patriarchal organization; the seed was there, and the mystery of feudalism is not quite as deep as it once seemed.

*

Another way of putting Maine's famous contrast was to say that in most societies, including that which he later saw in India, the community is very strong and the individual weak, while in mid-nineteenth-century Europe, the reverse was true. One of the major lessons, and one which it 'is often said that it takes two or three years' for a new visitor to India to learn, is that 'the vast Indian population is an aggregate of natural groups, and not the mixed multitude he left at home . . .'[12] He believed that this had once been the case in England and in Europe, in the Dark Ages. There had been a growth of 'Village Communities', and the 'historian of former days laboured probably under no greater disadvantage than that caused by his unavoidable ignorance of the importance of these communities . . .'[13] What, then, did Maine mean by 'community'?

There are a number of characteristics which, according to Maine, constitute a community. Communities are 'naturally organized', that is to say, the bond that unites people is a natural, rather than an artificial one. The two major bonds are kinship in tribal communities, and territory in village communities. The early bond of kinship had given place in both India and Europe to the bond of locality. The 'Indian Village-Community is a body of men held together by the land which they occupy: the idea of common blood and decent has all but died out.'[14] This is still a 'true Village-Community',[15] even though there had been a transition from the earlier form of 'the Village-Community, a brotherhood of self-styled kinsmen, settled on a space of land'.[16]

He believed that once upon a time the village community had been a collective entity in terms of landholding, both in India and early Europe. This collectivity manifested itself in terms of the absence of individual rights. Maine argued that there was no concept similar to the modern western one of inalienable human rights in the traditional village community. 'Nor, in the sense of the analytical jurists, is there *right* or *duty* in an Indian village-community; a person aggrieved complains not of an individual wrong but of the disturbance of the order of the entire little society.'[17] The growth of individual rights was one of the major transformations which had occurred in western Europe, and would soon break up the natural communities of India.

Another feature singled out by Maine was 'self-existing'. By this he probably meant 'self-sufficient'. He described how Indian villages were 'total' economies, not dependent for goods on the outside world. In fact, he envisaged in the earliest stage 'a territory occupied by village-communities, self-acting and as yet autonomous, each cultivating its arable land in the middle of its waste, and each,

I fear I must add, at perpetual war with its neighbour'.[18] These were little kingdoms. He described how the mixture of occupations in an Indian village seemed to cover all human needs, and wrote that it is 'the assignment of a definite lot in the cultivated area to particular trades which allows us to suspect that the early Teutonic groups were similarly self-sufficing'.[19]

Maine thus created a model of a village community, with the natural bonds of blood or locality, rather than artificial bonds of money and contract, with communal ownership of some form, with economic and political self-sufficiency, and with customary law. This he believed was a transitional form between tribal and modern society. He was aware, however, of certain limitations to the model: these village communities, for example, were neither homogeneous nor egalitarian: 'The brotherhood, in fact, forms a sort of hierarchy' in an Indian village, in which there are dominant families.[20] In fact, Indian village communities 'prove on close inspection to be not simple but composite bodies, including a number of classes with very various rights and claims'.[21] This was, in fact, the start of a departure of reality from the model. For Maine was quite aware that his description of the Indian village community was already an idealized model of what had faded away. In Bengal, 'from causes not yet fully determined, the village system had fallen into great decay'.[22] He believed that the concepts of private property and individual rights encouraged by British law would lead the village community to disappear;[23] already 'the Indian village-community is breaking to pieces'.[24]

Maine devotes less attention to the village community in the European sphere, but it is clear that he believed that early Germanic society had passed through this stage of village communities, a view shared by many of his contemporaries. This faced him with a very difficult problem. If all Indo-European societies went through a stage after tribalism of 'village communities', how did the curious privatized property of parts of western Europe emerge?

Maine believed that one could speak about 'communal' ownership of land, or perhaps the absence of any private ownership, as the original state out of which all societies have evolved. Thus he speaks of 'that collective ownership of land which was a universal phenomenon in primitive societies . . .'[25] He argues concerning India that 'there has been sufficient evidence to warrant the assertion that the oldest discoverable forms of property in land were forms of collective property . . .'[26] In this way, he believed that India followed the pattern of all early Aryan societies.[27] He believed that this was a system characteristic not only of ancient and oriental societies, but even of Scotland and Ireland into the seventeenth century.[28] The development of private, individual, property out of such communal property, 'the process by which the primitive mode of enjoyment was converted into the agrarian system, out of which immediately grew the land-law prevailing in all Western Continental Europe before the first French Revolution and from which is demonstrably descended our own existing property law', was, Maine declared, 'the great problem of legal history'.[29] How then did he attempt to solve this 'great problem'?

An oversimplified, single-word answer is 'feudalism'. In earlier societies and civilizations there had certainly been the concept of private property, in other words private, individual ownership of certain commodities. In Rome, for example, all things except slaves, land, oxen and horses could be treated by an individual as his private property.[30] But the great transformation, and the one to be explained, was the emergence of private property in land. This was inextricably linked to the development of the 'feud' or indivisible estate. Feudalism introduced the new notion of indivisibility, and the collapse of feudalism set the individual free to dispose of all objects on the market as his own. Without the collapse of feudalism, 'we should never have had the conception of land as an exchangeable commodity . . .'[31]

Maine saw a number of threads coming together to endow feudalism with this new arrangement. Partly it was the unrestrained power of manorial lords over their own demesne land. The 'emancipation of the lord within his own domains from the fetters of obligatory agricultural custom' suggested 'a plausible conjecture that our absolute form of property is really descended from the proprietorship of the lord in the domain . . .'[32] Other powerful forces were the development of written wills, encouraged by the Church, and the granting of land by 'book' to religious bodies. Gradually, rights to land came to be looked on as a personal commodity, which could be sold or exchanged just like any other commodity. He pointed out that in England titles to manorial estates, and to the copyholds within those estates, were conceived of as having been originally purchased or acquired.[33] Hence, they could be sold on to another. The internal dissolution of feudalism in England started as soon as feudalism itself, many centuries before the 'bastard feudalism' of the fourteenth and fifteenth centuries. Feudalism was the catalyst, and primogeniture was linked to 'the crucible of feudalism';[34] for instance, 'the Feudal law of land practically disinherited all the children in favour of one . . .'[35] This made it possible that 'the equal distribution even of those sorts of property which might have been equally divided ceased to be viewed as a duty'.[36]

Maine argued that the central feature of feudalism was that it 'mixed up or confounded property and sovereignty',[37] every lord of a manor having both economic and judicial rights. Political power and economic power were both delegated down the same hierarchical chain. A second feature was the ability to conceive of different layers of ownership or possession within feudal tenures: the 'leading characteristic of the feudal conception is its recognition of a double proprietorship, the superior ownership of the lord of the fief co-existing with the inferior property or estate of the tenant.'[38] A third feature is that the whole structure was based not on inherited relations of 'status', but on acts of will or 'contract'. In feudalism, the famous bridge from societies based on status to those based on contract was, perhaps for the first and only time, crossed. This point was memorably emphasized by Maitland.

> The master who taught us that 'the movement of the progressive societies has hitherto been a movement from Status to Contract', was quick to add that feudal society was governed by the law of contract. There is no paradox here. In the really feudal centuries men could do by a contract of vassalage or commendation, many things that can not be done now-a-days . . . Those were the golden days of 'free', if 'formal' contract.[39]

If the gateway from ancient to modern civilizations as Montesquieu, Tocqueville, Marx and Maine all believed, was feudalism, we are pushed back to considering the origins and nature of feudalism. Maine suggested primitive roots which led him back into widespread Indo-Aryan systems. The mixture of Roman and Germanic civilization was a particular branch of a tree which also had major branches in Celtic and Indian civilization. Yet he implied that in the other two branches, the major transition beyond a very early sort of quasi-feudalism had not occurred and might never have done so without the pressure of British civilization which had evolved in a particular manner.

Maine tried to sketch out the origins of feudalism in England, though his account was clouded for lack of accurate data. His view was that while it was the legal orthodoxy of his time that all that was important in feudalism dated from after the Norman invasion, much that was characteristic of fully developed feudalism was already present in Anglo-Saxon England. The court leet, he argued, arose from the old township assemblies rather than from royal (Norman or Angevin) grants, as lawyers had argued.[40] The common-field and three-field systems were present in Germanic societies; the 'three-field system was therefore brought by our own Teutonic ancestors from some drier region of the Continent'.[41] The whole manorial system was pre-Norman, both the concept of the manor and that of copyhold tenure.[42] Thus while 'the ordinary text-books . . . practically trace our land-law to the customs of the Manor, and assume the Manor to have been a complete novelty introduced into the world during the process which is called the feudalisation of Europe',[43] in fact, he argued, the Germanic landholding systems did not die out at the Conquest, but very greatly influenced subsequent land-law.[44] He argues that 'the primitive Teutonic proprietary system had everywhere a tendency, not produced from without, to modify itself in the direction of feudalism'.[45] This tendency was particularly marked in England because Germanic customs were not destroyed by the reintroduction of Roman law: 'English institutions have never been so much broken as the institutions of other Germanic societies by the overwhelming disturbance caused elsewhere by Roman law and Roman legal ideas.'[46] Yet there was some trace of Romanism, an essential ingredient, for the ground in England had been prepared by a previous Romanized population.[47]

Maine hoped to solve the riddle of what lay in early tribal property systems which would mean that, when mixed with Roman civilization, a new property law would emerge. He believed that he had found in early Irish law 'a feudal system (if we may so call it) dependent on cattle and kinship instead of land and tenure'.[48] The model of the central principle of feudalism, the 'Benefice or Feud', was, he argued, 'mainly taken from that which the men of primitive Aryan race had considered as appropriate to chiefships or sovereignties . . .'[49] The origins of private property thus arose from 'the ever-increasing authority of the Chief, first over his own domain and "booked" land, and secondarily over the tribe lands', a process which was beginning long before the Norman conquest.[50] The chiefs or kings then granted benefices, or permanent, indivisible blocks of land to others.[51] Thus feudal notions 'had somehow been introduced into the Western world by the barbarous conquerors of the Roman Imperial territories'.[52]

These are sweeping thoughts, but Maine was one of the first to examine these themes in a critical way. He specified very clearly what the important development had been, namely the emergence of contractual-based societies. Yet he was unable to solve the question of how such societies had emerged and, as Maitland would show, his grand theory of the movement from status to contract needs rethinking. Both the magnitude of his contribution and a specification of what qualities were needed to go further than Maine were summarized by Maitland. In his Inaugural Lecture, delivered on 13 August 1888, some six months after Maine's death, Maitland spoke as follows:

> Of the great man who when that science [comparative jurisprudence] exists will be honoured as its prophet, and its herald, of the great man whom we have lost, may I say this? His wonderful modesty, his dislike of all that looked like parade, or pedantry, the fascination of his beautiful style are apt to conceal the width and depth of his reading. He was much more than learned, but then he was learned, very learned in law of all sorts and kinds. It is only through learning wide and deep, tough and technical, that we can safely approach those world-wide questions that he raised or criticize the answers that he found for them.[53]

We may now turn to Maitland himself who accumulated that 'learning wide and deep, tough and technical' and hence put himself in a position to resolve some of the questions raised by Maine.

3
Life, Work and Methods

F.W. Maitland was born on 28 May 1850 at 53 Guilford Street, London. He was educated at Eton and Trinity College, Cambridge. There was no Law or History Tripos at that time so he started by reading Mathematics. He did badly in his first year exams and then, as Maitland tells us, 'the idle whim of an idle undergraduate' took him into Henry Sidgwick's lecture room in his second year at Trinity.[1] He changed to the new Moral and Mental Sciences Tripos and the result was that eighteen months later he was placed at the equal head of the First Class in his final exams. He was President of the Cambridge Union, a running Blue, a 'Sunday Tramp' and, like Sir Henry Maine before him, an 'Apostle'.

The major influence on his thought at that time was Henry Sidgwick, a disciple of John Stuart Mill. From Sidgwick he imbibed the agnosticism and love of liberty and equality which Mill had shared with Tocqueville. As we have seen, Maitland's dissertation considered the same themes as Montesquieu and Tocqueville and devoted several pages to considering Adam Smith's arguments for economic *laissez-faire*. Thus by the time he left Cambridge it was clear that Maitland's interest was in philosophy, and in particular the Enlightenment tradition of political philosophy. As Plucknett notes, 'His ambition was to lead an academic life as a political scientist' and it was only as a 'disappointed philosopher' that he left for London.[2] This is important not only because he 'brought to the law a mind exercised in the wide open spaces of philosophy', but because it helps us to recognize that his last ten years were really a return to philosophy in another guise. His translation of Gierke and writing on corporations and trusts which we shall examine later 'recall his early interest in political philosophy'.[3]

Maitland's failure to obtain a Trinity Fellowship forced him sideways and he moved to London. He lived with his sisters in Kensington and worked for seven years at the Bar. His legal training was thus a later specialization, though he was reputedly a good lawyer. As a pupil in chambers, his master wrote long after that 'He had not been with me for a week before I found that I had in my chambers such a lawyer as I had never met before. I have forgotten, if I ever knew, where and how he acquired his mastery of law; he certainly did not acquire it in my chambers; he was a consummate lawyer when he entered them.'[4] He became close friends with Leslie Stephen, father of Virginia Woolf, and later wrote the *Life of Leslie Stephen*. He married Stephen's sister-in-law, Florence.

It is clear that he wanted to return to academic life and he still hankered after philosophy. His first published work after leaving Cambridge was a review of A.J. Balfour's *A Defence of Philosophic Doubt* for the philosophical journal *Mind* in 1879 and in 1883 he published two further reviews of Herbert Spencer's work on 'The Ideal State' and 'The Law of Equal Liberty' in the same journal.[5] This interest may have been one of the reasons why the philosopher Henry Sidgwick helped to set up a Readership for him at Cambridge in 1884. It was a momentous year, for it was also when he discovered for himself the vast wealth of original materials for English history in the Public Record Office.[6] These documents would help him to pursue those questions concerning the origins of liberty and equality which he had first surveyed in his Trinity dissertation and which his predecessors had been unable to pursue in detail for lack of information. Thus his first substantial publication was the *Pleas of the Crown for the County of Gloucester*, which was dedicated to Paul Vinogradoff. He described the documents as

a picture, or rather, since little imaginative art went into its making, a photograph of English life as it was early in the thirteenth century . . . We have here, as it were, a section of the body politic which shows just those most vital parts, of which, because they were deep-seated, the soul politic was hardly conscious, the system of local government and police . . .[7]

These were just those areas which Tocqueville had suggested were most distinctive, important and unusual in the English political structure.

Three years later Maitland published an edition of the manuscript collection of cases which the great thirteenth-century lawyer Bracton had collected and used when writing his treatise *On the Laws and Customs of England*. These had been discovered by Vinogradoff and were published in three volumes as *Bracton's Note Books* (1887). In the following year Maitland was elected Downing Professor of the Laws of England at Cambridge. In his inaugural lecture on 'Why the History of English Law is Not Written'[8] he explained the enormous importance of editing the medieval yearbooks and other law sources to the highest standard before the history of law could properly be written. Here was a man who had taught himself palaeography, had the training in law, and saw the opportunity. He had discovered a vast repository of records, all of them bearing on exactly those unresolved problems to which his predecessors had pointed. Believing that 'hoarded wealth yields no interest', he founded the Selden Society for the publication of medieval documents.

A decade of publication of detailed legal records followed, including his *Select Pleas of the Crown* (1888) and *Select Pleas in Manorial and Other Seignorial Courts*, vol. i (1889). He also edited with Baildon, *The Court Baron* (1891) for the Selden Society and the *Memoranda de Parliamento* (1893) for the Rolls Society, as well as overseeing the editorial works of others. This immersion in the world of early law, plus an extensive knowledge of continental scholarship, put him in an ideal position to look at English law and politics from a wider perspective. He read and understood French, Latin and Greek and, thanks to early tutoring, was particularly fluent in German. This is important since much of the major progress in comparative and historical law during his lifetime was taking place in Germany. Maitland started on a translation of the major work of Savigny on Roman law, though he never completed it, and translated and published parts of Gierke's treatise on *Political Theories of the Middle Ages* from the German. In 1895 Maitland published his great masterpiece, more than 1,300 pages on *The History of English Law before the Time of Edward I*. Although known as 'Pollock and Maitland' after its two editors, in fact Maitland wrote all but the first chapter of the work. In this volume he synthesized the results of the detailed studies he and others were making, as he was also to do in *Domesday Book and Beyond* (1897), *Roman Canon Law in the Church of England* (1898), *Township and Borough* (1898) and *English Law and the Renaissance* (1901).

He also wrote numerous articles and reviews, many of which were published in *The Collected Papers of Frederic William Maitland* (1911) edited by H.A.L. Fisher in three volumes, comprising another 1,500 pages. Others which were omitted in this collection were published in *Selected Historical Essays of F.W. Maitland* (1957), edited by Helen Cam. His lectures were so polished that three sets of them could be published more or less verbatim. The first on *The Constitutional History of England* (1908) were delivered in Michaelmas 1887 and Lent 1888, when he was 37 and just before he became Downing Professor. They contain, in raw form, some of the seminal ideas that were to go into the *History of English Law*, and also contain 'several new and original ideas, which Maitland had no opportunity of expressing in his later work . . .'[9] Maitland lectured on *Equity* at Cambridge from 1892 until 1906, and these were also published, as were his seven lectures on *Forms of Action at Common Law*.

Thus Maitland's published work comprises well over 5,000 printed pages, much of it extremely detailed. This is all the more miraculous in that he only started the flow in 1888 and combined it with the usual administrative and teaching duties. In order to understand his achievement properly, we need to take this teaching context, the Fellowship at Downing College and University Professorship, into account.

From his letters we get a few glimpses of his work methods. He describes the other pressures on him from his full involvement as a teaching professor. On 16 February 1890 he wrote: 'I am now in the middle of our busiest term and lecturing daily; but the middle is past and I am beginning to look forward to Easter and pleasanter occupations.'[10] On 22 October 1905 he was still 'teaching six hours per week', but was 'hopeful of staying here through November – whereat I rejoice', rather than having to leave for the Canaries.[11] The following year he died. As well as the pressures of teaching and illness, there was the actual time spent searching for and copying out original documents at the Public Record Office. In June 1889 he wrote concerning the possible editing of Petitions to Parliament. He outlined the difficulty of finding them and thought that he could only transcribe 'five or six petitions per diem' and he himself 'cannot hope to give more than two months a year to work in the Record Office'. It would therefore take him five or six years to produce the quantity needed for an edited volume.[12]

The overwhelming nature, fascination and difficulty of the materials he was dealing with is well illustrated in several lectures as well as his letters. He was offered the Regius Professorship of History by Balfour in 1902 and turned it down. His official reason to Balfour was that 'For some time I have been compelled to do very little work and to absent myself from England for some months every winter. Twice I have offered to resign the professorship that I hold . . .'[13] But there were other reasons, explained after attending the inaugural of J.B. Bury who was appointed. 'The Regius Professor of Modern History is expected to speak to the world at large and even if I had anything to say to the W. at L. I don't think that I should like full houses and the limelight.' This again shows his reticence, but in the next sentence he showed where his real passion lay.

> So I go back to the Year Books. Really they are astonishing. I copy and translate for some hours every day and shall only have scratched the surface if I live to the age of Methusalem – but if I last a year or two longer I shall be a 'dab' at real actions. It was a wonderful game as intricate as chess and not like chess cosmopolitan. Unravelling it is an amusement not unlike that of turning the insides out of ancient comedies I guess.[14]

He was also increasingly ill. We are told that in the summer of 1887, aged 37, he was already seriously unwell. 'This was the first recorded attack of the tuberculosis which, together with diabetes, was to make the rest of his life precarious . . .' Thus in 1889 he wrote to Vinogradoff: 'I very much want to see you again and I don't know that I can wait for another year: this I say rather seriously and *only to you*. Many things are telling me that I have not got unlimited time at my command and I have to take things very easily.'[15] From 1898 he had to winter in the Canaries, carrying any books or copies of manuscripts with him to work on. He died prematurely of pneumonia on 20 December 1906, aged 56. During the 22 years of full production he transformed our understanding of the early history of England and solved many of the puzzles which his great predecessors had left only partially resolved.

*

So Maitland set out to probe deeply into the previous 1,000 years of English history. Yet the task seemed overwhelming. Glimpses of his working methods are shown in relation to the great *History of English Law*. On 24 November 1889 he wrote to Bigelow, 'Yes, Pollock and I have mapped out a big work, too big I fear for the residue of our joint lives and the life of the survivor. Vol. I. is to bring things down to the end of Henry III. I am already struggling with a chapter on tenure but cannot make progress for the ground is full of unsuspected pitfalls.'[16] A few months later, on 23 March 1890, he had already realized that Pollock was not going to be much help and he felt even more overwhelmed:

> I have been plunged for some months past in a big job. Pollock and I had a hope of turning out a historical book, but I am not sure now that he will be able to give his time, and if that be so I shall hardly get very much done in my lifetime. However, I have set to work on the more public side on the law of cent. XII and XIII, and am struggling with tenures and scutages and such like ... Some day I hope to get free of tenures and villeinage and so on, and to tackle the pure private law of ownership, possession etc ... I hope that this time may come; but have my doubts – for the topic of 'Jurisdiction' stares me in the face and looks even more threatening than 'Land Tenure'.[17]

On 18 October 1890 he wrote to Pollock:

> And now I will write about the size of our book. I go on writing and writing, for I have so arranged my lectures that I have little else to do. Thus matter accumulates at a great rate. I know that some of it deals with rather minute points; but the more I see of cents. XII and XIII the more convinced am I that their legal history must be written afresh with full proof of every point.[18]

At this stage he envisaged two volumes, one on public, one on private law. Among the subjects in the former would be 'our say about the genesis of feudalism. This means a great pile of stuff. For example, for six weeks past I have had "juristic persons" on my mind, have been grubbing for the English evidence and reading the Germans, in particular Gierke's great book (it is a splendid thing though G. is too metaphysical).'[19] He concluded that 'Tenure is practically finished. A large part of Jurisdiction is written but requires re-arrangement. In Status I have done the baron, the knight, the unfree. I am prepared to deal with monks and the clergy, and have opinions about corporations. Aliens will not take me long but Jews I have hardly yet thought.'[20] Thus within a year of starting he had written about 200 pages of the most difficult part of volume I.

On 29 May 1892 he wrote to Vinogradoff,

with me the matter stands thus – F.P., who is now in the West Indies and may go to India in the winter, has written an Anglo-Saxon chapter. *Between ourselves* I do not like it very much, partly because it will make it very difficult for me to say anything about A-S law in any later part of the book. My effort now is to shove on with the general sketch of the Norman and Angevin periods so that my collaborator may have little to do before we reach the Year Book period – if we ever reach it. So I am half inclined to throw aside all that I have written – it is a pretty heavy mass – about Domesday and the A-S books.[21]

In July 1894 Maitland explained in detail how he had gradually taken over the writing of the whole work:

The original scheme would have divided the work into approximately equal shares – but I soon discovered – that I wanted one thing while my yoke-fellow wanted another . . . the discrepancy was but slowly borne in upon me and, when it was becoming apparent, I pushed on my work in order that as much as possible might be done in the way which – rightly or wrongly – I like . . . you see therefore that I cannot accuse him [F. Pollock] of not doing his fair share, for I did not want him to do it. What I have always been fearing was not that he would get any credit that would belong to me but that he would take chapters out of my hand.[22]

The contract with the University Press was made with Maitland alone.

The two great volumes seem to have been written by the end of 1894, despite his work as editor of many other works alongside them, and in the preface of 21 February 1895 it was stated that

The present work has filled much of our time and thoughts for some years. We send it forth, however, well knowing that in many parts of our field we have accomplished, at most, a preliminary exploration. Oftentimes our business has been rather to quarry and hew for some builder of the future than to leave a finished building. But we have endeavoured to make sure, so far as our will and power can go, that when this day comes he shall have facts and not fictions to build with.

A separate note by Pollock stated that 'It is proper for me to add for myself that, although the book was planned in common and has been revised by both of us, by far the greatest share of the execution belongs to Mr. Maitland, both as to the actual writing and as to the detailed research which was constantly required.'[23]

*

Maitland developed a particular way of writing through which he might explore and explain the immensely complex interconnections of English history through the centuries. The style is one of our clues to the man, so it is worth pausing for a moment on this. G.O. Sayles tried to summarize it thus: 'As an artist in words, Maitland followed no conventions and is himself inimitable . . . He seems to take the reader into his confidence and to converse with him, charming him with his exquisite sense of the perfect word and phrase, the happy epigrams; his gay humour.'[24] In a section on Maitland's way of writing and style, Zutshi provides some important clues. He writes that 'Maitland's style is so individual, compelling, seductive and, at times, beautiful that many of those who have written about him have drawn attention to it.' The 'conversational quality' is partly explained by the fact that 'As he composed sentence and paragraph for book or lecture, he said the words aloud so that he might hear as well as see them.' He wrote 'as if he were speaking'.[25] He is said to have invariably written standing at the lectern which is still preserved at Downing College, Cambridge.

This last point is particularly interesting. All his writing has the quality of directness, simplicity and elegance, as if the author were talking in his ordinary voice. The fact that Maitland wrote as if he were trying to explain complex matters to an audience of undergraduates, and the fact that a lectern is confined so that one has to put the mass of data in one's notes to one side and concentrate on the central issues, is significant. Maitland himself explained his method to Lord Acton: 'According to my habit I made a rush at it, writing chiefly from memory, in order that I might see the general outlines of my chapter.'[26] Thus he wrote 'fast, and with relish, in a sinewy style that has engaged generations of readers' producing 're-creations of medieval life that convinced by their range, coherence and imaginative zest'.[27] His style and genius in writing is well captured by one of his foremost disciples, K.B. McFarlane: 'Here was a writer who could be highly technical and a delight to read, a fine artist with a powerful analytical mind and a remarkable flair for the concrete instance that made the past live.' In his later writings, 'There was the same learning, weighty but winged, the sparkle, the lucidity, the same sureness of finger in disentangling historical knots.' Thus in his twenty years of writing there are few pages which 'do not bear the stamp of Maitland's highly individual and, it would seem, effortless genius. He wrote like a brilliant talker; we are told that his talk was brilliant and that his public speeches were long remembered and quoted.'[28]

A little of the quality of his lectures is captured by one of those who attended them:

> Maitland lectured on English law . . . as though he were some saintly medieval monk reciting the miracles of his order. His tall gaunt figure was restless with animation; his voice would . . . pass into a sort of liturgic rhythm as he completed his outline of some large cycle of legal development . . . Yet even at a moment of what seemed genuine enthusiasm . . . a sudden shaft of humour would flash into the lecture and, though the tense face hardly relaxed, the eyes in an instant were all play . . .[29]

The editors of a set of his lectures on 'Equity' described how 'Those who heard them delivered – amongst whom we are – with all Maitland's gaiety, and with all his charm of manner and his power of making dry bones live, will not easily forget either the lectures or the lecturer.'[30]

The freshness of the lecturing and writing also undoubtedly lay in the fact that Maitland was always exploring new subjects, explaining them as much to himself as to his audience, thinking aloud in another's presence. History particularly interested him since he knew so little about it until quite late in his life. In another letter to Lord Acton who had asked him to write a chapter on sixteenth-century religion for the *Cambridge Modern History*, he explained his innocence and ignorance, the basis of his curiosity and wonder. Maitland wrote that he would try to do so, 'though you may guess a good deal, you can not know the depth of my ignorance – I have hardly so much as heard that there was a Queen Elizabeth. Until I was thirty years old and upwards I rarely looked at a history – except histories of philosophy, which don't count – and since then I have only "mugged up", as the undergraduates say, one subject after another which happened to interest me.'[31]

Maitland's work has often been likened to a piece of music. It is difficult to describe this, but one example of the tribute to his mind and style by his greatest legal historian contemporary and friend, Paul Vinogradoff, captures something of the effect: 'In every special case, in the treatment of any great doctrine, or institution, or epoch, Maitland has a manner of starting with disconcerting critical observations and of noticing at the outset contradictions and confusion, but then he feels his way, as it were, like a musician running his fingers over the keys in an improvised prelude, towards leading ideas and harmonious combinations.' Hence numerous apparently dry and difficult subjects become 'curiously attractive through the reflection of a kind of organic process in the mind of the scholar creating order and sense in the midst of confusion'.[32] It is not difficult to think of Bach, Handel or even Maitland's beloved Wagner, after whom he named his daughters Ermengard and Fredegond.

Maitland was a very private person. Although a number of biographical studies have been written about him, and though two volumes of his letters have been published, it is not easy to obtain a picture of Maitland the man. We know of his 'gaiety' in lecturing. From the lives and letters he appears to be an upright, moral man. He was Liberal in politics; an early advocate of degrees for women at Cambridge, agnostic in religion; committed above all to his family, friends and students. He was clearly deeply loved by his family. He was a workaholic and may have suffered a mental breakdown and contemplated suicide.[33] Thin and increasingly emaciated, he was frugal and energetic. To learn more about him we have to examine his voluminous writings.

Theoretical methodology

We have seen that one of Maitland's deepest interests was in the development of liberty. In pursuing this topic his training as a lawyer was obviously central and links him to his illustrious ancestors, Montesquieu, Adam Smith and Tocqueville. 'He had an unerring instinct for seeing the pattern behind a mass of details and the skill to weave the facts once linked into a persuasive case.' Furthermore, as S.F.C. Milsom writes, 'I am also pretty sure that the extraordinary immediacy of Maitland's writing has to do with his background as a lawyer and law teacher . . . A main ingredient is the habit of bringing situations to life in terms of the dialogues of real people.'[34] It seems likely that there was more to the legal training than this, for as in the other cases, it gave him that ability to see into the very essence or structure of things, to approach them in a *relational* way, seeing the balance of forces, to be able to measure the facts against an ideal-type model. Like Montesquieu, Smith and Tocqueville, he combined induction and deduction. Few had so many new 'facts' at their disposal and he clearly had an immensely good memory. Yet he shaped the facts into new imaginative patterns through inspiration. He took nothing for granted and questioned everything. Thus with his brilliance, energy and insight he created a new paradigm, or rather completed the one which had begun with Montesquieu.

His approach was both holistic and relational, treating all the different aspects of the past within one framework. By 'envisaging the history of English law as an aspect of the whole stream of English life he brought legal history into close relationship to political, constitutional, social, economic and religious history'.[35] In fact, what he did was to see that by taking law, the central English institution, as the thread he could show the *relations* between all the different features of English society. He concentrated on the medieval period, but lectured and taught on the whole period from the Anglo-Saxons to the nineteenth century. He was thus able to provide the first great, document-based, analysis of the patterns or spirit of English culture over the 1,000 years leading up to the industrial revolution.

Maitland's aim was to understand the development of later Victorian wealth and liberty. He was convinced that the answer lay buried in the mounds of hitherto unused legal records:

> Think for a moment what lies concealed within the hard rind of legal history. Legal documents, documents of the most technical kind, are the best, often the only evidence that we have for social and economic history, for the history of morality, for the history of practical religion. Take a broad subject – the condition of the great mass of Englishmen in the later middle ages, the condition of the villagers. That might be pictured for us in all truthful detail; its political, social, economic, moral aspects might all be brought out; every tendency of progress or degradation might be traced; our supply of evidence is inexhaustible . . .[36]

Or again he wrote more briefly: 'speaking broadly we may say that only in legal documents and under legal forms are the social and economic arrangement of remote times made visible to us.'[37]

Yet the difficulties were immense. There was the obvious fact that the hand-writing, the dog latin and law-french, the abstruse forms of procedure and technical terms all had to be mastered, requiring immense dedication and energy. He had not only to read the documents, but reconstruct a largely vanished world-view in order to understand them. This was particularly the case in certain branches of law which had faded out. For instance, in relation to the ecclesiastical court records, as he described:

> A detailed history of our ecclesiastical courts is at present impossible. Very few attempts have been made to put into print the records out of which that history must be wrung. They are voluminous . . . Those who achieved the task would have to learn much that has not been taught in England during the past three centuries and, it may be, to unlearn a good deal that has been taught too often.[38]

Related to this was the problem of anachronism. Here Maitland introduced one of his key concepts, the idea that one should write history both backwards and forwards. It is worth quoting the passage fully both as an example of his style and also his realization of the aims and the dangers of historical reconstruction. He pointed out that '[t]he history of law must be a history of ideas. It must represent, not merely what men have done and said, but what men have thought in bygone ages. The task of reconstructing ancient ideas is hazardous and can only be accomplished little by little. If we are in a hurry to get to the beginning we shall miss the path.' In particular, one had to beware of intellectual anachronism.

> Against many kinds of anachronism we now guard ourselves. We are careful of costume, of armour and architecture, of words and forms of speech. But it is far easier to be careful of these things than to prevent the intrusion of untimely ideas. In particular there lies a besetting danger for us in the barbarian's use of a language which is too good for his thought. Mistakes then are easy, and when committed they will be fatal and fundamental mistakes. If, for example, we introduce the *persona ficta* too

soon, we shall be doing worse than if we armed Hengest and Horsa with machine guns or pictured the Venerable Bede correcting proofs for the press; we shall have built upon a crumbling foundation.

How could one avoid this danger? 'The most efficient method of protecting ourselves against such errors is that of reading our history backwards as well as forwards, of making sure of our middle ages before we talk about the "archaic", of accustoming our eyes to the twilight before we go out into the night.'[39]

If one were successful, one might achieve the ultimate goal of imaginative reconstruction, that is to say the revealing of other worlds and other times, not just a distorted reflection of our own. Not only, for example, will the 'villages and hundreds which the Norman clerks tore into shreds' be 'reconstituted and pictured in maps', but 'Above all, by slow degrees the thoughts of our forefathers, their common thoughts about common things, will have become thinkable once more.'[40]

Another aspect of this anachronism or bias was caused by the historian's own convictions and often unexamined political orientation. Maitland recognized this when he wrote, for example, that 'the English believer in "free communities" would very probably be a conservative, I don't mean a Tory or an aristocrat, but a conservative'. 'On the other hand with us the man who has the most splendid hopes for the masses is very likely to see in the past nothing but the domination of the classes. Of course this is no universal truth – but it comes in as a disturbing element.'[41] Since Maitland became deeply immersed, as we shall see, in questions of 'free village communities', as well as liberty and equality, it is important that he recognized the problem and that we remember his pedigree and inspiration from Tocqueville by way of Mill and Sidgwick.

Another key was to start in the right place, to find the essence of the structure. This was Maitland's equivalent to Tocqueville's comprehension of the American pattern when he realized that equality was the starting point from which everything else flows. For Maitland, it was the understanding of the medieval concept of tenure which unlocked the rest:

In any body of law we are likely to find certain ideas and rules that may be described as elementary. Their elementary character consists in this, that we must master them if we are to make further progress in our study; if we begin elsewhere, we are likely to find that we have begun at the wrong place . . . as regards the law of the feudal times we can hardly do wrong in turning to the law of land tenure as being its most elementary part.[42]

Not elementary in the sense of simple, for it was immensely complex, but elementary in the sense of basic. For Maitland was also well aware that there was no correlation between 'elementary' or early forms and simplicity:

> Too often we allow ourselves to suppose that, could we get back to the beginning, we should find that all was intelligible and should then be able to watch the process whereby simple ideas were smothered under subtleties and technicalities. But it is not so. Simplicity is the outcome of technical subtlety; it is the goal, not the starting point. As we go backwards the familiar outlines become blurred; the ideas become fluid, and instead of the simple we find the indefinite.[43]

A further key lay in placing England in a comparative perspective. As Maitland wrote: 'History involves comparison, and the English lawyer who knew nothing and cared nothing for any system but his own hardly came in sight of the idea of legal history.'[44] Maitland's knowledge of German and French law was very extensive and he was deeply knowledgeable about Roman law.[45] Thus, like his great predecessors, he was able to see clearly what was unusual and what was in common in the English case. He was certainly no 'Little Englander', and, as Patrick Wormald notes, 'would bend over backwards to disabuse Englishmen of misplaced faith in the uniqueness of their Island Story'.[46] On the other hand, as we shall see, if he felt that England was different, he did not shrink from saying so.

*

One of the most difficult tasks for a historian is to balance change and continuity and it is in this theoretical area that we can learn most from Maitland. From Montesquieu to Tocqueville there had been a feeling that England had witnessed a peculiarly continuous and increasingly unusual history by the standards of the rest of Europe. To what extent did Maitland also find a continuity in the structure, and to what extent was there some kind of dramatic revolution in the early modern period? In Maitland's many works we look in vain for any sign of a belief that a vast and revolutionary change had occurred at some specific point in English history, dividing off 'medieval' from 'modern' England. Instead, his view that the legal and social structure of England, in its basic principles, was already laid down by the thirteenth century is shown in many passages.

By the death of Henry II (1271), 'English law is modern in its uniformity, its simplicity, its certainty.'[47] Lawyers from the fourteenth century onwards believed that 'the great outlines of criminal law and private law seem to have been regarded as fixed for all time. In the twentieth century students of law will still for practical purposes be compelled to know a good deal about the statutes of Edward I.'[48] This continuity, he believed, had been of great advantage to English historians, setting them off from those of continental nations where it had not occurred.

> So continuous has been our English legal life during the last six centuries, that the law of the later middle ages has never been forgotten among us. It has never passed utterly outside the cognizance of our courts and our practising lawyers. We have never had to disinter and reconstruct it in that laborious and tentative manner in which German historians of the present day have disinterred and reconstructed the law of medieval Germany.[49]

This continuity is shown in the treatment of particular subjects. For instance, when analysing the forms of action at common law, Maitland took the period 1307–1833 as one period. He admitted that this was 'enormously long', yet wrote: 'I do not know that for our present purpose it could be well broken up into sub-periods.'[50]

The most important area was property law. Here were the deepest continuities. This 'most salient trait', the 'calculus of estates which, even in our own day, is perhaps the most distinctive feature of English private law', Maitland thought very old. It had been a characteristic for six centuries, having taken a 'definite shape' in the second half of the thirteenth century, drawing on much older customs. This continuity was not merely to be found in the Common Law, which was 'one of the toughest things ever made'. In his *Constitutional History of England*, which covered the period from Anglo-Saxon England up to the 1880s, Maitland made no substantial modifications to Stubbs's general vision of continuity. For instance, he wrote:

'take any institution that exists at the end of the Middle Ages, any that exists in 1800 – be it parliament, or privy council, or any of the courts of law – we can trace it back through a series of definite changes as far as Edward's reign.'[51] It was because English constitutional and legal principles had been laid down so early that in the *History of English Law* he did not take the story beyond the thirteenth century.

Maitland's research did not just go back to the twelfth century. He was deeply knowledgeable about the Anglo-Saxon period. In his lectures on the *Constitutional History of England* he stressed the continuity between Anglo-Saxon and late eleventh-century England. He explains that though the Norman Conquest was of great importance, we 'must not suppose that English law was swept away or superseded by Norman law. We must not suppose that the Normans had any compact body of laws to bring with them. They can have had but very little if any written law of their own; in this respect they were far behind the English.'[52] After all, 'They were an aristocracy of Scandinavian conquerors ruling over a body of Romance-speaking Celts.' Thus, we 'must not therefore think of William as bringing with him a novel system of jurisprudence.'[53] Maitland then shows in detail how little changed in the legal framework until the mid-twelfth century. After all, William merely came to England, as he claimed, as the rightful heir to Edward the Confessor, 'William succeeded to Edward's position.'[54] Thus the 'valuable thing that the Norman Conquest gives us is a strong kingship which makes for national unity'.[55]

This view of the continuity of English law over the Norman invasion was not undermined by the next ten years of Maitland's research and was repeated in the *History of English Law*. He describes how it is only very slowly that the consequences of the Norman invasion came to be felt. 'Indeed if we read our history year by year onwards from 1066, it will for a long time seem doubtful whether in the sphere of law the Conquest is going to produce any large changes. The Normans in England are not numerous. King William shows no desire to impose upon his new subjects any foreign code. There is no Norman code.'[56] Thus 'we may safely say that William did not intend to sweep away English law and put Norman law in its stead. On the contrary, he decreed that all men were to have and hold the law of King Edward – that is to say, the old English law ... So far as we know, he expressly legislated about very few matters.'[57] Undoubtedly, the 'conquest, the forfeiture, the redistribution of the land gave to the idea of holding land from others a dominance that it could not obtain elsewhere', but this was an unintended consequence, as was that of the germ of the idea of the jury system which Maitland thought came from France.[58] But in general, as he shows in detail, the Normans and Angevins built on and then adapted, simplified, strengthened an earlier tradition of Anglo-Saxon laws.[59]

Maitland, in fact, managed to capture the mixture of continuity with change over the 700 years up to the time in which he was writing:

> Hardly a rule remains unaltered, and yet the body of law that now lives among us is the same body that Blackstone described in the eighteenth century, Coke in the seventeenth, Littleton in the fifteenth, Bracton in the thirteenth, Glanvill in the twelfth. This continuity, this identity, is very real to us if we know that for the last seven hundred years all the judgments of the courts at Westminster have been recorded, and that for the most part they can still be read . . . eventful though its life may have been, it has had but a single life.[60]

Maitland follows the trail back to the edge of the 'German woods'.

> Beyond these seven centuries there lie six other centuries that are but partially and fitfully lit, and in one of them a great catastrophe, the Norman Conquest, befell England and the law of England. However, we never quite lose the thread of the story. Along one path or another we can trace back the footprints, which have their starting-place in some settlement of wild Germans who are invading the soil of Roman provinces, and coming in contact with the civilization of the old world. Here the trail stops, the dim twilight becomes darkness; we pass from an age in which men seldom write their laws to one in which they cannot write at all. Beyond lies the realm of guesswork.[61]

It is this which 'gives to English legal history a singular continuity from Alfred's day to our own'.[62]

In lectures which constituted the *Constitutional History of England* Maitland described the early Anglo-Saxon law codes in England. Those of Ethelbert in about 600 'seem to be the earliest laws ever written in any Teutonic tongue'. It was already far from 'primitive', being influenced by Christianity. The later law codes of Ine in 690 and Alfred in about 890 'show us that during the last two centuries there had been no great change in the character of law or the legal structure of society'.[63] From then there was a continuous set of laws up to the Norman conquest. If we look at these, one thing is very clear, 'namely that the influence of Roman jurisprudence was hardly felt', even though the influence of Christianity was present, for example in the introduction of the written will.[64] Then came the Normans, 'a race whose distinguishing characteristic seems to have been a wonderful power of adapting itself to circumstances, of absorbing into its own life the best and strongest institutions of whichever race it conquered . . .'[65]

Thus the earlier Germanic invaders probably introduced the important division into 'hundreds'[66] and the central concept of feudalism, namely the loyalty to a chief. Maitland argues that the 'personal relation between land and man which is one ingredient of feudalism, is indeed old; we may see it in the first pages of the history of our race. It can be traced to the relation between the German *princeps* [prince] and his *comites* [counts] described by Tacitus'.[67] This developed into the territorial Anglo-Saxon thegn, and the principle expands so that 'This relation of man and lord we find in all parts of the social structure.'[68] Furthermore, while 'Nothing, I believe is more of the essence of all that we mean when we talk of feudalism than the private court – a court which can be inherited and sold along with land', 'jurisdiction, the right to hold courts, had been passing into private hands' for 'some time before the Norman Conquest'.[69] He suggested that 'in the eighth or even in the seventh century' there were in England people who had jurisdiction within their territories' and that 'a royal grant of land in the ninth and tenth centuries generally included, and this as a matter of "common form", a grant of jurisdiction'.[70] Thus in conclusion, 'The facts of feudalism seem to be there – what is wanting is a theory which shall express those facts. That came to us from Normandy.'[71]

Ten years later, in the *History of English Law*, Maitland had not changed his views on the basically Germanic origins of English law. The law that prevailed in England before the Norman Conquest was 'in our opinion . . . in the main pure Germanic law.'[72] Thus 'Coming to the solid ground of known history, we find that our laws have been formed in the main from a stock of Teutonic customs, with some additions of matter, and considerable additions or modifications of form received directly or indirectly from the Roman system.'[73] The original Anglo-Saxon impetus was increased by later waves of other Teutonic sources. 'Now each of these Germanic strains, the purely Anglo-Saxon, the Scandinavian, the Frankish' was important, and it is difficult to measure their relative influence.[74] Thus the picture that is painted fits very well with that of Maitland's predecessors. There are Montesquieu's early Germanic roots. There is Tocqueville's 'prodigious similarity', earlier than Tocqueville argues, namely in the eleventh century between England and northern France. Maitland's vision is balanced, providing both a picture of continuity and change, similarity and difference. The early Germanic origins are particularly important, as we shall see, for Maitland was able to show that Germanic law and social structure contained unusual attitudes towards property and family relations.

In this vision of a mixture of continuity and change, Maitland explicitly attacked the increasingly dominant evolutionary paradigm of the post-Darwinian era, which, perverting Darwin's central ideas, suggested a set of necessary 'stages' through which all societies had to move. The rejection of this framework helps to explain how he followed the undogmatic and open-minded tradition of Montesquieu, Smith and Tocqueville. In his *History of English Law* he writes that

> To suppose that the family law of every nation must needs traverse the same route, this is an unwarrantable hypothesis. To construct some fated scheme of successive stages which shall comprise every arrangement that may yet be discovered among backward peoples, this is a hopeless task. A not unnatural inference from their backwardness would be that somehow or another they have wandered away from the road along which the more successful races have made their journey.[75]

He explicitly rejected a unilineal, or single set of stages, of progress, the late nineteenth-century gospel, writing, for instance, in relation to the question of women's status in society that he could not start the investigation 'until we have protested against the common assumption that in this region a great generalization must needs be possible, and that from the age of savagery until the present age every change in marital law has been favourable to the wife'.[76]

Maitland's central attack on the doctrine of evolutionary stages comes in *Domesday Book*. He points out that the anthropologists of the time are divided on the question, but

Even had our anthropologists at their command materials that would justify them in prescribing a normal programme for the human race and in decreeing that every independent portion of mankind must, if it is to move at all, move through one fated series of stages which may be designated as Stage A, Stage B, Stage C and so forth, we still should have to face the fact that the rapidly progressive groups have been just those which have not been independent, which have not worked out their own salvation, but have appropriated alien ideas and have thus been enabled, for anything that we can tell, to leap from Stage A to Stage X without passing through any intermediate stages. Our Anglo-Saxon ancestors did not arrive at the alphabet, or at the Nicene Creed, by traversing a long series of 'stages'; they leapt to the one and to the other.[77]

He continued:

in truth we are learning that the attempt to construct a normal programme for all portions of mankind is idle and unscientific. For one thing, the number of portions that we can with any plausibility treat as independent is very small. For another, such is the complexity of human affairs and such their interdependence that we can not hope for scientific laws which will formulate a sequence of stages in any one province of man's activity. We can not, for instance, find a law which deals only with political and neglects proprietary arrangements, or a law which deals only with property and neglects religion. So soon as we penetrate below the surface, each of the cases whence we would induce our law begins to look extremely unique, and we shall hesitate long before we fill up the blanks that occur in the history of one nation by institutions and processes that have been observed in some other quarter. If we are in haste to drive the men of every race past all the known 'stages', if we force our reluctant forefathers through agnatic *gentes* [groups based on the male line] and house-communities and the rest of it, our normal programme for the human race is like to become a grotesque assortment of odds and ends.[78]

What alternative model of change, then, can Maitland offer? He does not usually address the problem directly, but often indicates obliquely how one might use an organic growth model, yet without any *necessity* for things to have occurred in a certain way. An illustration of this approach is shown in his treatment of one of the central and enduring features of English history, the system of local government. Maitland writes that 'Certainly, to any one who has an eye for historic greatness it is a very marvellous institution, this Commission of the Peace, growing so steadily, elaborating itself into ever new forms, providing for ever new wants, expressing ever new ideas, and yet never losing its identity . . . we shall hardly find any other political entity which has had so eventful and yet so perfectly continuous a life.'[79] Maitland describes here, in a delicate balance, both 'newness' and 'identity' over time, an institution whose history is both 'eventful' and yet 'continuous'. Such an approach allows us the flexibility to admit that by a strange paradox things can both remain the same and also change.

The effect of this approach was to make it possible to examine both continuity and change without being forced to project back a necessary course of 'stages'. For example, this dissolved the 'great break' theory of the change between the thirteenth and nineteenth centuries. In Maitland's hands the supposed structural transformation between a 'feudal/peasant' 'stage' of English history, which then was replaced by a 'modern/capitalist' stage through the 'revolution' of the sixteenth and seventeenth century evaporated. He pushed back the deeper structural continuity to the thirteenth century and earlier. He thus documented and expanded Tocqueville's insight that England was a quite 'modern' society by the seventeenth century by showing how it was similarly 'modern' back to the thirteenth century and before.

4
Power and Property

The unusual nature of English feudalism

The crucial period for the Enlightenment theories concerning the divergence of England from much of continental Europe was between the tenth and fifteenth centuries. This is the classic period when European feudalism gradually turned into something else. Thus if we are to understand Maitland's solution to the question of how modern English society emerged, we have to follow him into a fairly technical discussion of the nature and peculiarity of English feudalism and how it differed from that of its continental neighbours. Although this is complex, it is at the heart of his analysis. He shows the peculiar nature of the arrangement which emerged on this island, both centralized and decentralized, and he explains how this happened. By taking part of the feudal tie to its logical extreme, England benefited from great cohesion; by devolving power to the locality the country enjoyed flexibility and a certain amount of proto-democracy. Thus Maitland explains in detail what Tocqueville, Maine and others had only guessed and sketched out.

Maitland first lamented the difficulty of defining feudalism: 'the impossible task that has been set before the word *feudalism* is that of making a single idea represent a very large piece of the world's history, represent the France, Italy, Germany, England, of every century from the eighth or ninth to the fourteenth or fifteenth.'[1] The result is confusion. Maitland attempted to clarify the situation. The central feature of feudalism was the strange mixture of ownership, the relationship between the economic and political. The *fee* or *beneficium* was

45

a gift of land made by the king out of his own estate, the grantee coming under a special obligation to be faithful ... To express the rights thus created, a set of technical terms was developed:- the beneficiary or feudatory holds the land of his lord, the grantor – *A tenet terram de B*. The full ownership (*dominium*) of the land is as it were broken up between A and B; or again, for the feudatory may grant out part of the land to be held of him, it may be broken up between A, B, and C, C holding of B and B of A, and so on, *ad infinitum*.[2]

Maitland believed that 'the most remarkable characteristic of feudalism' was the fact that 'several different persons, in somewhat different senses, may be said to have and to hold the same piece of land'.[3] But there are other equally characteristic and essential features. In some mysterious way power and property have been merged. Feudalism is not just a landholding system, but also a system of government. While many have seen 'the introduction of military tenures' as the 'establishment of the feudal system', in fact, when 'compared with seignorial justice, military tenure is a superficial matter, one out of many effects rather than a deep seated cause'.[4] He describes as 'that most essential element of feudalism, jurisdiction in private hands, the lord's court'.[5] The merging of power and property, of public and private, is well shown elsewhere in Maitland's work.[6]

It is worth quoting one of his definitions in full. Feudalism is

A state of society in which the main bond is the relation between lord and man, a relation implying on the lord's part protection and defence; on the man's part protection, service and reverence, the service including service in arms. This personal relation is inseparably involved in a proprietary relation, the tenure of land – the man holds lands of the lord, the man's service is a burden on the land, the lord has important rights in the land, and (we may say) the full ownership of the land is split up between man and lord. The lord has jurisdiction over his men, holds courts for them, to which they owe suit. Jurisdiction is regarded as property, as a private right which the lord has over his land. The national organization is a system of these relationships: at the head there stands the king as lord of all, below him are his immediate vassals, or tenants in chief, who again are lords of tenants, who again may be lords of tenants, and so on, down to the lowest possessor of land. Lastly, as every other court consists of the lord's tenants, so the king's court consists of his tenants in chief, and so far as there is any constitutional control over the king it is exercised by the body of these tenants.[7]

Maitland stressed that English 'feudalism', though originating from a common ancestor, had developed into something peculiar and different by at least the twelfth century. He commented that 'we have learnt to see vast differences as well as striking resemblances, to distinguish countries and to distinguish times' when we discuss feudalism. Thus 'if we now speak of the feudal system, it should be with a full understanding that the feudalism of France differs radically from the feudalism of England, that the feudalism of the thirteenth is very different from that of the eleventh century.' For England, 'it is quite possible to maintain that of all countries England was the most, or for the matter of that the least, feudalized.'[8] The paradox is resolved when we remember that there are two central criteria whereby we measure feudalism. In terms of land law, England was the most perfectly feudalized of societies. All tenures were feudal. Maitland wrote, 'in so far as feudalism is mere property law, England is of all countries the most perfectly feudalized.'[9] Thus: 'Owing to the Norman Conquest one part of the theory was carried out in this country with consistent and unexampled rigour; every square inch of land was brought within the theory of tenure: English real property law becomes a law of feudal tenures. In France, in Germany, allodial owners might be found: not one in England.'[10] For instance, the 'absolute and uncompromising form of primogeniture which prevails in England belongs, not to feudalism in general, but to a highly centralized feudalism, in which the king has not much to fear from the power of his mightiest vassals ...'[11] Thus, in terms of tenure, England was the most feudal of societies.

On the other hand, in the even more important sphere of public and private law and political power, that is, in terms of government, England went in a peculiar direction, towards some centralization of power, rather than the dissolution of the state. Maitland points out that 'our public law does not become feudal; in every direction the force of feudalism is limited and checked by other ideas; the public rights, the public duties of the Englishman are not conceived and cannot be conceived as the mere outcome of feudal compacts between man and lord'.[12] Maitland outlines the major features of this limitation of public feudalism. 'First and fore-most, it never becomes law that there is no political bond between men save the bond of tenure ... whenever homage or fealty was done to any mesne lord, the tenant expressly saved the faith that he owed to his lord the king.'[13] Thus a man who fights for his lord against the king is not doing his feudal duty; he is committing treason. Over-mighty subjects could not draw on justification from this system. This point is so important that Maitland elaborates it in various ways.

'English law never recognizes that any man is bound to fight *for* his lord. The sub-tenant who holds by military service is bound by his tenure to fight for the king; he is bound to follow his lord's banner, but only in the national army: – he is in nowise bound to espouse his lord's quarrels, least of all his quarrels with the king. Private war never becomes legal – it is a crime and a breach of the peace.'[14] A 'man can hardly "go against" anyone at his lord's com-mand ... without being guilty of "felony"'. As Maitland wrote, 'Common law, royal and national law, has, as it were, occupied the very citadel of feudalism.'[15] To bring out the full peculiarity of this, Maitland tells us, 'you should look at the history of France; there it was definitely regarded as law that in a just quarrel the vassal must follow his immediate lord, even against the king'.[16] In England, 'military service is due to none but the king; this it is which makes English feudalism a very different thing from French feudalism'.[17]

There are a number of other differences which make this central feature possible and flow from it. In England there is an alternative army for the king, which helps to protect him against an over-dependence on his feudal tenants. 'Though the military tenures supply the king with an army, it never becomes law that those who are not bound by tenure need not fight. The old national force, officered by the sheriffs, does not cease to exist ... In this organization of the common folk under royal officers, there is all along a counterpoise to the military system of feudalism, and it serves the king well.'[18] Another source of strength for the centre is the fact that 'Taxation is not feudalized'. Maitland tells us that the 'king for a while is strong enough to tax the nation, to tax the sub-tenants, to get straight at the mass of the people, their lands and their goods, without the intervention of their lords.'[19] Thus he is not entirely dependent on powerful lords for soldiers or money.

Nor is he entirely dependent on them for advice. We are told that the King's Court (*Curia Regis*) 'never takes very definitely a feudal shape . . . It is much in the king's power to summon whom he will.'[20] Finally, the king is not forced to delegate judicial powers to the barons. 'The administration of justice is never completely feudalized. The old local courts are kept alive, and are not feudal assemblies.'[21] As a result of this the 'jurisdiction of the feudal courts is strictly limited; criminal jurisdiction they have none save by express royal grant, and the kings are on the whole chary of making such grants. Seldom, indeed, can any lord exercise more than what on the continent would have been considered justice of a very low degree.'[22] Starting with considerable power, the king 'rapidly extends the sphere of his own justice: before the middle of the thirteenth century his courts have practically become courts of first instance for the whole realm – from Henry II's day his itinerant justices have been carrying a common law through the land'.[23]

The contradiction is thus resolved. By taking one aspect of the feudal tie, the idea that each person is linked to the person above him, both in terms of tenure and power, to its logical limits, the English system developed into something peculiar. By the standards of Marc Bloch's French model of feudalism, England was the least feudal of countries. Looked at in another way, England was the ideal-typical feudal society, with an apex of both landholding and justice and power in the chief lord, and it was other feudal systems which, through the devolution of too much power, were defective. Both are tenable views.

What Maitland argued was as follows. Most of the important elements of feudalism were present in England before the Norman Conquest, in particular the superiority of the contractual relationship with a lord over the birth relationship with kin. Then for about a century after the Norman Conquest there was a real system of military tenures. 'Speaking roughly we may say that there is one century (1066–1166) in which the military tenures are really military . . .'[24] In this same period there are powerful local courts. This is the period when, though much more centralized, English and French 'feudalism' looked most alike. But after that the system moves away to that which is described above. By about 1266 at the latest 'the military organization which we call feudal has already broken down and will no longer provide either soldiers or money . . .' for the Crown.[25] Likewise, various devices are used to circumvent the feudal principle of separate courts for Lords.[26] 'Slowly but surely justice done in the king's name by men who are the king's servants becomes the most important kind of justice, reaches into the remotest corners of the land.'[27] Everything became permeated by centralized law, and a law which was in its turn permeated by the unusual concept of tenure, that is to say a contractual relationship of holding something or another by a non-blood relationship. Thus 'In the Middle Ages land law is the basis of all public law ... the judicial system is influenced by tenure, the parliamentary system is influenced by tenure.'[28]

Many great thinkers have concluded that the politico-economic relations are central to our puzzle. If Maitland is right that England developed an unusual form of centralized feudalism, building something unique on top of roots which were in themselves unusual and confined to western Europe, we would have found the key to some of the problems facing many of his intellectual predecessors.

Yet, like all mysteries, Maitland's answer just pushes the puzzle back further. If English feudalism was different, both in its nature and in how it evolved, why was this the case? Here we need to follow him into another fairly technical discussion, this time concerning the relationship between kinship and politics. The relations of institutions is the key to the mystery and one of the most powerful of these is the blending of kinship, power and property.

Kinship and property in England

Marc Bloch suggested that the development of feudalism in western Europe after the fall of Rome was linked to a peculiarly flexible and 'weak' kinship system. He wrote that kinship ties were 'by their very nature foreign to the human relations characteristic of feudalism.'[29] The 'relative weakness' of kinship in western Europe 'explains why there was feudalism at all'.[30] Or 'More precisely feudal ties proper were developed when those of kinship proved inadequate.'[31] His hypothesis is amply anticipated by Maitland's earlier account.

Maitland was well aware that the current anthropological orthodoxy, for instance in the work of Sir Henry Maine, was that all societies, including the Teutonic peoples, had gone through a period of agnatic kinship, that is, descent flowing through the male gender, leading to the formation of powerful clans or, as anthropologists call them, unilineal descent groups.[32] Yet detailed study of Tacitus and the codes of the Anglo-Saxons and other materials did not bear out this evolutionary sequence. Maitland first worked back to the thirteenth-century text of Bracton, which showed a system of tracing descent through both males and females which is identical to that which is used in England today.[33] He then took the analysis back to the Anglo-Saxon period. In a section on 'Antiquities' he showed that Anglo-Saxon kinship was bilateral or cognatic, tracing descent through both genders, and hence the formation of exclusive groups or clans, which could have been the basis for political and legal action, was impossible.

He pointed out that from the very earliest rules, we find that the blood-feud payments show that those who share the payment 'consist in part of persons related to him through his father, and in part of persons related to him through his mother'. Such a concept 'ties the child both to his father's brother and to his mother's brother' and hence 'a system of mutually exclusive clans is impossible, unless each clan is strictly endogamous'. As he puts it in a marginal note, 'No clans in England'.[34] Thus 'we ought not to talk of clans at all' for 'our English law does not contemplate the existence of a number of mutually exclusive units which can be enumerated and named; there were as many "blood-feud groups" as there were living persons.'[35] Such groups could not act as the bedrock of the politico-legal system. Whatever the earliest unrecorded history, 'What seems plain is that the exclusive domination of either "father-right" or "mother-right" ... should be placed for our race beyond the extreme limit of history.'[36] The absence of the patriarchal or patrilineal family, he argued, had nothing to do with Christianity – its emergence 'we certainly cannot ascribe to the influence of Christianity'.[37] The Germanic method of calculating descent through both male and female lines, preserved in England, was very different from the method of calculating through the male line alone, characteristic of the later Roman Empire even after the spread of Christianity.[38]

Two years later Maitland reiterated his central conclusion, namely that Anglo-Saxon kinship being cognatic could not provide the basis for political allegiances. Those who settled down in England at the fall of the Roman Empire may have been kinsmen,

> But (explain this how we will) the German system of kinship, which binds men together by the sacred tie of blood-feud, traces blood both through father and through mother, and therefore will not suffer a 'blood-feud-kin' to have either a local habitation or a name.

Thus the 'village community was not a *gens* [group based on the male line]. The bond of blood was sacred, but it did not tie the Germans into mutually exclusive clans.'[39]

As a number of subsequent anthropologists have confirmed, it is abundantly clear that as soon as the Anglo-Saxons appear in documented history, that is, from Tacitus' and Caesar's accounts of the first century AD, they appear to be tracing their descent simultaneously through the male and female line.[40] This made kinship, as Bloch had argued, too weak and fragmented to act as the basis for their legal and political system. Hence their development of elaborate alternatives through proto-feudalism, travelling judges and other devices.

Thus kinship did not provide the political infrastructure and hence, as both Maitland and Bloch argued, its weakness helped to create an environment in which the courts and the modern, territorial state could emerge out of 'feudalism'. Furthermore, its curiously fragmented nature had another important effect in relation to the economy and the subsequent development of an equally unusual system, to which we give the rough label of 'commercial capitalism'.

The essence of the property law in the majority of agrarian systems which we label 'peasant' is the link between the family and landed property. The 'domestic mode of production' is based on co-ownership by parents and children. All those born into a family have birthrights. They cannot be 'disinherited' for they are co-owners, members of a corporate group. The rise of individual ownership whereby parents or children have separate rights, is, as Marx and Weber rightly argued, the basis of modern capitalist property relations. It has often been thought that the destruction of familistic property rights occurred in England during a great transformation to capitalism from the later fifteenth century. For instance, Marx had argued that 'the legal view . . . that the landowner can do with the land what every owner of commodities can do with his commodities . . . arises . . . in the modern world only with the development of capitalist production.' Capitalism as a system 'transforms feudal landed property, clan property, small-peasant property' into modern, individualistic ownership.[41]

Maitland's work shows a striking absence of familistic ownership. In relation to freehold property, Maitland stated that 'In the thirteenth century the tenant in fee simple has a perfect right to disappoint his expectant heirs by conveying away the whole of his land by act *inter vivos* [between the living]. Our law is grasping the maxim *Nemo est heres viventis* [no one is the heir of a living person].'[42] Indeed, he believes 'that men were within an ace of obtaining such a power [i.e. of leaving real estate by will] in the middle of the thirteenth century.'[43] Although Glanvill produced some rather vague safeguards for the heir, Bracton in the thirteenth century omitted these and the King's Courts did not support a child's claim to any part of his parent's estates. The only major change between the thirteenth and sixteenth centuries was that, by the Statute of Wills in 1540, a parent could totally disinherit his heirs not only by sale or gift during his lifetime, but also by leaving a will devising the two-thirds of his freehold estate which did not go to his widow. The situation had in fact been formalized in the Statute *Quia Emptores* of 1290, which stated that 'from henceforth it shall be lawful for every freeman to sell at his own pleasure his land and tenements, or part of them . . .', with the exception of sales to the Church or other perpetual foundations.[44] In this crucial respect, English common law took a totally different direction from Continental law. As Maitland put it, 'Free alienation without the heir's consent will come in the wake of primogeniture. These two characteristics which distinguish our English law from her nearest of kin, the French customs, are closely connected . . . Abroad, as a general rule, the right of the expectant heir gradually assumed the shape of the *restrait lignager* [restraint of the line]. A landowner must not alienate his land without the consent of his expectant heirs unless it be a case of necessity, and even in a case of necessity, the heirs must have an opportunity of purchasing.'[45]

Thus by English common law children had no birthright and could be left penniless. Strictly speaking it is not even a matter of 'disinheritance'; a living man in the sixteenth century has no heirs, he has complete seisin or property. The only restriction is the right of his widow to one third of the real estate for life. A son, in effect, has no rights while his father lives and they are not co-owners in any sense. In the case of freehold real estate, in the sixteenth century the children had no automatic rights. The custom of primogeniture might give the eldest child greater rights than other children; but ultimately even the eldest son had nothing except at the wish of his father or mother, except where the inheritance had been formally specified by the artificial device of an entail. Even such entails could be broken quite easily in the sixteenth and seventeenth centuries.[46] As a result, as Chamberlayne put it in the seventeenth century, 'Fathers may give all their Estates un-intailed from their own children, and to any one child.'[47]

It would appear that 'Children had no stronger rights in the non-freehold property of their parents'.[48] This is particularly shown, as Maitland argues, in the absence of any *restrait lignager* in England, that is any custom that children could prevent their parents disposing of their property during their lifetime. The absence of this restraint is shown in numerous passages by Maitland.[49] He was puzzled by this unique feature, but in no doubt that it was present.[50] Even those restraints that there were, were probably not to keep land in the family.[51]

Another aspect of the oddity was the way in which inheritance worked. As Maitland explained:

> At the end of Henry III's reign [i.e. the 1270s] our common law of inheritance was rapidly assuming its final form. Its main outlines were those which are still familiar to us, and the more elementary of them may be thus stated:- The first class of persons called to the inheritance comprises the dead person's descendants; in other words, if he leaves an 'heir of his body', no other person will inherit.[52]

This may seem precocious, but not unexpected. But what Maitland realized was that it ruled out wider kin claims. For example, 'even though I leave no other kinsfolk, neither my father, nor my mother, nor any remoter ancestor can be my heir...'[53] We have 'the curious doctrine that the ascendants are incapable of inheriting'; inheritances must, acting by a law of social gravity, flow downwards.[54] Brothers, for example, were not each other's heirs. All that a child can claim is what has not been disposed of by his direct ancestor. 'An heir is one who claims by descent what has been left undisposed of by his ancestor; what his ancestor has alienated [disposed of] he cannot claim.'[55]

Thus Maitland had found no strong links between family and land. Nor did he find any restraint placed by the lord of the manor. In his earlier lectures he had argued that 'We can produce no text of English law which says that the leave of the lord is necessary to an alienation by the tenant... the royal judges, like all lawyers, seem to have favoured free alienation...'[56] In the *History* he confirms this view and shows how in this respect, as in relation to the crucial question of family ownership, what happened was that England retained the individualistic property system, while on the Continent it was abandoned and property and seigneurial rights grew. He concludes that in relation to lordly constraints, 'the tenant may lawfully do anything that does not seriously damage the interests of his lord. He may make reasonable gifts, but not unreasonable. The reasonableness of the gift would be a matter for the lord's court; the tenant would be entitled to the judgment of his peers.' Maitland is surprised that the system 'should have been so favourable to the tenants ... if we have regard to other countries', but suggests that 'the Norman Conquest must for a while have favoured "free trade in land"'.[57] The crux of the matter is that England in the first half of the thirteenth century began to diverge from the Continent:

> If the English lawyers are shutting their ears to the claims of the lords, they are shutting their ears to the claims of the kindred also, and this just at a time when in Normandy and other countries the claims of the lord and the claims of the expectant heir are finding a formal recognition in the new jurisprudence. Whether we ascribe this result to the precocious maturity of our system of royal justice, or to some cause deep-seated in our national character, we must look at these two facts together:- if the English law knows no *retrait feodal* [feudal restraint], it knows no *retrait lignager*.[58]

This crucial passage summarizes the great divide. Whatever the caveats of certain critics, there is no way round Maitland's argument.[59]

In the passages above, the argument is pushed back by Maitland to the time of the Norman invasions. In the period between about 1066 and 1200 England and much of the Continent had split the land from the lord's and the family's control: they were later united on the Continent but not in England. One central question is, then, where had this very unusual system originated? Was it something new in the eleventh century, or does it have earlier roots?

As Maitland explains, 'Seemingly what we mean when we speak of "family ownership", is that a child acquires rights in the ancestral land, at birth or, it may be, at adolescence; at any rate he acquires rights in the ancestral land, and this not by gift, bequest, inheritance or any title known to our modern law.'[60] He admits that there is some likelihood that some such rights may have existed in England and elsewhere in western Europe. Yet he argues that the earliest record we have of the peoples who conquered western

Europe at the fall of the Roman Empire, suggests that property was already treated as belonging to an individual.

> Tacitus told his Roman readers that the Germans knew nothing of the testament, but added that they had rules of intestate succession. These rules were individualistic: that is to say, they did not treat a man's death as simply reducing the number of those persons who formed a co-owning group. Again, they did not give the wealth that had been set free to a body consisting of persons who stood in different degrees of relationship to the dead man. The kinsmen were called to the inheritance class by class, first the children, then the brothers, then the uncles. The *Lex Salica* has a law of intestate succession; it calls the children, then the mother, then the brothers and sisters, then the mother's sister. These rules, it may be said, apply only to movable goods and do not apply to land; but an admission that there is an individualistic law of succession for movable goods when as yet anything that can be called an ownership of land, if it exists at all, is new, will be quite sufficient to give us pause before we speak of 'family ownership' as a phenomenon that must necessarily appear in the history of every race. Our family when it obtains a permanent possession of land will be familiar with rules of intestate succession which imply that within the group that dwells together there is mine and thine.[61]

This comes from the very early period.

The evidence for the Anglo-Saxon period in England is equally interesting and is summarized by Maitland as follows. 'Now as regards the Anglo-Saxons we can find no proof of the theory that among them there prevailed anything that ought to be called 'family ownership.' No law, no charter, no record of litigation has been discovered which speaks of land as being owned by a . . . family, a household, or any similar group of kinsmen. This is the more noticeable because we often read of *familiae* which have rights in land; these *familiae*, however, are not groups of kinsmen but convents of monks or clerks.'[62] But, further,

> the dooms and the land-books are markedly free from those traits which are commonly regarded as the relics of family ownership. If we take up a charter of feoffment [document investing an

individual with a fief or fee] sealed in the Norman period we shall probably find it saying that the donor's expectant heirs consent to the gift. If we take up an Anglo-Saxon land-book we shall not find this; nothing will be said of the heir's consent. The denunciatory clause will perhaps mention the heirs, and will curse them if they dispute the gift; but it will usually curse all and singular who attack the donee's title, and in any system of law a donee will have more to fear from the donor's heirs than from other persons, since they will be able to reclaim the land if for any cause the conveyance is defective. Occasionally several co-proprietors join to make a gift; but when we consider that in all probability all the sons of a dead man were equally entitled to the land that their father left behind him, we shall say that such cases are marvellously rare. Co-ownership, co-parcenary, there will always be. We see it in the thirteenth century, we see it in the nineteenth; the wonder is that we do not see more of it in the ninth and tenth than our Anglo-Saxon land-books display.[63]

Of course, expectant heirs may try to recover land which they feel they should have. But even here, Maitland found no greater power to do so in the Anglo-Saxon period than in the nineteenth century. 'In the days before the Conquest a dead man's heirs sometimes attempted to recover land which he had given away, or which some not impartial person said that he had given away. They often did so in the thirteenth century; they sometimes do so at the present day. At the present day a man's expectant heirs do not attempt to interfere with his gifts so long as he is alive; this was not done in the thirteenth century; we have no proof that it was done before the Conquest.'[64] In his 'Last words on family ownership', he concluded modestly: 'We have not been arguing for any conclusion save this, that in the present state of our knowledge we should be rash were we to accept "family ownership," or in other words a strong form of "birth-right", as an institution which once prevailed among the English in England. That we shall ever be compelled to do this by the stress of English documents is improbable.'[65] As far as I know, his view has not been controverted.

Maitland provides an overall scheme. From the earliest descriptions by Tacitus, individual ownership was the rule. Of course, there were rules of heirship, but these did not restrict the power of a living man who 'owned' the property to dispose of it. This very unusual, non-domestic mode of production may have prevailed over much of north-western Europe from the fifth to the twelfth centuries. Then, under pressure from kin and lords, it was transformed into seigneurial and family property over the Continent. In England alone it remained much as it had been – the basis for that capitalist, individualistic, system of property which was to lie behind much of later English development. The difference was largely due to the different balance of powers which existed in war-torn Europe and the relatively peaceful and nationally bounded island of Britain. Thus, once again, Maitland challenged the widespread view of a necessary set of stages which all societies had to go through, in this case from family to individual property.

5
Social Relations

The community and the individual

One of the great organizing ideas of social theorists of the later nineteenth century was the movement from Community to Association, as Tönnies put it. Much of the work of Marx, Morgan, Maine and others was centred on this supposed uniform movement. Again, if we examine Maitland's work, we shall see that by challenging this assumption he managed to resolve a number of the problems which had faced his predecessors.

As early as his lectures in 1883, published in the *Constitutional History*, he pointed to the 'very great difficulties which at the present moment cannot be explained' in relation to the theory of 'Recent historians' about the origins of the township. They argued that the township was 'a community which is far more ancient than the manor; a community which, so far as English history is concerned, we may call primitive; a group of men or of families bound together, very possibly by kinship, which cultivates land by a system of collective agriculture, which is or has been the owner of the land' but which, in course of time has 'fallen under the dominion of a lord'.[1] In an article in 1893 he showed even greater scepticism about the theory that 'land was owned by communities before it was owned by individuals'. Although he is not ready to attack the argument directly, he believes that 'this doctrine is as little proved and as little probable as would be an assertion that the first four rules of arithmetic are modern when compared with the differential calculus'.[2]

His full attack on the evolution from community to individual ownership occurs in later works. In the *History of English Law* he carefully defines the meaning of 'community' and concludes that while the county and the township constitute legal *communities* by the twelfth century,[3] the idea of the 'community' is more complex than this. 'The student of the middle ages will at first sight see communalism everywhere. It seems to be an all pervading principle. Communities rather than individual men appear as the chief units in the governmental system.' But this is deceptive. 'A little experience will make him distrust this communalism; he will begin to regard it as the thin cloak of a rough and rude individualism.'[4] Certainly the township is a 'communitas', but that does not mean that there is communalism.

For example, it looks on the surface as if there are rights 'in common' in the waste land and 'common' pasture. Yet are these rights 'of common' in any sense 'communal rights'? Of course there is an element of 'community' in it. 'A right of common is a right to enjoy something along with someone else, to turn out one's beasts on a pasture where the beasts of the lord and of one's fellow-tenants feed, to take sticks from a wood, turf from a moor, fish from a pond in which others are entitled to do similar acts.' Yet this does not imply communal ownership. 'But, for all this, the right may be an individual's several right, a right that he has acquired by a several title, a right that he can enforce against his fellow-commoners, a right that he without aid from his fellow-commoners, can enforce against strangers, a right over which his fellow-commoners have little or no control.'[5] Thus, having explained the matter further and in detail, Maitland concludes that 'This is not communalism; it is individualism *in excelsis*.'[6] Likewise, as a marginal note to further explanation put it succinctly: 'The manorial custom gives several rights not communal rights.' 'Rights of the township disappear when examined.'[7] He concludes that 'anything that even by a stretch of language could be called a communal ownership of land, if it had ever existed, had become rare and anomalous before the stream of accurate documents began to flow.'[8] There is no evidence back to the Conquest of 'common property'. Thus 'in this chapter we may have seen enough to give us pause before we assent to any grand dogma which would make "communalism" older than "individualism". The apparent communalism of old laws covers an individualism which has deep and ancient roots.'[9]

Another line of argument put forward by the defenders of the 'village community' theory was that open-field agriculture with its mingled strips necessitated communal management. If people had to act together to plant, let animals in to graze, and so on, surely there must have been some 'community organization'. Maitland answered this suggestion in several places. For instance, in an article on 'The Survival of Archaic Communities' he wrote as follows:

> It seems to me that some of our guides in these matters are in danger of exaggerating the amount of communalism that is necessarily implied in the open field system of husbandry. We have of course the clearest proof that the system can go on subsisting in days when manorial control has become hardly better than a name, that it can subsist even in the eighteenth and nineteenth centuries. We have also, so I think, fairly clear proof that it can subsist from century to century in many a village that has no court, no communal assembly. No communal bye-laws and indeed no legal recognition of the communal custom are absolutely necessary for the maintenance of the wonted course of agriculture; the common law of trespass maintains it.[10]

The effect is achieved 'not by the rights or the bye-laws of a community', but 'by the rights of other individuals'.[11] In other words, a person must behave like his co-cultivators and if he misbehaves he will either lose his crops or be disciplined by an ordinary common law writ of trespass. The 'community' does not come into it.[12]

In his *Domesday Book and Beyond* Maitland provided an analysis of the problem in a section on 'The Village Community' in 'England before the Conquest'. He started witheringly: 'A popular theory teaches us that land belonged to communities before it belonged to individuals. This theory has the great merit of being vague and elastic . . .' The theory 'seems to hint, and yet to be afraid to say, that land was owned by corporations before it was owned by men.' Maitland continues: 'The hesitation we can understand. No one who has paid any attention to the history of law is likely to maintain with a grave face that the ownership of land was attributed to fictitious persons before it was attributed to men.'[13] It is here that he attacks the 'normal sequence of stages' theory of 'the anthropologists'. He argues that

> To say the least, we have no proof that among the Germans the land was continuously tilled before it was owned by individuals or by those small groups that constituted the households. This seems to be so whether we have regard to the country in which

the Germans had once lived as nomads or to those Celtic and Roman lands which they subdued. To Gaul and to Britain they seem to have brought with them the idea that the cultivable land should be allotted in severalty. In some cases they fitted themselves into the agrarian framework that they found; in other cases they formed villages closely resembling those that they had left behind them in their older home. But to all appearance, even in that older home, so soon as the village was formed and had ploughed lands around it, the strips into which those fields were divided were owned in severalty by the householders of the village.[14]

Thus from the very start, land was owned by individuals or households, not by some larger entity. Thus 'our evidence, though it may point to some co-operation in agriculture, does not point to a communistic division of the fruits.' In a footnote, Maitland rejects Seebohm's ideas and explains how the Anglo-Saxon tithing system 'is compatible with the most absolute individualism'.[15]

Maitland continues: 'Thus, so far back as we can see, the German village had a solid core of individualism.'[16] He considers the 'commons' and again finds that the rights were attached to particular ownership of houses and arable strips so that 'such "rights of common" may take that acutely individualistic form which they seem to have taken in the England of the thirteenth century.'[17] Thus, repeating the material from the 1893 article, he puts as the side-heading 'Feebleness of the village community', for the 'village community' had 'no court, no jurisdiction'.[18] Nor was this system basically changed after 1066 with the elaboration of the manorial system. The evidence Maitland cites from the manor of Orwell 'brings to our notice the core of individualism that lies in the centre of the village. The houses and the arable strips are owned in severalty, and annexed to these houses and arable strips are pasture rights which are the rights of individuals . . .'[19] No more than the family, the 'village community' cannot provide a political, legal or economic foundation in the development of English society. In conclusion, therefore, he rejected the great hypothesis of the movement from Community to Individual, or even the reverse. 'In fine, is it not very possible that the formula of development should be neither "from communalism to individualism," nor yet "from individualism to communalism," but "from the vague to the definite"?'[20]

Maitland had thus shown some of the ways in which the individual was freed from the overwhelming power of kin or community. But he was well aware of other constraints that normally operated to tie the individual. One of these was the strength of structural inequality of status and power, which gave people a superior or inferior position at birth which could not be challenged. Having considered liberty of the individual at some length, he also paid attention to the closely related question of equality and inequality.

Social ranks

In relation to the higher ranks, Maitland's general case is put in the *Constitutional History of England.* In assessing the nature of the baronage, Maitland concludes that 'tenure is the quarter in which we must look: the idea of nobility of blood is not the foundation'.[21] He concedes that the idea of nobility of blood 'does occur all Europe over among the peoples of our own race if we go back far enough'. Thus 'The distinction between eorl and ceorl is a distinction between men who by birth are noble, and those who by birth are perfectly free but still not noble...' Yet, 'for a long time before the Conquest', that is, presumably, back into later Anglo-Saxon England, 'the nobility of birth had been supplanted by a nobility of tenure and of office.' Thus the 'thane is noble because of his relation to the king, a relation intimately connected with the holding of land...' Out of this one might have expected a 'nobility of tenants in chief, crown vassals'. But the Norman Conquest 'put difficulties in the way of the formation of such a nobility'. For the 'aggregate body of tenants in chief was a very miscellaneous mass, including very great men, and men who might relatively be called very small...' Hence the 'grades were many and small; there was no one place at which a hard line could be drawn; and probably it suited the king very well that none should be drawn, that he should not be hemmed in by a close aristocracy; against the greater feudatories he relies on the smaller tenants in chief.'[22]

Maitland is arguing that out of the power of the Crown and special circumstances, a separate nobility of birth failed to emerge in England. Comparing the situation with France, he wrote, 'Whatever social pre-eminence the families of peers may have, has no basis in our law: we have never had a *noblesse.*'[23] One symbol and key to this was the equality of all free men before the law, a central tenet of English law from at least the thirteenth century. As Milsom nicely summarizes Maitland's vision, 'The world into which Maitland's real actions fit is essentially a flat legal world, inhabited by equal neighbours. Lordship is little more than a servitude over the land of another, and its content is fixed and economic. The services and incidents are important, but the law relating to them is self-contained, unrelated to other questions...' Now this 'flat world' is the opposite of that hierarchical world, based on the premise of inequality, which was to develop over the rest of the continent. But when had such a flat world developed? Milsom is clear that 'There can be no doubt that by the end of the period covered by his book, the world was as Maitland saw it.'[24] Maitland's 'Book' ends in 1307; so Milsom is talking about the second half of the thirteenth century. Thus he agrees with Maitland that by the second half of the thirteenth century we are in a flat legal world.

As Maitland himself put it, 'if we could look at western Europe in the year 1272, perhaps the characteristic of English law which would seem the most prominent would be its precocity.' It was uniform over the country. It was also uniform over all the social statuses; 'in England the law for the great men has become the law for all men, because the law of the king's court has become the common law.'[25] Thus 'English law is modern in its uniformity, its simplicity, its certainty...'[26]

Law, ultimately, is based on contractual relationships, and not on status. This is the essence of feudalism – as Maine had realized. This can be found in all aspects of English life, for instance, as Maitland notes, 'In our English law bastardy can not be called a status or condition', a bastard 'is a free and lawful man... In all other respects he is the equal of any other free and lawful man' – a situation very different from that on the Continent.[27] The same is true of children – who, as we shall see, are not under 'patriarchal' power because of their age and status in the family, and women, who are not inferior because of their gender.

Two areas where status, birth, ascription usually operate are in relation to those above the normal law, with special privileges, namely the nobility, and those below it, the serfs. In each, Maitland notes some curious features. In his chapter on 'The Sorts and Conditions of Men', he starts by stating that in the thirteenth century, 'The lay Englishman, free but not noble, who is of full age and who has forfeited none of his rights by crime or sin, is the law's typical man, typical person.'[28] There are, of course, other special types – the 'noble men and unfree men', the clergy, Jews, aliens, etc. Yet, in relation to the lay order, 'it may seem to us that, when compared with the contemporary law of France or at any rate of Germany, our law of *status* is poor: in other words, it has little to say about estates or ranks of men. Men are either free men or serfs; there is not much more to be said. When compared with tenure, status is unimportant.'[29] Thus, 'our land law has been vastly more important than our law of ranks.'[30] He notes that English writers find it very difficult to translate the Latin word 'status'.

Turning specifically to the top, 'Our law hardly knows anything of a noble or of a gentle class; all free men are in the main equal before the law.'[31] As Maitland says, considering England had been conquered by the Normans, this is very strange: 'A conquered country is hardly the place in which we should look for an equality, which, having regard to other lands, we must call exceptional.'[32] Yet this equality is what there is. Under the powerful English kings, a small group emerged, 'an estate of temporal lords, of earls and barons'. But the 'principles which hold it together are far rather land tenure and the king's will than the transmission of noble blood.' The only privilege they have is political – they are consulted by the king. 'They have hardly any other privileges. During the baron's life his children have no privileges; on his death only the new baron becomes noble.' Among the 'extremely few' privileges was that of all free men to be judged by their peers – in this case other peers. Even this, as Maitland explains, was no great privilege and rather vague. Apart from this, 'There are a few little rules of procedure which distinguish the noble from the non-noble.'[33] Thus 'English *gentix hons* have no legal privileges, English counts and barons very few.'[34]

Turning to the knights, 'knighthood can hardly be accounted a legal *status*'.[35] There is a good deal of work which only they can do. 'In administrative law therefore the knight is liable to some special burdens; in no other respect does he differ from the mere free man. Even military service and scutage [tax paid in lieu of military service] have become matters of tenure rather than matters of rank...'[36]

At the other extreme of the social hierarchy, we may wonder about the serfs. 'In the main, then, all free men are equal before the law.' And, as Maitland continues, 'Just because this is so the line between the free and the unfree seems very sharp.' So what does Maitland make of the English serf? In a letter written in 1890, Maitland noted his difficulty in describing English serfdom. 'I have been writing about villeinage and have been puzzled by our law's way of treating the villein as "free against all men but his lord".'[37]

His central conclusion, though he does not quite put it in these words, is that just as nobility is a contractual relationship between king–lord–land (tenure), and not a status, so serfdom is a contractual relationship between two individuals. In this it contrasts with 'slavery' which is in most civilizations a 'status'. The conception of serfdom in medieval England according to contemporary texts 'at many points comes into conflict with our notion of slavery'. Thus Maitland says of the great English lawyer Bracton, 'In his treatment of the subject Bracton frequently insists on the relativity of serfdom. Serfdom with him is hardly a status; it is but a relation between two persons, serf and lord.' It is true that 'As regards his lord the serf has, at least as a rule, no rights; but as regards other persons he has all or nearly all the rights of a free man; it is nothing to them that he is a serf.' As Maitland says, 'Now this relative serfdom we cannot call slavery. As regards mankind at large the serf so far from being a mere thing is a free man.'[38]

Even in relation to the lord, the situation is not so clear cut. 'As against his lord the serf can have no proprietary rights.'[39] Yet, in practice, 'the lord in his court habitually treats them as owners of chattels, he even permits them to make wills . . .'[40] Maitland comments, 'So here again, when we look at the facts, the serf's condition seems better described as unprotectedness than as rightlessness . . .'[41] Or again, 'Yet another qualification of rightlessness is suggested. More than once Bracton comes to the question whether the lord may not be bound by an agreement, or covenant, made with his serf. He is inclined to say Yes.' Bracton argues that 'the serf may be made a free man for a single purpose, namely that of exacting some covenanted benefit . . .'[42]

As for other people, 'The serf's position in relation to all men other than his lord is simple: – he is to be treated as a free man. When the lord is not concerned, criminal law makes no difference between bond and free . . .'[43] This freedom is most graphically shown in relation to property: 'in relation to men in general, the serf may have lands and goods, property and possession, and all appropriate remedies.'[44] As for the manumission of the serf, for Bracton, it is simple. Since Bracton 'habitually regards serfdom as a mere relationship', he 'sees no difficulty; the lord by destroying the relationship destroys serfdom'.[45]

All this leaves us with a very curious half-way position; a strange mixture of status and contract. As Maitland notes, 'Its central idea, that of the relativity of serfage, is strange. It looks artificial: that is to say, it seems to betray the handiwork of lawyers who have forced ancient facts into a modern theory.'[46] They were faced with the 'juristic curiosity' of 'a merely relative serfdom'. Even the relative serfdom is complex. 'When a lord allows it to be recorded that on the death of his servile tenant he is entitled to the best beast, he goes very far towards admitting that he is not entitled to seize the chattels of his serf without good cause.' Thus Maitland writes, 'We hesitate before we describe the serf as rightless even as against his lord . . .'[47]

As to the number of serfs, it is very difficult to estimate, since 'tenure is so much more important than status', so that the contemporary surveys 'are not very careful to separate the personally free from the personally unfree',[48] an interesting admission. Furthermore, Maitland writes, 'it is highly probable that large numbers of men did not know on which side of the legal gulf they stood . . .'[49] A gulf of such hazy outlines is hardly a great gulf. Nevertheless, it would seem probable that 'the greater half of the rural population is unfree'[50] – whatever that means.

All this requires further investigation – for instance, though serfs could in theory be sold as chattels by their lord, how often did this happen? The economic historian Thorold Rogers wrote, 'In the many thousands of bailiffs and manor rolls which I have read, I have never met with the single instance of the sale of a serf.'[51] He also states that serfdom was a secure position and not at all rightless, even against the lord.[52] All this may help to explain one of the most curious silences in English history – the way in which, without any formal emancipation, without any noticeable activity of any kind, serfdom and villeinage faded away; they just seem to have sloughed off a skin and transformed themselves.

In conclusion, Maitland fully endorses the picture of English peculiarity which had been elaborated by Tocqueville and gives it historical precision. In that crucial period between the twelfth and fourteenth centuries when France and Germany moved from contract (feudalism) to status – or 'caste' in Tocqueville's language – England did not take this 'normal' path. This unusual divergence is crucial to the understanding of later class society. For example, Sugarman has recently noted, 'the English gentry were in this vital way institutionally different from the lesser nobilities of other nations. The fact that only the titular peers were a distinct sub-species, to be tried only by members of their own order, was surely a very important legal difference from countries where the whole of the second estate was privileged at law.'[53]

The inequalities of wealth and blood status are but two of the 'natural' inequalities which people often use to organize life in agrarian societies. Two others, age and gender, both finding their strongest expression within the family, are others. Maitland devoted considerable attention to family relations and again we may wonder how his picture fits with that of the earlier theorists.

Family relations

It is a characteristic of the majority of agrarian societies that, just as property is not owned by an individual, so the individual does not have distinct legal rights. Put crudely, the family is a single legal and political entity and the oldest male, the 'father', has fairly absolute rights over the others: men over women, parents over children, and the father over all. This is the patriarchal form, the *patria potestas* which we do not merely find in simple societies studied by anthropologists, but enshrined in Roman law and widespread in much of western Europe in the *ancien régime*. How does Maitland's analysis of English history compare with this simplified model?

In relation to the Saxon period, Maitland felt that 'It is by no means certain . . . that we ought to endow the English father with an enduring *patria potestas* over his full-grown sons, even when we are speaking of the days before the Conquest.'[54] As for the later period, the position is much clearer:

If our English law at any time knew an enduring *patria potestas* which could be likened to the Roman, that time had passed away long before the days of Bracton. The law of the thirteenth century knew, as the law of the nineteenth knows, infancy or non-age as a condition which has many legal consequences; the infant is subject to special disabilities and enjoys special privileges; but the legal capacity of the infant is hardly, if at all, affected by the life or death of his father, and the man or woman who is of full age is in no sort subject to paternal power . . . Our law knows no such thing as 'emancipation', it merely knows an attainment of full age.[55]

Equally significantly, an 'infant may well have proprietary rights even though his father is still alive'. This it explained as follows:

Boys and girls often inherit land from their mothers or maternal kinsfolk. In such case the father will usually be holding the land for his life as 'tenant by the law of England', but the fee will belong to the child. If an adverse claimant appears, the father ought not to represent the land in the consequent litigation; he will 'pray aid' of his child, or vouch his child to warranty, and the child will come before the court as an independent person. What is more, there are cases in which the father will have no right at all in the land that his infant son has inherited; the wardship of that land will belong to some lord.[56]

Furthermore, 'An infant can sue; he sues in his own proper person, for he can not appoint an attorney. He is not in any strict sense of the word "represented" before the court by his guardian, even if he has one.'[57] Some '"friend" of the infant sues out the writ and brings the child into court', but the 'action will be the infant's action, not the friend's action, and the court will see that the infant's case is properly pleaded.' When the procedure was regularized in the thirteenth century, 'How weak the family tie had become we see when we learn that this next friend need not be a kinsman of the infant.'[58] All of this is an extremely long way from the *patria potestas* model. The idea that infants could inherit separate property, could sue separately, that they were not responsible for their parent's crimes, or their parents for theirs after childhood is extraordinary by the standards of most civilizations.

Even more extraordinary is the relation between man and woman. Maitland treats their position in a number of key passages and throughout his account rejects the theory that female status had once been low and had 'evolved' upwards to his own time.[59] He showed that English law from very early on treated even husband and wife as separate persons, so that in England, 'Long ago we chose our individualistic path.'[60] He shows that almost immediately after the Norman Conquest women were able to inherit even property which required the holder to provide military service for the Crown.[61] He recognizes that within marriage from the thirteenth century, a married woman loses some rights: her husband by the common law is the wife's guardian, which 'we believe to be the fundamental principle', but he constantly needs her consent also.[62] Let us examine in a little more detail three sections where he describes the status of men and women.

In relation to female children's status in England before the

Conquest, Maitland writes, 'That women were subject to anything that ought to be called a perpetual tutelage we do not know. Young girls might be given in marriage – or even in a case of necessity sold as slaves – against their will; but for the female as well as for the male child there came a period of majority, and the Anglo-Saxon land-books show us women receiving and making gifts, making wills, bearing witness, and coming before the courts without the interven-tion of any guardians.'[63] 'After the Norman Conquest, the woman of full age who has no husband is in England a fully competent person for all the purposes of private law; she sues and is sued, makes feoffments, seals bonds, and all this without any guardian.' All this is very different from 'the "perpetual tutelage of women"', relics of which 'were to be found on the continent in times near to our own'.[64]

In relation to the complex relation of husband and wife, he found that a much more equal relationship had been partially undermined from the fourteenth to nineteenth centuries. Thus 'throughout the twelfth century and into the thirteenth we habitually find married women professing to do what according to the law of a later time they could not have done effectually.'[65] Yet through the system of the marriage settlement and the courts of equity 'the English wife, if she belonged to the richer class, became singularly free from marital control. Modern statutes have extended this freedom to all wives.'[66] Again, we see a divergence between England's common law and equity system and what happened from the fourteenth century on the continent where an apparently egalitarian system, where husband and wife pooled or completely shared their prop-erty, actually led women into a trapped position with no separable rights. Maitland explains how not only did the modern freedom of English women arise out of a reaction to harsh or unjust laws, but

we ought also to say that if our modern law was to be pro-duced, it was necessary that our medieval lawyers should reject that idea of community which came very naturally to the men of their race and of their age. We may affirm with some cer-tainty that, had they set themselves to develop that idea, the resulting system would have taken a deep root and would have been a far stronger impediment to the 'emancipation of the married woman' than our own common law has been. Elsewhere we may see the community between husband and wife growing and thriv-ing, resisting all the assaults of Romanism and triumphing in the modern codes.[67]

In relation to private law in the thirteenth century:

> Women are now 'in' all private law, and are the equals of men.
> The law of inheritance, it is true, shows a preference for males
> over females; but not a very strong preference, for a daughter
> will exclude a brother of the dead man, and the law of wardship
> and marriage, though it makes some difference between the male
> and the female ward, is almost equally severe for both. But the
> woman can hold land, even by military tenure, can own chat-
> tels, make a will, make a contract, can sue and be sued. She sues
> and is sued in person without the interposition of a guardian;
> she can plead with her own voice if she pleases; indeed – and
> this is a strong case – a married woman will sometimes appear
> as her husband's attorney. A widow will often be the guardian
> of her own children; a lady will often be the guardian of the
> children of her tenants.[68]

In relation to public functions, however, women were excluded
from almost all public roles. Thus Maitland again summarizes the
position: 'As regards private rights women are on the same level as
men, though postponed in the canons of inheritance; but public
functions they have none. In the camp, at the council board, on
the bench, in the jury box there is no place for them.'[69]

We thus have an intermediary status. In terms of the position of
spinsters and widows, their private position was as it is today. In
relation to married women, they were under the 'guardianship' of
their husband. In relation to public affairs, they were largely excluded. There are no grounds for thinking that their status had
improved since Anglo-Saxon times, and it probably deteriorated
between the thirteenth and nineteenth centuries, but much less so
than of many women in continental Europe. The relatively high
status of women which Tocqueville saw in America is a direct de-
scendant of this – even down to his analysis of the extreme separation
between the private and public role of women which exactly mirrors
Maitland's account.

From a consideration of Maitland's treatment of feudal, family
and community relations we can see that he elaborated a picture
that enriches and substantiates the guesses of Montesquieu, Smith
and Tocqueville. He showed some structural peculiarities in England. The individual was freer, the social structure was more flexible.
Above all, the vital separations between economy, kinship and polity,

which Maitland thought had been present in Anglo-Saxon England, had survived into a peculiar form of feudalism, which had then evolved in a different direction from that in most of the 'feudal' societies in continental Europe. Thus Maitland had outlined a narrative which filled in the earlier guesses, showing how the widespread tendency towards rigidity had not happened in England.

Maitland's solutions here lead us on to further questions and in particular lead us to wonder why it was that in the important period after about 1200, England retained its flexibility, its separation of powers, whereas much of continental Europe moved towards centralized power, the relinking of politics and economics, politics and religion, a growth of a status-based society. Maitland had shown that England was peculiar. He needed to explain why it had become different and, even more importantly, why it remained so.

6
The Divergence of Legal Systems

If we gather together all his discussions, Maitland's picture of what happened is, in essence, as follows. The legal, political and social systems of much of north-western Europe were alike in the long period between the collapse of the Roman Empire and about the twelfth century. There was nothing special about England except that, having been overrun by three waves of Teutonic peoples (Anglo-Saxons, Vikings, Normans), and having been less deeply Romanized than much of continental Europe, it was an extreme example, with northern Germany and Scandinavia, of the Germanic system. It was only in the twelfth century that the divergence between England and the Continent became clear, consisting largely in the fact that in England the relations between king, lords and people remained balanced, property was held by contract and the rights of kin were not re-established. In other words, while much of the continent began to move towards a 'peasant' and 'caste', that is highly stratified, system, England developed towards an individualized and open social structure. The similarity to Tocqueville's account is striking.

The question, of course, is why England did not follow the course of most continental countries? Ultimately, Maitland's answer seems to lie in the field of politics and law. At the heart of this was the issue of royal power. On the one hand it was the powerful, highly centralized, legal system focusing on the Crown which began to differentiate England. Yet Maitland also documents in great detail the numerous 'intermediary bodies' and checks and balances which prevented the judicial centralization from turning into the administrative centralization and political absolutism which Montesquieu and Tocqueville had seen emerge on the Continent. The Crown in

England was both immensely powerful, yet not absolutist. Following Stubbs, Maitland characterized its position on a number of occasions, in a series of paradoxical remarks which capture the essence of the fact that the Crown is both the font of power and law, yet not absolute. 'The king can do wrong; he can break the law; he is below the law, though he is below no man and below no court of law.'[1] Thus the 'rights of the king are conceived as differing from the rights of other men rather in degree than in kind.'[2] Magna Carta merely confirmed what was long the case, that 'the king is ... below God and the law ... the king is bound to obey the law', a view which Fortescue excellently elaborated in the fifteenth century, but had earlier been exemplified by Bracton.[3]

Thus there is a contradiction. England is the most centralized, rule-bound and highly governed country in Europe, with royal power penetrating right down to the level of every citizen, just as every citizen holds his property of the Crown. On the other hand, there is no large bureaucracy, no standing army, an enormous amount of delegated power and delight in powerful intermediary liberties. Maitland filled in the picture which Montesquieu and Tocqueville had sketched out, showing how it worked and evolved. Although he occasionally alludes to 'some cause deep-seated in our national character',[4] he pays little attention to such nebulous concepts. Instead, he focuses on a set of historical 'accidents'. The accident of islandhood, of the Norman Conquest, of the genius of the Angevin rulers, and so on. Nothing was to do with 'race', nothing was determined by Germanic origins. Yet origins and customs, and language and many other things were parts of that unusual chemistry which produced an increasingly odd situation on this small island.

In a sense, to understand why and how the peculiarity emerged through a mixture of structural and accidental causes, one would have to write a detailed history of England. Briefly, however, we can approach part of Maitland's answer to this question by looking at two themes that he pursued with increasing interest, that is the relations between English and Roman law, and the development of corporations and trusts. Both provide keys to his solution.

*

Maitland's remarks on the growing divergence between English and Roman law are scattered through his works. Although he had read deeply on continental law, carried on a correspondence with a number of leading Roman law scholars and even edited part of the work of one of the greatest comparative philosophers of law, Otto Gierke, Maitland's references are usually allusive and brief. It would have grossly inflated his work to have undertaken as detailed a survey of the legal traditions of each country as he did of England. His comparative remarks, therefore, have to be set in the context of the numerous other studies of the comparison of continental and English law which were available at the time and have been published since.[5] He looked at the English side of the differences, and took the continental side as given. Some may wonder whether he has thereby exaggerated or distorted the differences and it is for this reason that I later provide an assessment from the French side by the greatest of the later comparative historians, Marc Bloch. Maitland's work should also, obviously, be read in the context of the previous detailed comparative accounts by Montesquieu, Smith and Tocqueville with whom his analysis is essentially in agreement.

Maitland noted that during the twelfth to the sixteenth centuries much of northern Europe was reconquered by a renovated Roman law. As he put it, 'Englishmen should abandon their traditional belief that from all time the continental nations have been ruled by the "civil [i.e. Roman] law", they should learn how slowly the renovated Roman doctrine worked its way into the jurisprudence of the parliament of Paris, how long deferred was the "practical reception" of Roman law in Germany, how exceedingly like our common law once was to a French *coutume*.'[6]

By the thirteenth century, England was beginning to look distinctly different from the rest of Europe, not because England had changed, but because Roman law had made no conquest there: 'English law was by this time recognized as distinctly English.' This feeling of contrast was heightened because, although 'Roman jurisprudence was but slowly penetrating into northern France and had hardly touched Germany', by the thirteenth century many Englishmen thought that the whole of Europe now had written Roman law, which 'served to make a great contrast more emphatic'.[7] Certainly, by the sixteenth century England was an island carrying an old Germanic legal system, and lying off a land mass dominated by Roman law.

Examples of the growing divergence abound. For instance, in relation to the law of contract, 'it is plain that at latest in the thirteenth century our English law was taking a course of its own.'[8] In relation to inheritance, over much of Europe there was a partial 'reception' of Roman ideas, but 'during the middle ages the Roman system was not observed in England'.[9] The claims of wider kindred to family land were 'finding a formal recognition in the new jurisprudence' over much of Europe, but not in England.[10] When Normans and Angevins came to England, they re-enforced, modified and developed a system which was different from that which grew up in their homeland. 'Not upon the Normans as Normans can we throw the burden of our amazing law of inheritance, nor can we accuse the Angevin as an Angevin.'[11] Thus, 'In dealing with any century later than the thirteenth, the historian of English law could afford to be silent about Roman and Canon law, for... these laws appear in a strictly subordinate position, are administered by special courts, and exercise very little, if any, influence on the common law of England.'[12]

The effects of this difference were immense and among them, Maitland believed, was the reason why political absolutism did not develop in England.

> The English common law was tough, one of the toughest things ever made. And well for England was it in the days of Tudors and Stuarts that this was so. A simpler, a more rational, a more elegant system would have been an apt instrument of despotic rule. At times the judges were subservient enough: the king could dismiss them from their offices at a moment's notice; but the clumsy, cumbrous system, though it might bend, would never break. It was ever awkwardly rebounding and confounding the statecraft which had tried to control it. The strongest king, the ablest minister, the rudest Lord-Protector could make little of this 'ungodly jumble'.[13]

Or again, Maitland writes, 'our old law maintained its continuity... it passed scathless through the critical sixteenth century, and was ready to stand up against tyranny in the seventeenth... if we look abroad we shall find good reason for thinking that but for these institutions our old-fashioned national law... would have utterly broken down, and the "ungodly jumble" would have made way for Roman jurisprudence and for despotism.'[14] Instead, the common law with its vague but strong assumption that the king was under no man, but *was* under the law, was maintained.

Clearly the maintenance and development of an alternative legal system to Roman law was a key to England's peculiarity. How did this happen? Here we can only summarize a few of Maitland's widely spread hints. The first thing to look at, as Tocqueville would have said, was the 'point of origin'. Before the Norman invasion the differences were already marked. This was partly due to the fact that the effects of the Germanic invasions were different. In England the Roman civilization was swept away. But 'in the kingdoms founded by Goths and Burgundians the intruding Germans were only a small part of a population, the bulk of which was Gallo-Roman, and the barbarians . . . had made their entry as subjects or allies of the emperor . . .'[15] This partly helps to explain why Roman civilization, in the shape of law and religion and language, came back into France, Spain and Italy, whereas it did not do so in England. In England 'there was no mass of Romani, of people who all along had been living Roman law of a degenerate and vulgar sort and who would in course of time be taught to look for their law to Code and Digest'.[16]

The difference becomes clear if we contrast the continental and English situations:

> On the continent of Europe Roman law had never perished. After the barbarian invasions it was still the 'personal law' of the con-quered provincials. The Franks, Lombards, and other victorious tribes lived under their old Germanic customs, while the van-quished lived under the Roman law. In course of time the personal law of the bulk of the inhabitants became the territorial law of the country where they lived. The Roman law became once more the general law of Italy and of Southern France; but in so doing it lost its purity, it became a debased and vulgarised Roman law, to be found rather in traditional custom than in the classical texts, of which very little was known. Then, at the beginning of the twelfth century, came a great change. A law-school at Bologna began to study and to teach that Digest in which Justinian had preserved the wisdom of the great jurists of the golden age. A new science spread outwards from Bologna.[17]

In England the situation was different during the Anglo-Saxon period:

> Eyes, carefully trained, have minutely scrutinised the Anglo-Saxon legal texts without finding the least trace of a Roman rule out-side the ecclesiastical sphere. Even within that sphere modern

research is showing that the church-property-law of the Middle
Ages, the law of the ecclesiastical 'benefice', is permeated by
Germanic ideas. This is true of Gaul and Italy, and yet truer of
an England in which Christianity was for a while extinguished.
Moreover, the laws that were written in England were, from the
first, written in the English tongue; and this gives them a unique
value in the eyes of students of Germanic folk-law, for even the
very ancient and barbarous *Lex Salica* is a Latin document, though
many old Frankish words are enshrined in it. Also we notice –
and this is of grave importance – that in England there are no
vestiges of any 'Romani' who are being suffered to live under
their own law by their Teutonic rulers.[18]

Thus, by the time of the Norman invasion there was a significant difference, already, between, say, France and England. This
difference was made the greater by the fact of the size and geography of England. Thus Maitland writes that in accounting for the
unusually coherent legal and political system in England, 'we should
have to remember the small size, the plain surface, the definite
boundary of our country.' This continues as a very powerful background factor: 'This thought indeed must often recur to us in the
course of our work: England is small: it can be governed by uniform law: it seems to invite general legislation.' Again, we should
note that 'the kingship of England, when once it exists, preserves
its unity: it is not partitioned among brothers and cousins.' Furthermore, 'a close and confused union between church and state
prevented the development of a body of distinctively ecclesiastical
law which would stand in contrast with, if not in opposition to,
the law of the land.'[19]

The fact of geography meant that England became one nation
and one state. Referring to the twelfth and thirteenth centuries,
Maitland wrote that 'there was no need in England for that *recon-
stitution de l'unité nationale* which fills a large space in schemes of
French history, and in which, for good and ill, the Roman texts
give their powerful aid to the centripetal and monarchical forces.
In England the new learning found a small, homogeneous, well
conquered, much governed kingdom, a strong, a legislating kingship. It came to us soon; it taught us much; and then there was
healthy resistance to foreign dogma.'[20]

The reference to the 'much governed kingdom' takes us on to
his last two major theories. The effects of the Norman Conquest

and subsequent development of Angevin kingship were to make England even more homogeneous and united. For instance, in terms of law, 'The custom of the king's court is the custom of England and becomes the common law.'[21] Or even more graphically, 'our system is a single system and revolves around Westminster Hall.'[22] In England, the 'nation is not a system of federated communities; the king is above all and has a direct hold on every individual.'[23] Yet this direct hold is also a protection, for instance against the oppressions of the lords. By the statute of novel disseisin (new dispossession) of 1166, for example, the 'seisin of a free tenement, no matter of what lord it be holden, is protected by the king'.[24]

Thus part of the answer is that the Crown was so powerful that it 'protected' the individual, not only against his superiors, but against the strong claims of the Church, or of his family. 'Here in England old family arrangements have been shattered by seignorial claims.'[25] There is no overlap of family and law, just as the absence of defined kin groups broke any possible link between family and religion. This is reinforced by the religious system for 'the Christianity which the Germans have adopted . . . is not a religion which finds its centre at the family hearth . . . the heir could not offer the expiatory sacrifice, nor would it be offered in his house; no priesthood had descended upon him.'[26]

What then of the growing interest in Roman law that was spreading all over Europe in the twelfth century onwards? Here Maitland develops a very subtle argument which we might term the 'vaccination' theory. England did absorb some elements of Roman law, that is to say some systematization and clarity, enough to make its own law better. Yet it was enough to prevent the full version of Roman law being accepted at a later date.

*

Maitland was well aware that Roman Law had a considerable influence on English law in the twelfth and particularly the thirteenth centuries. All over Europe in the thirteenth century onwards Roman law swept all before it. 'In the thirteenth century the Parliament of Paris began the work of harmonising and rationalising the provincial customs of Northern France, and this it did by Romanising them. In the sixteenth century, after "the revival of letters," the Italian jurisprudence took hold of Germany, and swept large portions of the old national law before it. Wherever it finds a weak, because an uncentralised, system of justice, it wins an easy triumph.'[27]

To England 'it came early' so that 'very few are the universities which can boast of a school of Roman Law so old as that of Oxford'.[28] Thus 'for a short while, from the middle of the twelfth to the middle of the thirteenth century' the influence of Roman Law 'was powerful'. 'Some great maxims and a few more concrete rules were appropriated, but on the whole what was taken was logic, method, spirit rather than matter.'[29] The extent and limits of the influence can be seen in the work of the greatest of medieval English lawyers, Bracton. 'He was an ecclesiastic, an archdeacon, but for many years he was one of the king's justices. He had read a great deal of the Italian jurisprudence, chiefly in the works of that famous doctor, Azo of Bologna. Thence he had obtained his idea of what a lawbook should be, of how law should be arranged and stated; thence also he borrowed maxims and some concrete rules; with these he can fill up the gaps in our English system. But he lets us see that not much more can now be done in the way of Romanisation.'[30]

Bracton mainly drew on English common law, for he found that the numerous writs and precedents there showed a system where 'the king's court of professional justices – the like of which was hardly to be found in any foreign land, in any unconquered land – had been rapidly evolving a common law for England, establishing a strict and formal routine of procedure, and tying the hands of all subsequent judges.'[31] Consequently, his work, rather than ushering in Roman law, had the opposite effect: 'From Bracton's day onwards Roman law exercises but the slightest influence on the English common law, and such influence as it exercises is rather by way of repulsion than by way of attraction. English law at this early period had absorbed so much Romanism that it could withstand all future attacks, and pass scathless even through the critical sixteenth century.'[32] It was shortly after he wrote his treatise that Edward I's (1272–1307) reign saw 'English institutions finally take the forms that they are to keep through coming centuries.'[33]

Bracton's work and the unusual failure of Roman law to gain more than a small foothold in England were due to many other factors. One of them was the legislative ability of the Angevin kings and the expansion of royal justice. In his characteristically graphic way Maitland describes what happened. If the Anglo-Saxon laws had been maintained unaltered, the English legal system might have 'split into a myriad local customs, and then at some future time

Englishmen must have found relief from intolerable confusion in the eternal law of Rome'. This did not happen because, among other things, 'under Henry II the king's own court flung open its doors to all manner of people, ceased to be for judicial purposes an occasional assembly of warlike barons, became a bench of professional justices, appeared periodically in all the counties of England under the guise of the Justices in Eyre. Then begins the process which makes the custom of the king's court the common law of England.'[34] Thus 'in the middle of the twelfth' century Henry II 'concentrated the whole system of English justice round a court of judges professionally expert in the law. He could thus win money – in the Middle Ages no one did justice for nothing – and he could thus win power; he could control, and he could starve, the courts of the feudatories. In offering the nation his royal justice, he offered a strong and sound commodity. Very soon we find very small people – yeomen, peasants – giving the go-by to the old local courts and making their way to Westminster Hall, to plead there about their petty affairs.'[35] Maitland believed that 'King Henry and his able ministers came just in time – a little later would have been too late: English law would have been unified, but it would have been Romanised.'[36] There were disadvantages to the English system, 'But to say nothing of the political side of the matter, of the absolute monarchy which Roman law has been apt to bring in its train, it is probably well for us and for the world at large that we have stumbled forwards in our empirical fashion, blundering into wisdom.'[37]

For Maitland the story did not quite finish here. Impressed by the resurgence and spread of Roman law in the sixteenth century, particularly in Germany, he suggested that England narrowly avoided becoming Romanized again in that century.[38] It appears that his anxiety was exaggerated since numerous subsequent historians have examined the matter and have suggested that, short of actual conquest by Philip II, there was no real likelihood of such a reception taking place.[39] Thus by the end of the thirteenth century, he argued, the trajectories of England and much of continental Europe were decisively diverging.

The absence of the reception of Roman law had many implications in every sphere of life; it altered political relations, social relations, religion. In a late essay on 'The Body Politic' Maitland mused on some of the reasons for the divergence between England and the continent. He made a few further suggestions. Speaking of Italy, Spain, Germany, the Low Countries, France and England he wrote that 'Of all these countries at the critical time, say between 1150 and 1300, Britain was the only one in which there was no persecution of heretics, in which there were no heretics to perse-cute.' This influenced the law deeply. 'Everywhere else the inquisitory process fashioned by Innocent III for the trial of heretics becomes a model for the temporal courts.' He admitted that this was not the only reason for divergence: 'If I were to say more I should have to speak of the causes which made the England of the twelfth century the most governable and the most governed of all Euro-pean countries, for if a Tocqueville had visited us in 1200 he would have gone home to talk to his fellow-countrymen of English civiliz-ation and English bureaucracy.' Nevertheless, he continued that 'there can I think be no doubt that we have laid our finger on one extremely important cause of divergence when we have mentioned the Catharan heresy.' He notes that the Cathar or Albigensian heresies became 'endemic in the south of France' and in particular in Languedoc. Yet he decides to turn away from this and ends by asserting that the English history, though diverging, is as 'normal' as any other.

Nevertheless in considering the wider causes of the growing di-vergence, Maitland's mind did not rest with Roman law and religion or even islandhood. Rather, he began to see that it was possible to investigate a largely overlooked but enormously significant reason for the divergence.

7
Fellowship and Trust

In his consideration of the balance of liberty, equality and wealth through time, Maitland had effectively demolished one side of the famous nineteenth-century dichotomy which was the basis of most thought on the evolution of societies. He had shown that not all civilizations had started in a world where individuals were embedded within the community, where contract was entirely subordinate to status, and where hierarchy and patriarchy were universal. Yet his magnificent achievement would be incomplete if he were to be unable to reconstruct the other end of the famous supposed transformation. He needed to rethink the nature of the modern world as supposedly constituted by contract, individualism and absolute equality.

In the last few years of his life, Maitland sketched out a plan for how this rethinking might be done. He died without implementing the scheme in detail. But we can see in his hints the way in which he finally reconciled those great contradictions which he had wrestled with in his youthful fellowship dissertation on liberty and equality, namely how Adam Smith's 'self love' and 'social love' could be harmonized, and how Tocqueville's problem of how to reconcile equality with liberty could be achieved. Maitland did this through an exploration of what he came to believe was the greatest of all English legal contributions to the world, the Trust. This was an institution born by accident, not from Roman law, but which became the third great principle of social organization in the world, standing on the same level as Status and Contract. It was the Trust – and the trust which it engendered – which provided the foundations for modern liberty, wealth and equality.

*

Maitland asked himself what the link between political liberty, economic prosperity and the legal framework might be. Tocqueville had isolated parts of the solution. He had noted that there was a developing tendency in much of Europe for the central power to abolish all the intermediary bodies, that is to withdraw any franchises previously given to towns, local assemblies and parliaments. Any corporate group which derived its power from the state became a threat and was undermined. In the end, one had the state and the individual – with very little in between. There were very few ways in which individuals could associate without incurring the jealousy of the state. Since, among other things, religious and economic differentiation and development required the formation of sub-units – to worship, trade, manufacture – this tendency to eliminate the smaller grouping would finally abolish political, religious and economic liberty and also abolish progress towards wealth.[1]

Tocqueville also saw that one country seemed to have developed along a different path. He laid great stress in his work on America on the free associations which the Americans constantly set up. These associations were the essence of their religious, social and economic dynamism. Without them, wealth and liberty would again vanish. Thus Tocqueville had isolated the structural mechanism which linked social and legal forms through to religious and economic liberty. What he lacked was the training and deep knowledge of medieval European law to see what the 'point of departure' of this development was. He traced it back to England, as with other features, but was unable to pursue the matter further. It is from Maitland that we receive an answer.[2]

Maitland started his account of the development of the corporation based on Roman law with the universal need for some kind of group above the level of the individual. 'Every system of law that has attained a certain degree of maturity seems compelled by the ever-increasing complexity of human affairs to create persons who are not men, or rather (for this may be a truer statement) to recognize that such persons have come and are coming into existence, and to regulate their rights and duties.'[3] The essence of what has to be set up, the corporation or 'embodiment', he describes as follows:

> The core of the matter seems to be that for more or less numerous purposes some organized group of men is treated as a unit

which has rights and duties other than the rights and duties of all or any of its members. What is true of this whole need not be true of the sum of its parts, and what is true of the sum of the parts need not be true of the whole. The corporation, for example, can own land and its land will not be owned by the sum of the corporators; and, on the other hand, if all the corporators are co-owners of a thing, then that thing is not owned by the corporation. This being so, lawyers from the thirteenth century onwards have been wont to attribute to the corporation a 'personality' that is 'fictitious' or 'artificial'.[4]

We are told that 'Sinibald Fieschi, who in 1243 became Pope Innocent IV was, it is said, the first to proclaim in so many words that the *universitas* is *persona ficta* [the association is a fictive person]'.[5]
   The corporation thus has considerable power. The crucial question is where it derives this power from. In relation to English boroughs Maitland argued that 'Incorporation must be the outcome of royal charter . . . The king makes something. He constitutes and erects a body corporate and politic in deed, fact and name (in *re, facto et nomine*).'[6] Maitland gave a fuller account of the development of corporation theory on the Italian model.

   Its sacred texts were the law of an unassociative people. Roman jurisprudence, starting with a strict severance of *ius publicum* from *ius privatum*, had found its highest development in 'an absolutist public law and an individualistic private law.' . . . The theory of corporations which derives from this source may run (and this is perhaps its straightest course) into princely absolutism, or it may take a turn towards mere collectivism (which in this context is another name for individualism); but for the thought of the living group it can find no place; it is condemned to be 'atomistic' and 'mechanical'.[7]

He believed that

   If it be our task legally to construct and maintain comfortable homes wherein organic groups can live and enjoy whatever 'liberty of association' the Prince will concede to them, a little, but only a little, can be done by means of the Romanist's co-ownership (*condominium, Miteigentum*) and the Romanist's partnership (*societas, Gesellschaft*). They are, so we are taught, intensely individualistic categories: even more individualistic than are the parallel categories of English law, for there is no 'jointness' (*Gesammthandtschaft*) in them.[8]

This leads to what is known as the 'Concession Theory'. That is to say, 'The corporation is, and must be, the creature of the State. Into its nostrils the State must breathe the breath of a fictitious life, for otherwise it would be no animated body but individualistic dust.'[9] Thus 'the corporation does not grow by nature; it must be made, by the act of parliament, or of the king, or of the pope . . .'[10] Basically, 'If the personality of the corporation is a legal fiction, it is the gift of the prince.'[11] He quoted a classic definition that 'a Corporation is a Franchise' and commented that 'a franchise is a portion of the State's powers in the hands of a subject'.[12]

The absolutist element in this state derivation is spelt out by Maitland with clarity, for 'what was understood to be the Roman doctrine of corporations was an apt lever for those forces which were transforming the medieval nation into the modern state. The federalistic structure of medieval society is threatened. No longer can we see the body politic as *communitas communitatum*, a system of groups, each of which in its turn is a system of groups. All that stands between the State and the individual has but a derivative and precarious existence.'[13] Thus, paradoxically, rather than strengthening the individual in relation to the state, the corporation became an indirect way of weakening the subject. France provided a very good example, as Montesquieu and Tocqueville had earlier realized. In France,

I take it, we may see the pulverising, macadamising tendency in all its glory, working from century to century, reducing to impotence, and then to nullity, all that intervenes between Man and State . . . In this, as in some other instances, the work of the monarchy issues in the work of the revolutionary assemblies. It issues in the famous declaration of August 18, 1792: 'A State that is truly free ought not to suffer within its bosom any corporation, not even such as, being dedicated to public instruction, have merited well of the country.' That was one of the mottoes of modern absolutism: the absolute State faced the absolute individual.[14]

It is this view of the tendency to absolutism, and the way a Roman concept of corporations aided it, that explains remarks Maitland made in a letter to Henry Jackson in 1900. 'The subject of my meditation is the damnability of corporations. I rather think that they must be damned . . .' He ends the letter by looking forward to a great work. 'Then for the great treatise *De Damnabilitate Universitas.*'[15]

If, then, it was not the Roman law corporation that led towards the vibrant world of American associationalism, where did the key lie? Here, in the last ten years of his life, Maitland started to see the answer, and it was an accidental, unexpected and chance one. It lay in the development of a device that had no roots in Roman law, but was a by-product of many forces, in particular the inadequacies of Roman law and the structural tensions in English society in the thirteenth century. He had considered the theory that the origin of the Trust was in Roman law, but by 1894 could write that 'I have long been persuaded that every attempt to discover the genesis of our *use* [the device that led into the Trust] in Roman law breaks down . . .'[16] In his lectures on Equity, given up to the year of his death, he told his audience: 'I don't myself believe that the use came to us as a foreign thing. I don't believe that there is anything Roman about it. I believe that it was a natural outcome of ancient English elements.'[17] He expanded this remark later in the lectures, starting his assessment of the evidence as follows:

> Some have thought that this new jurisprudence of uses was borrowed from the Roman law; that the English use or trust is historically connected with the *fidei commissum*. I do not myself believe in the connexion. One reason for this disbelief I will at once state because it leads on to an important point. From the first the Chancellors seem to have treated the rights of the *cestui que use* [the person or persons on whose behalf the trust is undertaken] as very analogous to an estate in land. They brought to bear upon it the rules of the English land law as regards such matters as descent and the like.[18]

Maitland believed he might discover something special and powerful. He had, among other things, thrown light on the question of how it was possible to move from status-based societies to something other than pure, atomistic and individualistic contract. His excitement on discovering this key to the riddle of the peculiar nature of the modern world is palpable. In a letter to John Gray in 1902, he wrote of 'a matter of great historical importance – namely the extreme liberality of our law about charitable trusts . . . I think that continental law shows that this was a step that would not and could not be taken by men whose heads were full of Roman Law.'[19] The individual was acting like a king. '*Practically* the private man who creates a charitable trust does something that is very like the creation of an artificial person, and does it without asking leave of the State.'[20] The following year he also wrote to Gray: 'I am endeavouring to explain in a German journal how our law (or equity) of trusts enabled us to keep alive "unincorporated bodies" which elsewhere must have perished.'[21]

In the few years before his premature death he came to believe that the Trust was probably the most important of all English legal contributions. He wrote: 'The idea of a trust is so familiar to us all that we never wonder at it. And yet surely we ought to wonder. If we were asked what is the greatest and most distinctive achievement performed by Englishmen in the field of jurisprudence I cannot think that we should have any better answer to give than this, namely, the development from century to century of the trust idea.'[22] These words were echoed in a letter to John Gray in November 1903, 'Some one ought to explain our trust to the world at large, for I am inclined to think that the construction thereof is the greatest feat that men of our race have performed in the field of jurisprudence. Whether I shall be able to do this remains to be seen – but it ought to be done.'[23] Increasingly ill, Maitland was unable to perform the task and died within three years. But he has given us glimpses of how he would have approached the subject and why he thought it so very important.[24]

Through a series of reported conversations with his German lawyer friends, Maitland brought home the fact that the Trust was something unique to England and very important. The Trust, Maitland explained to his students in a series of lectures given up to the year of his death, 'perhaps forms the most distinctive achievement of English lawyers. It seems to us almost essential to civilization, and yet there is nothing quite like it in foreign law. Take up for instance the . . . Civil Code of Germany; where is trust? Nowhere. This in the eyes of an English practitioner is a big hole. Foreigners don't see that there is any hole. "I can't understand your trust," said Gierke to me.'[25] The size of the gap in Continental law is shown by another remark. Much of modern society, as many have argued, is based on Contract. Yet Maitland chides a German friend for not having anything equivalent to the Trust in their legal system and tells him: 'I have looked for the Trust, but I cannot find it; to omit the Trust is, I should have thought, almost as bad as to omit Contract.'[26] The German friend was obviously nettled by such remarks and others such as 'Foreigners manage to live without trusts. They must.'[27] He replied: 'Well, before you blame us, you might tell us what sort of thing is this wonderful Trust of yours.'[28] Maitland is more than happy to attempt this, and indeed published one of his longest analyses of Trusts and corporations in German. He was keen to do so because he believed that 'Of all the exploits of Equity the largest and the most important is the invention and development of Trust.'[29] Consequently, 'Anyone who wishes to know England, even though he has no care for the detail of Private Law, should know a little of our Trust.'[30] Nor was it just the concept of the Trust in itself that was so striking; many of the ideas which sprang out of it were equally remarkable. For example, 'That idea of the trust-fund which is dressed up (invested) now as land and now as current coin, now as shares and now as debentures seems to me one of the most remarkable ideas developed by modern English jurisprudence.'[31]

*

The idea of holding something in trust for someone else is a very old one and may have been found in a number of Germanic societies after the collapse of the Roman Empire. Certainly, Maitland found that the idea of the use, *opus*, was widespread in Anglo-Saxon England, for example, 'long before the Norman Conquest we may find a man saying that he conveys land to a bishop to the use of a church ...'[32] Well before the revival of Roman law with its idea of a corporation created by a higher power, there was a widespread idea of an unincorporated body of people who held some asset on behalf of themselves or others. 'Probably as far back as we can trace in England any distinct theory of the corporation's personality or any assertion that this personality must needs have its origin in some act of sovereign power, we might trace also the existence of an unincorporated group to whose use land is held by feoffees.'[33] The germ of the idea, holding to the use of another in trust and the creation of a non-governmental body, was thus already present. Its formal institutionalization on a large scale which was to change the world, began, however, in the thirteenth century.

One minor contribution to this development may have been religious. Several times Maitland draws attention to the effect of the peculiar vows of poverty undertaken by the new Franciscan orders, who came to England in the early thirteenth century. 'The law of their being forbade them to own anything . . . A remarkable plan was adopted.' This was that the benefactor would convey the property which they needed in order to survive 'to the borough community "to the use of" or "as an habitation for" the friars'.[34] The major contribution, however, came from another source.

Maitland pointed out that the institutionalized Trust emerged out of a dilemma:

> The Englishman cannot leave his land by will. In the case of land every germ of testamentary power has been ruthlessly stamped out in the twelfth century. But the Englishman would like to leave his land by will. He would like to provide for the weal of his sinful soul, and he would like to provide for his daughters and younger sons. That is the root of the matter. But further, it is to be observed that the law is hard upon him at the hour of death, more especially if he is one of the great. If he leaves an heir of full age, there is a *relevium* to be paid to the lord. If he leaves an heir under age, the lord may take the profits of the land, perhaps for twenty years, and may sell the marriage of the heir. And then if there is no heir, the land falls back ('escheats') to the lord for good and all.[35]

To get round the problem, the 'landowner conveys his land to some friends . . .' 'They are to hold it "to his use (*a son oes*)". They will let him enjoy it while he lives, and he can tell them what they are to do with it after his death. I say that he conveys his land, not to a friend, but to some friends. This is a point of some importance. If there were a single owner, a single *feoffatus*, he might die, and then the lord would claim the ordinary rights of a lord . . . Enfeoff five or perhaps ten friends . . . ("as joint tenants"). When one of them dies there is no inheritance; there is merely accrescence. The lord can claim nothing.'[36] This idea came out of Anglo-French law, 'it is not in Roman books that Englishmen of the fourteenth century have discovered this device.'[37]

The desire of the landowners to avoid the strict implications of primogeniture and royal power would have failed if they had not coincided with the developing interest of one of the very strongest of royal officials, the Chancellor, to provide a new legal flexibility to supplement the Common Law, through the system of equity.

'The Chancellor began to hold himself out as willing to enforce these honourable understandings, these "uses, trusts or confidences" as they were called, to send to prison the trustee who would not keep faith. It is an exceedingly curious episode. The whole nation seems to enter into one large conspiracy to evade its own laws, to evade laws which it has not the courage to reform. The Chancellor, the judges, and the Parliament seem all to be in the conspiracy. And yet there is really no conspiracy: men are but living from hand to mouth, arguing from one case to the next case, and they do not see what is going to happen.'[38] These trustees were not a perpetual corporation. They were not set up or "incorporated" by the State. Yet they had 'a jointness about them so that they could act as one body.' They were a 'fictitious person', recognized by the law, but nothing to do with the state.

The growth of this device proceeded apace, both nourishing and being protected by the growth of 'equity'.[39] The royal power as well as the lawyers turned a blind eye to this development, which seemed at first so innocuous. Like the custom of primogeniture, what had started as an upper class device spread through the large middling ranks of the population and began to widen its purposes in so doing. 'And then, if I may so speak, the "settlement" descended from above: descended from the landed aristocracy to the rising monied class, until at last it was quite uncommon for any man or woman of any considerable wealth to marry without a "marriage settlement."'[40] In due course, 'the trust became one of the commonest institutes of English law. Almost every well-to-do man was a trustee . . .'[41]

When it became clear that the Trust was developing into a major threat to royal power and finances, Henry VIII tried to crush it in the Statute of Uses (1535). But the horse had already bolted. Maitland summarizes a complex story in a few lines:

> Too late the king, the one person who had steadily been losing by the process, saw what had happened. Henry VIII put into the mouth of a reluctant Parliament a statute which did its best – a clumsy best it was – to undo the work. But past history was too strong even for that high and mighty prince. The statute was a miserable failure. A little trickery with words would circumvent it. The Chancellor, with the active connivance of the judges, was enabled to do what he had been doing in the past, to enforce the obligations known as trusts.[42]

The Trust continued on its way. By the late sixteenth century an alternative set of methods to form meaningful, enduring associations of citizens in pursuit of a common goal, for it was widening out from just passing property across the generations, had been developed. It was becoming particularly important for the setting up of charities and good works.

*

Maitland drew attention to some of the structural benefits of this development, in particular as a supplement to the idea of corporations or *universitas*. 'The trust has given us a liberal substitute for a law about personified institutions.'[43] More generally he outlined the situation thus, describing the period roughly from 1500 to 1900. 'For the last four centuries Englishmen have been able to say, "Allow us our Trusts, and the law and theory of corporations may indeed be important, but it will not prevent us from forming and maintaining permanent groups of the most various kinds: groups that, behind a screen of trustees, will live happily enough, even from century to century, glorying in their unincorporatedness. If Pope Innocent and Roman forces guard the front stairs, we shall walk up the back."'[44] Whereas under Roman law all could be threatened by the state, in England it was different: what for Roman lawyers was a 'question of life and death was often in England a question of mere convenience and expense, so wide was that blessed back stair. The trust deed might be long; the lawyer's bill might be longer; new trustees would be wanted from time to time; and now and again an awkward obstacle would require ingenious evasion; but the organized group could live and prosper, and be all the more autonomous because it fell under no solemn legal rubric.'[45] The diversity and vagueness of what a Trust could be helped it in its flourishing diversity. 'In dealing with charitable trusts one by one, our Courts have not been compelled to make any severe classification.'[46] Whatever was useful and broadly 'charitable', in the words of mutual benefit to those involved (other than the trustees) and not illegal, could be pursued.

Thus the Trust enabled the development of unincorporated bodies, protected from the prying eyes of the State or others. The *Genossenschaft* (Fellowship) 'has to live in a wicked world: a world full of thieves and rogues and other bad people. And apart from wickedness, there will be unfounded claims to be resisted: claims made by neighbours, claims made by the State. This sensitive being must have a hard, exterior shell. Now our Trust provides this hard, exterior shell for whatever lies within.'[47] Thus, 'we come upon what has to my mind been the chief merit of the Trust. It has served to protect the unincorporated *Genossenschaft* against the theories of inadequate and individualistic theories.'[48] Yet there was something mysterious to foreigners about 'the most specifically English of all our legal institutes... the trust'. There was a kind of paradox; here was a non-body, or nobody, that was yet embodied. Maitland tried to explain the contradiction to his continental friends as follows. In the Trust there is 'the device of building a wall of trustees', which 'enabled us to construct bodies which were not technically corporations and which yet would be sufficiently protected from the assaults of individualistic theory. The personality of such bodies – so I should put it – though explicitly denied by lawyers, was on the whole pretty well recognised in practice. That something of this sort happened you might learn from one simple fact. For some time past we have had upon our statute book the term "unincorporate body."'[49]

Maitland readily admitted that this was mysterious, even illogical, yet it worked. 'Some day the historian may have to tell you that the really fictitious fiction of English law was, not that its corporation was a person, but that its unincorporate body was no person, or (as you so suggestively say) was nobody.'[50] Yet this 'nobody' was much more than a mere partnership in pursuit of short-term profit. It was something different from what looked like equivalent devices under the revived Roman law: 'we may notice that an Englishman will miss a point in the history of political theory unless he knows that in a strictly legal context the Roman *societas*, the French *société*, and the German *Gesellschaft* should be rendered by the English *partnership* and by no other word.'[51] A partnership for practical, money-making ends did not create much mutual confidence, trust or commitment, but a Trust did. 'It has often struck me that morally there is most personality where legally there is none. A man thinks of his club as a living being, honourable as well as honest, while the joint-stock company is only a sort of machine into which he puts money and out of which he draws dividends.'[52]

The Trust was, as Maitland realized, something very peculiar, somehow bridging the gap between status and contract, between people and things. Although it forms people into powerful groups, 'It has

all the generality, all the elasticity of Contract.'[53] 'It is an "institute" of great elasticity and generality; as elastic, as general as
contract.'[54] In order to blend two contradictory principles, a sleight
of hand had to be performed which puzzled continental lawyers
and is difficult to explain. Probably once again referring to Gierke,
Maitland wrote:

> 'I do not understand your trust,' these words have been seen in
> a letter written by a very learned German historian familiar with
> law of all sorts and kinds. Where lies the difficulty? In the terms
> of a so-called 'general jurisprudence' it seems to lie here: – A
> right which in ultimate analysis appears to be *ius in personam*
> (the benefit of an obligation) has been so treated that for prac-
> tical purposes it has become equivalent to *ius in rem* and is
> habitually thought of as a kind of ownership, 'equitable owner-
> ship.' Or put it thus: If we are to arrange English law as German
> law is arranged in the new code we must present to our law of
> trust a dilemma: it must place itself under one of two rubrics; it
> must belong to the Law of Obligations or to the Law of Things. . . .
> It was made by men who had no Roman law as explained by
> medieval commentators in the innermost fibres of their minds.[55]

Maitland explains roughly how the Chancellor somehow managed
to muddle the two:

> We know what happened. No sooner had the Chancellor got to
> work than he seems bent on making these 'equitable' rights as
> unlike mere *iura in personam* and as like *iura in rem* as he can
> possibly make them. The ideas that he employs for this purpose
> are not many; they are English; certainly they are not derived
> from any knowledge of Roman law with which we may think fit
> to equip him. On the one hand as regards what we might call
> the internal character of these rights, the analogies of the com-
> mon law are to be strictly pursued.[56]

Maitland seems to have conceived the Trust as combining two
principles. On the one hand, the way it was held, protected, entered into and enforced was according to voluntaristic, not contractual
methods. 'No, there is no "obligatory" language: all is done under
cover of "use"; a little later of "confidence" and "trust".'[57] Or again
he writes: 'Let me repeat once more . . . that use, trust or confidence

originates in an agreement. As to the want of valuable consideration for the trustee's promise, it might, I think, fairly be said that even if there is no benefit to the promisor, the trustee, there is at all events detriment to the promisee, the trustor, since he parts with legal rights, with property and with possession.'[58] From this voluntaristic external viewpoint all that is created is a set of personal rights, between the trustor, trustee and person for whom the trust is made. It is quite clear that 'the trustee is the owner, the full owner of the thing, while the *cestui que trust* has no rights in the thing.' Yet this is not quite the whole story, for a personal relationship not of contract but of trust or obligation has been set up, not enforceable by law but by equity. 'The specific mark of the trust is I think that the trustee has rights, which rights he is bound to exercise for the benefit of the *cestui que trust* or for the accomplishment of some definite purpose.'[59] Thus, considered from one viewpoint we are talking about those interpersonal relations which belong to rights in persons. This is the essence of the Trust:

> Men ought to fulfil their promises, their agreements; and they ought to be compelled to do so. That is the principle and surely it is a very simple one. You will say then that the Chancellor begins to enforce a personal right, a *jus in personam*, not a real right, a *jus in rem* – he begins to enforce a right which in truth is a contractual right, a right created by a promise. Yes, that is so, and I think that much depends upon your seeing that it is so. The right of *cestui que use* or *cestui que trust* begins by being a right *in personam*. Gradually it begins to look somewhat like a right *in rem*. But it never has become this; no, not even in the present day.[60]

Yet while the frame is, so to speak, an enforcement of personal rights, the content is modelled on and filled with the highly sophisticated system of contractual land law which Maitland in his earlier works had shown to have developed in England by the thirteenth century and which spelt out rights against the whole world in 'things'. Thus Maitland explains that 'as regards estates and interests the common law of land is to be the model ... The new class of rights is made to look as much like rights *in rem* (estates in land) as the Chancellor can make them look – that is in harmony with the real wish of the parties who are using the device ... Thus we get a conversion of the use into an incorporeal thing – in which estates and interests exist – a sort of immaterialized piece of land. This is a perfectly legitimate process of "thing making" and one that is always going on.'[61] Thus the content of the Trust, the 'use', came to have all that strange flexibility and multiplicity which was the great contribution to a new kind of property system developed under common law. In Maitland's words, 'the use came to be conceived as a sort of metaphysical entity in which there might be estates very similar to those which could be created in land, estates in possession, remainder, reversion, estates descendible in this way or in that.'[62]

The result is a hybrid, which is neither straight status nor contract, neither pure rights in a person, nor rights in a thing. Such a system, Maitland believed, would not have emerged in Roman law, where the distinction between these two was very firm; 'the Trust could hardly have been evolved among a people who had clearly formulated the distinction between a right *in personam* and a right *in rem*, and had made that distinction one of the main outlines of their legal system.'[63] This is what mystified Maitland's continental colleagues, heirs of many centuries of Roman law. 'Jurists have long tried to make a dichotomy of Private Rights: they are either *in rem* or *in personam*. The types of these two classes are, of the former, *dominium*, ownership; of the latter the benefit of contract – a debt. Now under which head does trust – the right of *cestui que trust* – fall? Not easily under either. It seems to be a little of both. The foreigner asks – where do we place it in our code – under Sachnrech or under Obligationenrecht?'[64] In fact, it straddles both, bridging those great divides between Community and Association, Status and Contract, Mechanical and Organic solidarity which were supposed to divide the 'modern' world from the 'ancient'. If asked whether it is a system based on status or contract, one has to give a mixed answer. 'The best answer may be that in history, and probably in ultimate analysis, it is *jus in personam*; but that it is so treated (and this for many important purposes) that it is very like *jus in rem*. A right primarily good against *certa persona*, viz. the trustee, but so treated as to be almost equivalent to a right good against all – a *dominium*, ownership, which however exists only in equity. And this is so from a remote time.'[65]

By bridging this gap, by uniting the great dichotomy, Maitland had implicitly refuted his predecessor Maine and subverted much of the classic sociology of the later nineteenth century. He had suggested that there was not just a binary opposition between two forms of civilization, and a movement from one to another. He showed that much of modern dynamism came through mixing the two principles, thereby creating a tolerable balance of interpersonal warmth and trust and commitment, with a reasonable amount of flexibility and voluntary association. Alluding to Maine's famous thesis, he was able to argue that the Trust was indeed as important as that other great legal institution, the contract, and that modernity was based on it. 'The march of the progressive societies was, as we all know, from status to contract. And now? And now... there are many to tell us that the line of advance is no longer from status to contract, but through contract to something that contract cannot explain, and for which our best, if an inadequate, name is the personality of the organised group.'[66] What was set up through the device of the Trust was an entity which has been created by ordinary citizens and not by the state. In other words, a personal right had been turned into a property right. This was totally against the spirit of Roman law. 'In truth and in deed we made corporations without troubling king or parliament though perhaps we said that we were doing nothing of the kind.'[67]

The effect of Trusts

The effects of this revolutionary innovation of a new legal device, the Trust, were diverse. One was in contributing to political freedom. Here Maitland assumes the voice of a continental lawyer, who speaks as follows.

> There is much in your history that we can envy, much in your free and easy formation of groups that we can admire. That great 'trust concept' of yours stood you in good stead when the days were evil: when your Hobbes, for example, was instituting an unsavoury comparison between corporations and ascarides [intestinal worms, thread worms], when your Archbishop Laud (an absolutist if ever there was one) brought Corporation Theory to smash a Puritan Trust, and two years afterwards his friend Bishop Montague was bold enough to call the king's attention to the shamelessly unincorporate character of Lincoln's Inn. And your thoroughly un-Roman 'trust concept' is interesting to us.[68]

Since much of Maitland's work was concerned with the relations between the individual and the state it is worth examining his various hints in a little more depth. One benefit of the Trust was to help keep the judiciary independent. Lawyers were trained, and found their social and moral life sustained, by the Inns of Court.[69] If these had been appropriated by the Crown through incorporation, for example, the great struggle between Sir Edward Coke and the common lawyers and the Crown in the seventeenth century might have turned out differently. More generally, the constraints which the law put on the tendency for power to grow were dependent on the independence of the judiciary as Montesquieu and Tocqueville had noted. The fact that among the 'great and ancient, flourishing and wealthy groups' which were based on the Trust were the Inns of Court was significant.[70] This was by choice. 'Our lawyers were rich and influential people. They could easily have obtained incorporation had they desired it. They did not desire it.'[71] They retained their independence.

Another important area was in the right to political associations. There were the various political clubs, essential to the balance of British politics. There were also numerous other political associations set up for particular purposes. Maitland only mentioned in passing 'those political societies which spring up in England whenever there is agitation: a "Tariff Reform Association" or a "Free Food League" or the like'.[72] But on several occasions he mentions Trade Unions as one of the fruits of the right of free association arising from the idea of the Trust.[73] He brought out their importance by way of contrast with the Continent. He noted that many of his examples were taken from the eighteenth century, when Montesquieu and others were making a similar contrast. This was 'a time when, if I am not mistaken, corporation theory sat heavy upon mankind in other countries. And we had a theory in England too, and it was of a very orthodox pattern; but it did not crush the spirit of association. So much could be done behind a Trust, and the beginnings might be so very humble.'[74] But the contrast did not end then. Maitland noted that during the French Revolution, despite all the talk of freedom, although business partnerships were maintained, 'Recent writers have noticed it as a paradox that the State saw no harm in the selfish people who wanted dividends, while it had an intense dread of the comparatively unselfish people who would combine with some religious, charitable, literary, scientific, artistic purpose in view.' In France, even 'at the beginning of this twentieth century it was still a misdemeanour to belong to any unauthorised *association* having more than twenty members.'[75] The idea of a legal, unincorporated, association of free people pursuing political ends was essential to democracy.

Another effect Maitland noted was on one of Tocqueville's main themes, the decentralization of power and the autonomy of local and regional bodies. He believed that the 'English county' was one example of an unincorporated, yet existing, body.[76] It was this which prevented it becoming merely a servant of the central government. So that 'if the English county never descended to the level of a governmental district, and if there was always a certain element of "self-government" in the strange system that Gneist described under that name, that was due in a large measure (so it seems to me) to the work of the Trust.'[77]

Perhaps deepest of all was an effect that spread outwards through all of political life. All power tends to corrupt, but it does so far less if the power is not looked on as the personal property of the powerful, but rather as a temporary force held 'in trust' for others. This, Maitland, suggests, is what the idea of the Trust and the trust it entailed performed. He explains that 'In the course of the eighteenth century it became a parliamentary commonplace that "all political power is a trust"; and this is now so common a commonplace that we seldom think over it. But it was useful.'[78] Above all it permeated the delicate relationship between the king and the people, enabling a new kind of constitutional monarchy to emerge. 'Possibly the Crown and the Public are reciprocally trustees for each other; possibly there is not much difference now-a-days between the Public, the State, and the Crown, for we have not appraised the full work of the Trust until we are quitting the province of jurisprudence to enter that of political or constitutional theory.'[79] This was an established fact by the later nineteenth century and Maitland briefly suggests how the application of the concept of Trust had spread and influenced events in a somewhat disguised way in the aftermath to the confrontations between king and people of the seventeenth century. 'Applied to the kingly power it gently relaxed that royal cord in our polity which had been racked to the snapping point by Divine right and State religion. Much easier and much more English was it to make the king a trustee for his people than to call him officer, official, functionary, or even first magistrate. The suggestion of a duty, enforceable indeed, but rather as a matter of "good conscience" than as a matter of "strict law" was still possible; the supposition that God was the author of the trust was not excluded, and the idea of trust was extremely elastic.'[80]

Having established a concept of trust between monarchy and people by the eighteenth century, the idea found a further extension and application as a metaphor to hold together the largest Empire the world has ever known. Maitland explained that 'when new organs of local government are being developed, at first sporadically and afterwards by general laws, it is natural not only that any property they acquire, lands or money, should be thought of as "trust property," but that their governmental powers should be regarded as being held in trust. Those powers are, we say, "intrusted to them," or they are "intrusted with" those powers.'[81] A political example of how this worked was in relation to India. Maitland alludes to the way in which the delicate matter of the absorption of the East India Company was handled. 'When a Statute declared that the *Herrschaft* which the East India Company had acquired in India was held "in trust" for the Crown of Great Britain, that was no idle proposition but the settlement of a great dispute.'[82] He expands on this as follows: 'the English Trust . . . has played a famous part on the public, the world-wide, and world-historic stage. When by one title and another a ruler-ship over millions of men in the Indies had come to the hands of an English Fellowship, this corporation aggregate was (somewhat unwillingly) compelled by Acts of Parliament to hold this precious thing, this "object of rights," this rulership, upon trust for a so-called corporation sole, namely, the British Crown.'[83]

This was just part of that wider concept that all power was held in trust. The whole of the British Empire came to be seen as held 'in trust' for the peoples themselves, until they were ready to take over. 'Open an English newspaper, and you will be unlucky if you do not see the word "trustee" applied to "the Crown" or to some high and mighty body. I have just made the experiment, and my lesson for today is, that as the Transvaal has not yet received a representative constitution, the Imperial parliament is "a trustee for the colony." There is metaphor here.'[84] Maitland noted government ministers of his and earlier times saying that Victoria's government 'is a trustee for "the whole empire"'.[85] Perhaps this is part of the explanation for Tocqueville's question as to how such a small country as England could hold such a large Empire with such apparent lack of strain. The mechanism of the Trust both gave the metropolitan government confidence and an easy conscience and allowed elastic forms of delegation of power without posing a direct clash between the centre and the periphery.

Equally important, as Maitland realized, were the effects of the possibility of having non-incorporated bodies in the field of religion. Maitland shows how the Trust became a key defence of religious nonconformity and the sects. Any religious organization needs to form itself into some kind of permanent group. For instance, it needs a place of worship. Since such buildings had to be funded and maintained, how was this to happen? The state, associated with a Catholic or Anglican settlement, was hardly likely to give them corporate status. What the Methodists, Baptists, Quakers and others did was to set up Trusts. Groups of trustees ran their affairs and were recognized by the law. As Maitland pointed out, it is likely that without this legal loophole, the whole of nonconformity would have been crushed. Religious liberty and the Trust were closely linked.

This is how Maitland himself puts the case. 'All that we English people mean by "religious liberty" has been intimately connected with the making of trusts. When the time for a little toleration had come, there was the Trust ready to provide all that was needed by the barely tolerated sects. All that they had to ask from the state was that the open preaching of their doctrines should not be unlawful.'[86] All that was required by the state was minimal. For

> if the State could be persuaded to do the very minimum, to repeal a few persecuting laws, to say 'You shall not be punished for not going to the parish church, and you shall not be punished for going to your meeting-house,' that was all that was requisite. Trust would do the rest, and the State and *das Staatskirchenthum* [the Established Church] could not be accused of any active participation in heresy and schism. Trust soon did the rest. I have been told that some of the earliest trust deeds of Nonconformist 'meeting-houses' say what is to be done with the buildings if the Toleration Act be repealed. After a little hesitation, the courts enforced these trusts, and even held that they were 'charitable'. And now we have in England Jewish synagogues and Catholic cathedrals and the churches and chapels of countless sects. They are owned by natural persons. They are owned by trustees.[87]

Maitland illustrated this with the case of the Wesleyans, whose chapels were set up as Trusts. 'Now-a-days we see Wesleyan chapels in all our towns and in many of our villages. Generally every chapel has its separate set of trustees . . .'[88] Even large religious organizations could be tolerated in the form of Trusts. 'Behind the screen of trustees and concealed from the direct scrutiny of legal theories, all manner of groups can flourish: . . . a whole presbyterian system, or even the Church of Rome with the Pope at its head.'[89]

That England and later America were lands of toleration and sectarianism, exhibiting that mysterious relation between private and public which puzzled Tocqueville but which he saw as a central feature of America, is partly explained by the device of the Trust. The presence of the Trust explained why, if one searched through the voluminous records of common law, 'in the hope of discovering the organization of our churches and sects (other than the established church) you will find only a few widely scattered hints'.[90] It was equity and the Trust that provided the infrastructure for the distinctive Protestant sectarianism of England and America. Maitland sums up the finding thus: 'If we speak the speech of daily life, we shall say that in this country for some time past a large amount of wealth has "belonged" to religious "bodies" other than the established church, and we should have thought our religious liberty shamefully imperfect had our law prevented this arrangement. But until very lately our "corporation concept" has not stood at the disposal of Nonconformity, and even now little use is made of it in this quarter: for our "trust concept" has been so serviceable.'[91]

Linked to religious freedom was economic liberty. In terms of economic development, a device was needed which would allow people to come together to cooperate in some venture of a new kind. This was the era when new insurance facilities were needed. It was a time when traders and manufacturers needed to form themselves into joint-stock arrangements and to issue shares. The law of Trusts made all this possible, providing a 'wedge' which allowed in joint-stock arrangements and limited liability.[92] In all these cases the entity was recognized by the law, yet did not draw its strength directly from the Crown. It was a free association of individuals who had bound themselves together.

Again, let us look at Maitland's account of some of the effects. Two examples Maitland describes in some detail may be given. He traces the history of the development of a late seventeenth-century coffee house owned by Edward Lloyd, embodied in the mid-eighteenth century in a small trust fund and later, in 1811, a trust deed with 1,100 signatures. Thus was developed the great insurance firm of Lloyds.[93] Maitland could easily have added numerous other examples of banks or mutual (or building) societies. But his second example was the London Stock Exchange. He describes how it grew from people meeting in an eighteenth-century coffee house into a group of trustees. By the later nineteenth century it was vast and wealthy. In 1877 some people recommended that after all these years as a Trust it should be incorporated. 'And so the Stock Exchange was incorporated? Certainly not. In England you cannot incorporate people who do not want incorporation, and the members of the Stock Exchange did not want it.'[94] As for insurance companies, Maitland noted that a number of insurance companies, including the 'Sun' had been set up as unincorporated bodies by the early eighteenth century and had continued so until the time of Maitland's writing.[95]

One of the advantages of the fact that many of the pivotal economic institutions in England from the sixteenth century developed as Trusts would have been appreciated by Adam Smith. New economic enterprises, for example long-distance trade, or marine insurance, or making a new product, are risky. The individual needs protection, some limitation of liability, mutual assurance. Yet if the protection is given by the government, it very often takes the form of a monopoly. As Smith pointed out, this could easily turn out over time into something that would inhibit creative development. But it was of the essence of Trusts that they were not state monopolies. If someone else wanted to set up a marine insurance company or a building society the trustees could not prevent them. It provided a protection for the members without inhibiting newcomers. It was thus the ideal situation for competition with protection, for uniting individuals in a way that did not inhibit other individuals. It is difficult to see how the wealth of industrial England could have been created without the Trust concept.

The later development of Trusts, from the second half of the nineteenth century, is more complex. On the one hand, some have argued that, particularly in America, they later became an impediment to economic growth by creating *de facto* monopolies.[96] On the other hand, Maitland was right to draw attention to the way in which the Trust also formed the foundation for dynamic growth in America. 'It is a big affair our Trust. This must be evident to anyone who knows – and who does not know? – that out in America the mightiest trading corporations that the world has ever seen are known by the name of "Trusts."'[97] He was not sure why the Americans should have used the Trust form, rather than the corporation, 'when they were engaged in constructing the greatest aggregations of capital that the world had yet seen', but he believed that it was because 'the American corporation has lived in greater fear of the State than the English corporation has felt for a long time past'.[98]

A third, equally important area which Maitland touched on was in relation to social and intellectual liberties. He noted that a foreigner thinking of England would have noted 'you have been great makers of clubs'.[99] Many were of pivotal importance in political, legal and social life. For instance, 'every judge on the bench is a member of at least one club'.[100] Maitland took as an example the Jockey Club.

> I believe that in the eyes of a large number of my fellow-countrymen the most important and august tribunal in England is not the House of Lords but the Jockey Club; and in this case we might see 'jurisdiction' – they would use that word – exercised by the *Verein* [club] over those who stand outside it. I must not aspire to tell this story. But the beginning of it seems to be that some gentlemen form a club, buy a race-course, the famous Newmarket Heath, which is conveyed to trustees for them, and then they can say who shall and who shall not be admitted to it.[101]

Newmarket Heath had been purchased by the Jockey Club without asking the king's or the state's permission.[102] He also referred to 'your clubs and those luxurious club-houses which we see in Pall Mall'.[103] But there were numerous others. Clubs were also closely related to intellectual activities, for example the Royal Society, British Academy and numerous working men's clubs were of enormous importance in furthering science and learning. He noted that 'many learned societies', including the one he had founded, the Selden Society, were run by trustees, as were key institutions such as the London Library.[104] While it struck Tocqueville that America was notable for its associations, it has struck many that one of the great peculiarities of England is its creativity in the field of inventing quasi-groups: its charitable, social, scientific and literary, 'clubs' and associations.

A final area which Maitland sees as important is what he calls 'social experimentation' and which we might roughly term innovation. He writes as follows:

> First and last the trust has been a most powerful instrument of social experimentation. To name some well-known instances:

– It (in effect) enabled the landowner to devise [leave] his land by will until at length the legislature had to give way, though not until a rebellion had been caused and crushed. It (in effect) enabled a married woman to have property that was all her own until at length the legislature had to give way. It (in effect) enabled men to form joint-stock companies with limited liability, until at length the legislature had to give way. The case of the married woman is specially instructive. We see a prolonged experiment. It is deemed a great success. And at last it becomes impossible to maintain (in effect) one law for the poor and another for the rich, since, at least in general estimation, the tried and well-known 'separate use' has been working well. Then on the other hand let us observe how impossible it would have been for the most courageous Court of Common Law to make or to suffer any experimentation in this quarter.[105]

Thus the device of the Trust affected not only individuals, but categories – married women, the poor (through Boards of Guardians, Poor Law funds and charity), the young, and so on. The way it raised the status of married women by protecting their property particularly impressed Maitland.[106] In general it allowed a flexibility and vagueness which allowed change: 'let us observe that Englishmen in one generation after another have had open to them a field of social experimentation such as could not possibly have been theirs, had not the trustee met the law's imperious demand for a definite owner.'[107]

Of course, this is not to say that continental-style corporations were completely neglected. They were available as well. But as Maitland points out, the fact that an alternative mechanism also existed took the strain off the corporation route. If a group of people could get a better deal out of being incorporated, they might at a later point seek one – as Oxford and Cambridge did in the seventeenth century. But they had a choice and thus were not wholly dependent on royal whim. This was tremendously important. He singled out as one of the great achievements of the Trust idea that it 'has given us a liberal supplement for a necessarily meagre law of corporations'.[108] In Germany, where Roman law had conquered in the sixteenth century, there had lingered on various earlier forms of associations which were different. Much of Maitland's interest in German historical law was in the academic attempts to revise these alternatives, in particular the research on *Genossenschaft* which he thought was best translated as 'Fellowship', which 'with its slight flavour of an old England may be our least inadequate word'.[109] But while the Germans had to try to revive or reinvent such associations, they had become a rich and multifarious species in England by the seventeenth century.

*

Summarizing Maitland's illuminating insight into the solution to Tocqueville's puzzle concerning the origins of associations, we can say that in England from about the thirteenth century there began to develop a society which had various essential constituents. It had a powerful Crown and a ruling group in parliament. The centre was strong – but it was limited in its power by two other levels. In the middle was a crowd of unincorporated bodies, to a certain extent 'nobodies', in Maitland's phrase, but nobodies which are the essence of what would now be called 'Civil Society'. The secret, anti-state organizations (mafia, triads) which have been the bane of most governments were not necessary. The rights of association, so important later for the trades union and the labour movement, allowed people to associate. They were encouraged to put their energies into open activity.

Thus through the widening development of the concept of the Trust, there also, indirectly, developed a world of trust and openness, which is the basis not only of capitalism but also for modern science.[110] Maitland points out that this is such a large feature of the development of English civilization that it has become invisible. 'Now we in England have lived for a long while in an atmosphere of "trust," and the effects that it has had upon us have become so much part of ourselves that we ourselves are not likely to detect them. The trustee ... is well known to all of us, and he becomes a centre from which analogies radiate.'[111] The whole system is based on trust, both presuming a widespread level of trustability and, by that assumption, creating it. 'If I convey land to you as a trustee for me, or as a trustee for my wife and children, there is not merely what our law calls a trust, there really is trust placed by me in you; I do trust you, I do place confidence, faith, reliance in you.'[112] In many civilizations such trust in unrelated individuals would not be easy. Nor would it be easy to find people who were prepared, for no obvious reward, to carry out such duties, for 'a very high degree not only of honesty but of diligence has been required of trustees'.[113] The whole wide concept of public and disinterested service for others and for the community is related to the development of the Trust. It is indeed a peculiar development and, if we combine Tocqueville with Maitland, one of the keys to the making of the modern world.

8
Maitland and Durkheim

Although they were almost exact contemporaries (Emile Durkheim was born six years after Maitland in 1856), and although they both worked on an almost identical problem, I know of no evidence that Maitland and Durkheim knew of each other. Yet I think it is helpful to set Durkheim alongside Maitland for three reasons. First, Durkheim's work indicates something of the mental climate and set of problems which formed a much wider, European, context for Maitland's investigations towards the end of the nineteenth century. Second, the deep similarity of the problems they addressed adds force to the argument that Maitland was not just a legal historian, but rather a political theorist, or even a comparative sociologist. Most importantly, comparing him to Durkheim gives some idea of Maitland's stature. Durkheim is a household name in the social sciences, one of the great triumvirate with Marx and Weber, while even well-read historians and social scientists often know little of Maitland. Durkheim's life's work, as I shall show, was centrally concerned with the problem which Maitland addressed in his last years in relation to corporations and Trusts. He exerted all his efforts to solve the question of what held societies together in the modern world. We shall see to what extent he succeeded in a puzzle which, as we have already noted, Maitland made a singularly able attempt to solve. Maitland's work is often effortless and it is easy to forget how difficult the problems he tackled were. By looking at Durkheim's contemporary attempt we can better judge Maitland's achievement.

Durkheim's central problem was that of order: 'the recurring theme in all of Durkheim's writings is the problem of order', for society is fragile and always on the edge of collapse.[1] Sociology as a discipline was the tool which would help one to solve this fundamental question; what is it that unites people in the modern, industrial, world? As he wrote to a colleague, 'the object of sociology as a whole is to determine the conditions for the conservation of societies'.[2] If traditional societies had been held together by various institutions such as the family, religion, communities, what holds industrial societies together? Basically, Durkheim's work is part of the great effort by a number of thinkers from Tocqueville onwards to come to terms with the political revolution in France in 1789, and the industrial revolution in Britain starting around the same date.

Durkheim started in his characteristic way by eliminating alternative ways to create social order. One of these was the family. The loss of unity created by the family in earlier agrarian civilizations was the result of the change in mode of production to industrial, factory, urban civilization.[3] Mixed units which combined religion and the family, such as the Indian castes, were also all collapsing.[4] The family could no longer be relied on to tie humans together, to organize or give meaning to their lives.

Another collapsed source of authority and integration was religion. Durkheim put forward a straightforward evolutionary scheme here. He wrote that 'if there is one truth that history teaches us beyond doubt, it is that religion tends to embrace a smaller and smaller portion of social life. Originally, it pervades everything; everything social is religious ... Then, little by little, political, economic, scientific functions free themselves from the religious function ... God, who was at first present in all human relations, progressively withdraws from them; he abandons the world to men and their disputes.'[5] Thus religion, like the family and education, cannot help to overcome modern atomization. The total result is that contemporary civilization is in constant crisis, unstable, volatile and composed of egotistic individuals.

In many ways Durkheim's ideas could be aligned with those of earlier thinkers such as Tönnies, Maine and Morgan; from *Gemeinschaft* to *Gesellschaft* (Community to Association), from status to contract, from sacred to profane (secularization and disenchantment), social atomization. In particular, his thinking on the cumulative effects of all this on the central problem of egotistical individualism is almost identical to the insights of Tocqueville. Thus he describes the erosive effects of hyper-individualism on any form of social association or community. Like Tocqueville, or like Benjamin Constant who believed that 'when all are isolated by egoism, there is nothing but dust, and at the advent of a storm, nothing but mire', he thought society without anything except individuals would be a monstrosity.[6]

Durkheim's original contribution to all this fairly standard exposition is to apply the theory, in depth, to one example. His work on *Suicide* is thus the documentation of the dimensions and nature of the malaise. He believed that suicide was the individualistic opposite of social solidarity. His central thesis was that the crucial variable in differential suicide rates was the degree of integration of individuals into society. Where there was high integration, through family, religion or some other means, suicide rates were low. Lukes summarizes his theory as follows: 'that under adverse social conditions, when men's social context fails to provide them with the requisite sources of attachment and/or regulation, at the appropriate level of intensity, then their psychological or moral health is impaired, and a certain number of vulnerable, suicide-prone individuals respond by committing suicide.'[7]

So what was his solution to the problem of how one could create social solidarity in an industrial civilization? The first thing to do was to eliminate unsatisfactory alternatives, to leave the way clear for his own solution. As we have seen, he eliminated the family, religion and education as solutions. He also rejected Rousseau's totalitarian solution of the state as representing the General Will. So what was left?

The major contender in the field was contract. The particular target for Durkheim was the set of nineteenth-century economists and thinkers who believed that individualism could be tamed by contract, especially Herbert Spencer. Of Spencer and others he wrote: 'They suppose original, isolated, and independent individuals who, consequently, enter into relationship only to cooperate, for they have no other reason to clear the space separating them and to associate. But this theory, so widely held, postulates a veritable *creatio ex nihilo*. It consists indeed in deducing society from the individual.'[8] Durkheim's basic point was that dyadic contracts are too unstable to hold a society together. He writes that where 'interest is the only ruling force each individual finds himself in a state of war with every other since nothing comes to mollify the egos, and any truce would not be of long duration. There is nothing less constant than interest. Today, it unites me to you; tomorrow, it will make me your enemy. Such a cause can only give rise to transient relations and passing associations.'[9]

In fact, the paradox of the fact that modern society seemed to be based more and more on contract, yet more and more unified, was because contract was not what it seemed. 'In effect, the contract is, *par excellence*, the juridical expression of co-operation.'[10] There is an underpinning which is necessary, but invisible. 'In sum, a contract is not sufficient unto itself, but is possible only thanks to a regulation of the contract which is originally social.'[11] Contract, in fact, 'forces us to assume obligations that we have not contracted for, in the exact sense of the word, since we have not deliberated upon them . . . Of course, the initial act is always contractual, but there are consequences, sometimes immediate, which run over the limits of the contract. We co-operate because we wish to, but our voluntary co-operation creates duties for us that we did not desire.'[12]

In a broad way, Durkheim is right. Contracts are indeed only the surface and cannot easily work without a state, without a shared morality, judicial system, and so on. Although his historical account is questionable in a number of respects, he does almost stumble onto Maitland's central discovery. This was that the opposition behind 'from status to contract' put forward by Maine is wrong, that in reality most relations are much more mixed.

Durkheim's first major attempt to solve the problem of how to achieve social solidarity in modern civilizations was put forward in *The Division of Labour in Society*. His answer is encapsulated in his well-known distinction between the two forms of solidarity, mechanical and organic. Traditional, pre-industrial societies were held together by mechanical solidarity. 'If we try to construct intellectually the ideal type of a society whose cohesion was exclusively the result of resemblances, we should have to conceive it as an absolutely homogeneous mass whose parts were not distinguished from one another.'[13] These are 'segmental societies with a clan-base', so-called 'in order to indicate their formation by the repetition of like aggregates in them, analogous to the rings of an earthworm . . .'[14] In contrast to this is the form of solidarity in modern societies, organic solidarity, like the 'organs' of a body which are functionally integrated. These are constituted 'by a system of different organs each of which has a special role, and which are themselves formed of differentiated parts'.[15]

Thus what binds people together is their interdependence. 'Mechanical' was used because of 'the cohesion which unites the elements of an inanimate body, as opposed to that which makes a unity out of the elements of a living body.' The paradox was that modern society, as it advanced, became more and more integrated: 'the unity of the organism increases as this individuation of the parts is more marked'.[16] Thus the division of labour produces solidarity, 'not only because it makes each individual an *exchangist*, as the economists say', but at a deeper level.[17] It is the division of labour which itself holds people together, just as an arm and a leg and a head are functionally interdependent and need each other.

Now there are some fundamental flaws in this idea. One is that it assumes that the division of labour is spontaneous and voluntary. Durkheim admits that 'the division of labour produces solidarity only if it is spontaneous and in proportion as it is spontaneous.'[18] Of course, in practice, workers and others are forced against their will into such a division of labour. Another weakness is Durkheim's unconvincing answer to the question why people who work in a sphere where there is a high division of labour, for example in a factory conveyor belt production unit in the post-Fordian world, or as a checkout worker in a supermarket, should feel a moral involvement with each other. His solution is that alienation will disappear if the management explain to the workers their important role and place in the total process. Parkin quotes Durkheim to the effect that the worker is 'not therefore a machine who repeats movements the sense of which he does not perceive, but he knows that they are tending in a certain direction, towards a goal that he can conceive of more or less distinctly. He feels that he is of some use' and that 'his actions have a goal beyond themselves.'[19] It is fairly clear that this is very unrealistic.

The goal which comforts the workers is the creation of social solidarity. This is related to Durkheim's argument that integration, rather than economic efficiency, is the true function (i.e. goal) of the division of labour. The 'economic services' which the division of labour provides are small when 'compared to the moral effect that it produces, and its true function is to create in two or more persons a feeling of solidarity'. It is clear that Durkheim is not talking about manifest and latent function, but goal, for he goes on that 'In whatever manner the result is obtained, its aim is to cause coherence among friends and to stamp them with its seal.'[20] It is not self-evident that the owner of a supermarket has social solidarity as his foremost consideration when he places twenty girls in a row at the checkout tills and twenty others filling the shelves. Adam Smith and Tocqueville, who lamented the terrible effects of the division of labour, were much closer to the actual consequences.

Durkheim's failure in his first attempt to solve the question of what holds modern societies together is widely recognized by later critics. The failure was clearly recognized by Durkheim himself, for he never referred with any seriousness to the theory of organic solidarity in his later works.

Another indication of his failure is in Durkheim's main support-ive evidence for the supposed cohesive nature of modern societies. This he found in the contrast between two types of legal system. He argued that 'In lower societies, law . . . is almost exclusively penal; it is likewise almost exclusively very stationary.'[21] Law in modern societies, on the contrary, is restitutive rather than repressive. As Parkin summarizes the contrast, 'Repressive laws are those which punish the offender by inflicting injury upon him or causing him to suffer some loss or disadvantage.' He quotes Durkheim to the effect that 'Their purpose is to harm him through his fortune, his honour, his life, his liberty, or to deprive him of some object whose possession he enjoys.' 'Restitutive laws, by contrast, do not bring down suffering on the head of the offender. Instead, they aim at "restoring the previous state of affairs".'[22] In fact, as almost every anthropologist since Durkheim has pointed out, this is back to front.[23] Many of the simpler societies have a mainly restitutive system, while most modern societies use penal and repressive measures.

Having failed in his first attempt he moved to a new projected work on occupational groups. The subject was first raised in a lec-ture in 1892, and his last major publication on the subject took place in 1902. It will be remembered that this was exactly the same period when Maitland became especially interested in corporations and Trusts. What Durkheim intended to do in the book on the subject which he never wrote can be reconstructed from various sources. In various parts of *Suicide* he laid out the need for moral and political integration through new forms of grouping. In the preface to the second edition of *The Division of Labour* he dealt with this particular problem in relation to a new form of grouping. And in the lectures, originally delivered between 1890 and 1900, and published as *Professional Ethics*, he gave his most detailed out-line of what needed to be done. As Nisbet points out, this is not just a wayward side-issue in his work, but rather 'in these proposals lies the origin and the very essence of his theoretical approach to the problem of authority and power, not merely in modern Euro-pean society, but in ancient as well as medieval groups, Eastern as well as Western'.[24] Let us therefore consider this second theory.

Durkheim's work was a response to what were considered to be the two great revolutions of modern times and their consequences – the political revolution (the French revolution and democracy) and the industrial revolution (the division of labour, factories, mass society, the loss of community). We can see that these were the two major areas where Durkheim thought his new organizational forms would solve the problem.

In relation to the political revolution, there seem to be two strands to Durkheim's argument. First, in almost identical terms to Montesquieu and Tocqueville, Durkheim realized that in order to prevent the state from becoming over-powerful and despotic, it needed to be balanced by what Montesquieu had called 'intermediary institutions'. His ideas of pluralism and countervailing secondary groups were just like those of Tocqueville. 'It is the nature of every form of association to become despotic unless it is restrained by external forces through their competing claims upon individual allegiance.'[25] 'Every society is despotic, at least if nothing from without supervenes to restrain its despotism'.[26]

In a number of places Durkheim writes about the necessity for there being cooperative and corporate groups between the state and the citizen.

> A society composed of an infinite number of unorganised individuals, that a hypertrophied State is forced to oppress and contain, constitutes a veritable sociological monstrosity . . . A nation can be maintained only if, between the State and the individual, there is intercalated a whole series of secondary groups near enough to the individuals to attract them strongly in their sphere of action and drag them, in this way, into the general torrent of social life.[27]

One needs a multiplication of centres. 'What liberates the individual is not the elimination of a controlling centre, but rather the multiplication of such centres, provided that they are co-ordinated and subordinated one to another.'[28] Although the state was essential for liberating individuals in the first place, it also needed to be checked. Unlike Rousseau, Durkheim believed that 'it is out of this conflict of social forces that individual liberties are born'.[29]

His second theme was that of moral integration. The state could not provide this for it is too far removed from the citizen. Since the state

is far from them, it can exert only a distant, discontinuous influence over them; which is why this feeling has neither the
necessary constancy nor strength ... Man cannot become attached
to higher aims and submit to a rule if he sees nothing above
him to which he belongs ... While the state becomes inflated
and hypertrophied in order to obtain a firm enough grip upon
individuals, but without succeeding, the latter, without mutual
relationships, tumble over one another like so many liquid mol-
ecules, encountering no central energy to retain, fix and organize
them.[30]

Durkheim's great fear was of social disintegration, of egotistical
and anomic behaviour culminating in such pathological forms as
suicide. He believed the new forms he would recommend would
check this. These groups would create warmth and break down narrow
egotism. An individual 'must feel himself more solidarity with a
collective existence which precedes him in time, which survives
him, and which encompasses him at all points. If this occurs, he
will no longer find the only aim of his conduct in himself and,
understanding that he is the instrument of a purpose greater than
himself, he will see that he is not without significance. Life will
resume meaning in his eyes, because it will recover its natural aim
and orientation.'[31] Thus he argued that 'What we especially see in
the occupational group is a moral power capable of containing individual egos ...'[32]
   In very early societies, he believed, this integration had been
provided by the family, but the new groups would take over from
this. 'Up to now, it was the family which, either through collective
property or descendence, assured the continuity of economic life,
by the possession and exploitation of goods held intact ... But if
domestic society cannot play this role any longer, there must be
another social organ to replace its exercise of this necessary function ... a group, perpetual as the family, must possess goods and
exploit them itself ...'[33] In the medieval period 'the occupational
guild was the basis of social solidarity', creating genuine moral
communities.[34] His new forms would provide the same function in
a modern, industrial society. But what, exactly, was to be set up? If
the family, religion, education and the state could not provide a
model, what could? And what could one learn from previous civilizations about how such entities work?
   Durkheim provides a potted history of occupational associations

and their history in France. This is a narrow account, for he does not deal with all the other important earlier corporations, in particular towns and cities, universities, religious orders, and so on. This weakens the argument. He describes the rise of the medieval occupational guilds in the eleventh and twelfth centuries and their quasi-religious character.[35] He then notes their destruction, which he mainly dates to the eighteenth century and the French revolution. This is again a distortion, since, as Montesquieu and Tocqueville had shown, the process had started much earlier. He notes Rousseau's hatred of all intermediary institutions and sides with him in that context. 'Since the eighteenth century *rightfully* suppressed the old corporations . . .',[36] there has been nothing to replace them. His studies showed the French Revolution levelling all the intermediary institutions. The effects of modernity 'is to have swept away cleanly all the older forms of social organization. One after another they have disappeared either through the slow erosion of time or through great disturbances.' 'Only one collective form survived the tempest: the State.'[37] Indeed, such was the force of the revolution that it was only in 1901, after much of Durkheim's work on the subject was formulated, that the Law of Congregations allowed freedom of association for all secular purposes in France.

Durkheim clearly felt that the medieval corporations were rightly brushed away. Not only were they selfish, with their conservative mysteries and craft traditions, but they were not adapted to modern industrial conditions.[38] His animus against the medieval guilds was the same as his dismissal of the trade unions. They were retrograde, putting their members' interests above the common good. So what was to be set up? For 'it remains to study the form the corporative bodies should have if they are to be in harmony with present-day conditions of our collective existence... The problem is not an easy one.'[39]

Basically the new entities, like the medieval guilds, would be based on the professions. They were to be the craft and artisan guilds restored in a new way. What Durkheim 'wished for was a type of guild that had a natural compatibility with modern industrialism'.[40] But what precisely would they do? One of the most detailed descriptions was as follows. 'To them, therefore, falls the duty of presiding over companies of insurance, benevolent aid and pensions . . .' They would also allocate rewards to their members. 'Whenever excited appetites tended to exceed all limits, the corporations would have to decide the share that should equitably revert to each of the cooperative parts. Standing above its own members, it would have all necessary authority to demand indispensable sacrifices and concessions and impose order upon them.'[41] They would be property-owning, perpetual corporations. Thus they would act as a kind of surrogate family, village community and caste group rolled into one.

They would also bridge the gap between the individual citizen and the state by 'becoming the elementary division of the State, the fundamental political unity'. Thus 'Society, instead of remaining what it is today, an aggregate of juxtaposed territorial districts, would become a vast system of national corporations.'[42] These associations 'will be units of society – recognized equally by the state, its members and their families'.[43] They would become 'the true electoral unit'.[44]

This is what they would do, but how exactly? Here all is obscure. As Parkin comments, 'Durkheim is characteristically vague when it comes to the organizational structure of the guilds.'[45] A thousand questions crowd into one's mind. Why should the state allow these rivals to political allegiance to emerge at all? Why should they be more altruistic than the medieval guilds or trades unions? Indeed, what is the structural difference? What would the role of women, and especially women working in the home, be in these new guilds? What of the many people who had professions which were highly mobile (sailors, travelling salesmen), low status (rubbish collectors), semi-legal (prostitutes), scattered (lighthouse keepers), part-time (shelf-fillers), and so on? How would other corporations – universities, clubs, sects, and so on – fit in?

There are innumerable problems with his ideas and it is not surprising that he never got beyond a very vague blueprint. What is more surprising is that Durkheim never paid any attention (unlike Montesquieu and Tocqueville) to the very extensive associational and corporative groups which would have provided him with working models of what he hoped to set up, and which were flourishing in America and had flourished for many centuries in England. Yet there is an even graver problem than the fact that the solution he proposes is so unformed and so filled with practical difficulties. This lies in the nature of what he proposed, namely state-dependent corporations.

Durkheim was frightened of the power of secondary groups and approved of their destruction in the eighteenth century. He tells us that in a properly constituted political state 'there must be no forming of any secondary groups that enjoy enough autonomy to allow of each becoming in a way a small society within the greater'.[46] This explains why he basically saw the professional groups as extensions of the state, holding delegated powers, on licence or by charter. The state must control all the sub-groups: it 'must even permeate all those secondary groups of family, trade and professional association, Church, regional areas and so on ... which tend, as we have seen, to absorb the personality of their members. It must do this, in order to prevent this absorption and free these individuals, and so as to remind these partial societies that they are not alone ... The State must therefore enter into their lives, it must supervise and keep a check on the way they operate and to do this it must spread its roots in all directions.'[47]

Indeed, the state needed to think on their behalf. As Parkin summarizes his view, 'civil society needs the state to think on its behalf because the common consciousness is not up to the job.' Indeed, in an echo of so many totalitarian thinkers from Hobbes onwards, Parkin suggests that Durkheim believed that the 'state saves civil society from itself'.[48] This is because the state has a higher intelligence. Thus the growth of the state automatically expands the individual, for 'liberty is the fruit of regulation'.[49]

It is in this context that we can understand why he foresaw no conflict between the state and civil society. The state allows civil society to exist, and indeed, at a deeper level, there is really no civil society in the full sense. What happens is that the state sets up sub-units, corporations, which it can manipulate, close, alter at will. It thinks for them, and permeates them. It can save them from themselves. And we can also understand the extraordinary footnote in which Durkheim said it did not really matter whether corporations were set up by the state or not. 'All we say of the situation of the corporations entirely leaves aside the controversial question as to whether, originally, the State intervened in their formation. Even if they had been under State control from the very beginning (which does not appear likely) it still is true that they did not affect the political structure. That is what is important for us.'[50] As Maitland brilliantly showed, corporations are always set up by the state, that is their essence. They can have no other source of authority. Durkheim does not seem to have grasped this most elementary point, nor its consequences, so well spelt out by Maitland, that is to say the totalitarian tendency which he only vaguely glimpses.

Now a number of writers on Durkheim have pointed to his unrealistic view of the benevolence of states and state bureaucracies.[51] But this is really only a very small part of the problem. The whole point of civil society is that it arises spontaneously outside the state. Montesquieu, Tocqueville and Maitland had all realized this and documented it. Durkheim does not seem to have understood this basic fact or else, in his fear of disorder, had ignored it. Siding with the destroyers of intermediate institutions in the eighteenth century, and showing a very impoverished idea of what medieval corporations had been, he was not well placed to develop a robust theory of civil society. The greater threat, he believed, were the insubordinate associations. The state should think for them, regulate them and crush them 'for the greater good' when it deemed it was necessary.

Durkheim's assumption undermines his whole endeavour. The professional associations, if they had ever been set up along lines sketched out by Durkheim, would never have worked as a protection for the individual. Nor would it have led to the affective warmth and moral integration he hoped to produce if the professional associations were merely cells of the central Party. His weakness also reflects a deeper lack of perception.

Unlike Tocqueville or Maitland, Durkheim paid no attention, as we have seen, to the rich history of civil society in the West. He did not show any interest in the development of those numerous associational mechanisms which had developed alongside the trade guilds. Nor did he show any interest in examining how they worked in other parts of Europe (e.g. Germany or England) or the world (e.g. America) in his day. If he had done so he might have begun to understand the very curious blend of status and contract which gave them their special character. He might have seen how they generated emotion, long-term commitment, loyalty and trust. He might have seen how they really solved exactly his problem, combining the flexibility needed in modern society, with the warmth needed in human relations. It would not have been easy for him to understand. As Maitland explains, the greatest of German thinkers, like Gierke, who had devoted their whole lives to the subject, coming from a corporative tradition based on Roman law, found it almost impossible to understand it. But Montesquieu and Tocqueville had gone a long way. Durkheim hardly made a start. Despite this being his largest question – solidarity in an industrial age – and despite feeling that groups of some kind were the answer, his answer is unsatisfactory.

His second effort had failed. He may have sensed this also, since he lost interest in this topic as well. He turned away to the study of what he considered to be the origins and function of religion in the simplest societies in his *Elementary Forms of the Religious Life*. He never returned to a sustained discussion of the unsolved problem of cohesion in modern society.

Durkheim's life's work had been a failure. He had specified the problem, namely what could create solidarity and democratic civilization. He had examined the effects of loss of integration in relation to suicide. But as far as providing an understanding of his own times as a remedy for rootlessness, his solutions were hardly helpful. We may compare this to the work of Maitland who was working at exactly the same period, the 1890s and first few years of the twentieth century, on the same problem.

What Maitland had done was to answer this fundamental question of integration by solving a whole set of questions left open by previous thinkers. He had shown how the peculiar relation of economics and politics worked, how feudalism mixed status and contract, how liberty fed back into a strengthened civil society, hence increasing political and economic power. He showed how civil society and the strength of intermediary powers had emerged in England and how this was related to a powerful middle class. He explained how the English property system worked and evolved, and the role of private property. He showed how modern atomistic individualism was matched by the social glue of associations.[52] He explained how Tocqueville's balance between centralization and decentralization worked and avoided the tendency to bureaucratic centralization. He explained that the evolution from 'Community' to 'Individual' was a gross over-simplification and how a system without birth-given statuses, either of rank or family, had long been present in England. And throughout this he delicately showed the role of legal institutions in preserving the balances and contradictions which are the essence of the modern condition. All this profound sociological and philosophical analysis was covered over with a veneer of technical legal history which has deceived subsequent historians into thinking of him just as a historian or legal historian.

9
Maitland Assessed

Maitland died over 90 years ago and a huge amount of research has been undertaken along the lines he sketched out. Before we accept his account of the making of the modern world it is worth briefly summarizing the modifications and corrections to his work since his death.

There have been a number of detailed assessments which summarize the modifications. James Cameron's *Frederick William Maitland and the History of English Common Law* (1961), points out that Maitland's theory of the origin of English boroughs is no longer accepted and that in relation to Roman law, Bracton was probably a better Romanist than Maitland believed. He also notes that as Holdsworth and others have shown, Maitland exaggerated the danger of a 'Reception' of Roman Law in England in the sixteenth century. Yet, in relation to 95 per cent of Maitland's work, Cameron suggests that the interpretations he put forward are still trustworthy. H.E. Bell's *Maitland, a Critical Examination and Assessment* (1965) echoes the above three criticisms and adds minor modifications in relation to three particular topics.[1] Otherwise, again, he leaves almost all the findings intact, for instance pointing out that in the debate about the pre-Norman roots of feudal relations, scholarship has swung back in favour of Maitland's interpretation.[2] Bell generally endorses the vision of a man he describes as 'the greatest English historian'.[3] In relation to Maitland's *History of English Law*, Bell places it as the third of the great syntheses of English law, alongside Bracton and Blackstone, and notes 'how very much later scholars have depended on Maitland's groundwork, and, second, how rarely, in matters of great importance, they have found serious fault with it'.[4]

More recently, G.R. Elton's *F.W. Maitland* (1985) summarizes the

same set of minor criticisms. To these he adds three other technical criticisms.[5] Elton also draws attention to one other area of
challenge. This was a view put forward by S.F.C. Milsom in his
introduction to the reprint of *The History of English Law* (1968).
Milsom suggested quite tentatively that while Maitland's picture of
a flat, two-dimensional world in law was correct by the later thirteenth
century, possibly Maitland underestimated the strength of feudal
power relations between about 1160 and 1260.

It is worth pointing out that even if Milsom turns out to be
right, this only makes a small difference to one sub-aspect of
Maitland's work. Milsom himself recognizes this when he writes:
'if all this is right, and if the modifications required now seem
important, they are not important when compared with the original picture.'[6] When he returned to the same allegations 14 years
later, Milsom remained diffident about whether his 'heresy' was right
at all and concluded with the words, 'And now the dwarf must
stop grumbling about his vantage-point on the giant's shoulder . . .'[7]
Elton considers Milsom's claim that 'Maitland failed to give proper
weight to the social structure of a feudal or seigneurial world'.[8] He
summarizes Milsom's view that 'Maitland antedated the settled and
sophisticated state of the law by a hundred years at least, whereas
in his view the feudal relationship predominated down to the end
of the twelfth century over the King's rule . . .'[9] As Elton writes, 'In
the end, the two pictures differ in emphasis rather than essentials . . .'[10]
In any case, even this minor heresy may be wrong: 'No attempt
has yet been made to assess this new interpretation, and for all I
know Milsom may not in the end prevail.'[11] That the heresy has
gained so little ground either from its original proponent or others
in the 18 years of its life leads one to wonder as to its importance
and plausibility.

When we consider that some 5,000 pages of detailed findings,
written about 100 years ago, have been modified in only a few
minor emphases and one or two facts, and that the bulk of Maitland's
edifice still stands, we can begin to understand why he has an almost god-like status among historians who know the problems he
faced and the elegance of his solutions.

The great legal historian Vinogradoff disagreed with Maitland on
some specific points, but shortly after Maitland's death wrote of
him as 'the greatest legal historian of the law of England' and as a
man to whom lawyers, historians and sociologists were equally

indebted: 'lawyers because of his subject, historians because of his methods, sociologists because of his results.'[12]

J.H. Hexter referred to Maitland as 'the greatest of English historians' in his book on modern historians.[13] R.G. Collingwood referred to the 'best historians, like Mommsen and Maitland'.[14] Denys Hay, in his overview of western historiography, describes him as a 'giant' who, with Marc Bloch, is one of the 'two greatest historians of recent times'.[15] Bloch himself referred to 'the great English jurist Maitland'.[16] The medievalist Helen Cam ends her preface to his *Selected Essays* by concluding 50 years after his death. 'Let us say with Powicke, "Maitland is one of the immortals" and leave it at that.'[17] G.O. Sayles wrote that 'In the range of his interests, the fineness of his intellect, and the considerable bulk of what he wrote in barely twenty-five years, Maitland has no match among English historians.'[18] Part of the reason he has not been more generally appreciated is explained by John Burrow. Comparing him to the great William Stubbs, Burrow writes that 'Maitland's was a comparable mind, sharper, finer, more theoretical and impressionable, but in Maitland's case . . . there is no single work which is so obviously the summation of his talents and learning.'[19]

K.B. McFarlane wrote in 1965 that if when Seccombe talked in his obituary of Maitland of 'the shallowness of the ripple caused by the passing of England's greatest historian since Gibbon and Macaulay', he

means to suggest that Maitland's greatness as a historian fell short of the heights attained by Gibbon and Macaulay, he did his friend an injustice. Probably he wished only to indicate how select was the company to which Maitland belonged. Few with any right to an opinion would find fault with that estimate for claiming too much. As we look back over the whole range from a distance, we can see that the summit of Mount Maitland overtops them all. What other English historian has combined such exact scholarship with so much imaginative insight, intellectual grasp, and brilliance in exposition. Outside Britain his only rival is Mommsen.[20]

Even his most learned critic, Milsom, writes of him as 'a still living authority'. Maitland, he wrote, 'would probably wish his work to be superseded. There is little sign that this will happen soon.'[21]

In a recent symposium, a number of distinguished medieval historians and two lawyers have combed through his great work on the *History of English Law* 100 years after its publication. They have found very little to quibble with, making only minor technical adjustments to his account.[22] Often where they do differ in interpretation, this merely lends weight to Maitland's more general argument. For example, Patrick Wormald suggests three 'heresies', but concludes that 'one outcome of what I am arguing would be to buttress a central plank in Maitland's case', namely that 'the history of law in England and in other European countries differed because the king of England was in command of his courts... To me that seems an essential truth...'[23] Likewise, in a foreword to a new edition of *Domesday Book and Beyond*, J.C. Holt has pointed to some technical errors in the book, yet still recommends it as 'the greatest single book on English medieval history'.[24]

Subsequently, Wormald has produced the first volume of his magisterial two volume work on *The Making of English Law*. He pays tribute to Maitland as 'the greatest legal historian of all time', an 'Immortal'.[25] He suggests that Maitland believed that the common law had sprung with 'marvellous suddenness' from the head of King Henry II (1154–89) and that this indicates that Maitland underestimated the importance of its roots in the Anglo-Saxon period.[26] Since, as I have argued above, I do not interpret Maitland in this way, but rather as stressing the Anglo-Saxon origins of English civilization at a wider level, I do not find it necessary to correct Maitland. Everything that Wormald argues merely reinforces what I think Maitland was more generally arguing. For example, Wormald writes that 'Henry II made law like no other twelfth-century king, because he inherited a system of royal justice that was already uniquely old and active'.[27] Or again he writes: 'the kingdom where something singular happened to law in the twelfth century was also one where something without European parallel was happening in the tenth and eleventh. Henry II legislated as Alfred, Aethelstan, Edgar and Cnut had, but as the last Carolinginans, Ottonians and Capetians had not.'[28]

Thus it may well be true that Wormald has spotted an inconsistency in Maitland's presentation of his argument, but the general thrust of Wormald's enterprise serves only to reinforce the story which Maitland told about the peculiar nature of English history. The theme of the projected second volume is announced on the back cover of the first and again fits extremely well with what I take to be Maitland's more general argument. We are told that the book will show 'how a formidable system of formal and informal control was established by England's first kings in the fields of Church law, crime and punishment, law-courts and property.' The achievements of Henry II and his successors would have been impossible without this. I believe that Maitland would have been delighted with Wormald's conclusion that 'England has a unique legal history because it is the oldest continuously-functioning state in the world.'

Another very recent work which basically endorses much of the argument for continuity and Anglo-Saxon origins which Maitland advanced is James Campbell's *The Anglo-Saxon State*. In a number of reprinted essays he argues, for example, that the 'individual' characteristics which I detected in medieval and early modern England, on the basis of reading Maitland and other sources, 'existed earlier'. He relates this to other phenomena in Anglo-Saxon England: 'a high proportion of land transfers were by sale; women had very considerable rights; legal procedures rather than being, as used to be argued, archaic and irrational by our standards, have been powerfully argued to be perfectly sensible and rational in a modern sense, with much stress on written evidence: there was a lot of literacy in that society.'[29]

He stresses again and again the commercial sophistication, the strong sense of national unity, the powerful state apparatus, the relative weakness of kinship, the seeds of democratic politics and other factors which fit perfectly with Maitland's account. Maitland's work is very frequently cited and almost always endorsed. That arguably the most learned Anglo-Saxon and early medieval scholar of his generation should continue to support the Stubbs–Maitland vision in a publication nearly a hundred years after Maitland's death is worth noting.

*

We have seen that Maitland took the argument on a stage by documenting the theories suggested by Tocqueville and others. They put forward a hypothesis of what had happened based on some historical research, but were unable to go deeply into the most important case, England, for lack of sources and training. Maitland had the training and sources and was one of the leaders of the great movement of the last quarter of the nineteenth century which opened up the public records and printed selections for the first time. He was a great editor and student of original documents, from Anglo-Saxon times onwards. His intuitions were checked against, and also arose from, a deep understanding of historical documents. Yet he only had a few years of healthy life in which to do this, and there were some tasks he bequeathed to his successors. We earlier saw the fruits of this labour in various publications and the founding of the Selden Society.

Maitland was well aware that he was just scratching the surface. In the introduction to *Select Pleas in Manorial and Other Seignorial Courts* he wrote that 'A few sets of rolls completely printed beginning in the thirteenth and ending in, let us say, the sixteenth century, would be of inestimable value, especially if they began with surveys or 'extents' and ended with maps.'[30] He was well aware that vast treasures awaited the social and legal historian in areas of local records which he could only touch on.

His own work was mainly on early manorial records and those of the central courts of the common law. He was unable to explore thoroughly whole ranges of other documents, the rich records of equity jurisdiction, local ecclesiastical records, and so on. And although he did make a more detailed study of some of the Cambridgeshire area, he never really undertook a detailed study of one village or set of manors which would bring together the records.

Maitland was the leading figure in the first archival revolution, when the central records became usable and used for the first time. The second archival revolution took place roughly in the quarter of a century after 1950 when local history and the reorganization of the local record offices revealed an immense new set of materials.[31] These materials allow us to see how far Maitland's still somewhat intuitive conclusions were substantiated by microscopic work on how the system he postulated actually worked at the local level. This forms a fascinating case rather similar to a biologist predicting certain things would be found when the microscope becomes strong enough. The work I briefly summarize below allows us to test his conclusions.

Large quantities of historical materials at the local level have been published since Maitland died, particularly by record societies. There have also been a number of well-known studies of villages and manors. The study I have been engaged on since 1970 with my colleagues, and particularly Sarah Harrison, is somewhat different from these. First, we have endeavoured to track down all the records for a particular parish, Earls Colne in Essex, over the period from the earliest records through to 1850, some 500 years. Second, all these records have been typed into a computer, published on microfiche and are now available on the World Wide Web.[32] We thus have available, for the first time, very long runs of manor court rolls, which can be combined with other excellent manorial records including a detailed map of 1598, to reconstruct landholding over half a millenium. This material is complemented by the extensive records generated by the ecclesiastical authorities, including parish registers and wills, and by the central courts, in particular the rich and hitherto largely unused records of the equity courts (for example, Chancery). At one period we are also taken down to the personal level through the diary of Ralph Josselin, the vicar of Earls Colne, through the middle part of the seventeenth century.[33]

All this material has been indexed very extensively and family histories and land patterns have been reconstructed. This has taken a team effort involving several computer programmers and many person-years of work. It is unlikely that it will ever be repeated, but it does give us a chance to see how well Maitland's vision works.

It is not possible to do more than summarize some impressions from this dense mass of material. In relation to some of Maitland's major arguments, it would seem that his preliminary hunches fit the data very well. The Earls Colne documents show that English law and society had a continuous evolution from 1200 onwards and that there was no great break, no 'transformation' from one kind of civilization ('feudal', 'peasant') to another ('capitalist', 'individualist'). Anyone who reads through the documents for Earls Colne, and who investigates how the system worked which generated them, will endorse Maitland's vision. There is change, but the deeper structures have great force and evolve without any revolutionary break. Even if we go behind the documents as much as we can, we can see no shadow of the Marxist or other transformations.

Maitland had argued that the English system feels very different from what one reads about in relation to France or much of 'peasant' Europe during the period between the fourteenth and eighteenth centuries. For example, that the attachment to the land in England is far weaker than in France and the strength of the family–land bond is never the same. The conclusion of Maitland concerning the English case again seems fully borne out by the Earls Colne documents.

Maitland had argued that the system in England was never based on the idea of a 'village community', with 'community' ownership of land or other assets and a deeply immobile society where blood and neighbourly relations formed people into a 'Gemeinschaft'. Maitland's description of the mixture of individualism and association appears to capture how the system worked in Earls Colne very well indeed, and there is no sign between 1350 and 1850 of the movement from community to individualism.

Maitland had suggested that the English system consisted of a complex web of rights and duties which was both centralized and decentralized, and which nested people in levels and layers. A study of the land and other records of Earls Colne is beautifully illuminated by Maitland's account of how feudalism worked, and in particular the detailed descriptions in some of the large court cases in Earls Colne, involving such notables as the Earl of Oxford and Lord Treasurer Burleigh, illustrate the immensely sophisticated links between power and property which Maitland analysed so well.

Maitland presented a picture of an unstable, meritocratic and mobile social structure, in which people were constantly jockeying for wealth. In other words, there were no castes, no hereditary blood ranks; rather wealth could buy status. This is illustrated throughout the history of Earls Colne, with property changing hands, with new rich London merchants entering the village, with children of the same parents rising and dropping in wealth and rank.

Maitland suggested that the family system was based on negotiation and a basic premise of equality, for instance that there was an absence of patriarchal male power over children and women. There is abundant evidence in Earls Colne, again especially in the equity records, but also in wills and other records, of the relative autonomy and power of women and children. There is, as Maitland argued, no evidence of a gradual improvement in women's status over the centuries and, if anything, the women of the fourteenth to sixteenth centuries appear more autonomous than those of the nineteenth.

Maitland documented the power and ubiquity of law and due process. This is everywhere apparent; the heart of the system in Earls Colne was the multiplicity of courts, the respect for law, the widespread knowledge of and involvement of people down almost to the bottom of the society in the legal system. It was, as Maitland realized, a society steeped in law, but law of a curiously confrontational, customary and rights-based kind.

Maitland suggested that what held the system together was the ability of non-related persons to work together in small associations and units based on the concept of the Trust. Even at the local level of Earls Colne we can see his ideas reflected, often indirectly, in a thousand ways. We can see it in the organization of the school, the church, the manor, the county administration; the way in which the clergy, the teachers, the jurors in the manorial courts, the small nonconformist sects worked. All this and many other signs show us a world where people collaborated to run their own activities with their neighbours, friends, co-religionists or whatever in numerous informal associations. Many of these were based on trust and honesty, on time freely given to benefit not the community as a whole, but either the association or something at a higher level, though it was not yet called the state. Thus the individualism was curbed by the proliferation of associations and by the obligations to work with others.

In a book such as this, all this can only really be asserted. I can only affirm that in studying Earls Colne over the last 30 years, in comparing it to another English parish in the north of England, Kirkby Lonsdale, and by comparing both of these to what I have read about as an anthropologist, and a long study of a Himalayan village and the history of Japan, I have found that Maitland's vision fits and illuminates the English case beautifully.[34] I did not undertake the village study to test Maitland, but after the event, when we compare his hypothetical model against the superb documentation for one English parish for 500 years, it is impossible to find anything that he seems seriously to have misjudged. This is more than can be said for many of those who have come after him and it is another hint that we can have some confidence in his conclusions. Inspired by Maitland's heritage, we have made available many thousands of pages of original documents against which his vision can be tested.[35]

*

Since Maitland's account, if correct, would be such an elegant demonstration of the accuracy of the guesses of Montesquieu, Smith and Tocqueville, it is worth assessing his authority by one further test. Although he was deeply knowledgeable about continental law and far from being a 'little Englander', we may wonder whether England was really so odd, and whether the divergence during the twelfth to fifteenth centuries is as real as Maitland argued. In order to pursue this, we can look at the problem from another angle, through the eyes of arguably the only other medievalist who can vie with Maitland in width and depth, namely Marc Bloch. What did Bloch think of that comparison between continental and English development which was at the centre of the theories of all these thinkers?

In relation to England, Bloch seems to have developed a three-period model which is in many respects parallel to Maitland's. The Anglo-Saxon period constituted the first phase. In his great work on *Feudal Society*, Bloch noted that from Anglo-Saxon times there was something independent and different about England, it was 'a society of a Germanic structure which, till the end of the eleventh century, pursued an almost completely spontaneous course of evolution'.[36] Part of the reason for its oddness, as Maitland had argued, was that 'Britain lacked that substratum of Gallo-Roman society which in Gaul . . . seems clearly to have contributed to the development of class distinctions.'[37]

Then, as Maitland had argued, there was about a century and a half of considerable overlap between about 1100 and 1250. 'Despite its distinctive features, the course of development in England presented some obvious analogies with that in the Frankish state.'[38] Thus the 'evolution of the *de facto* nobility at first followed almost the same lines as on the continent – only to take a very different direction in the thirteenth century.'[39]

The divergence began pretty soon for, again echoing Maitland, Bloch argued that from about the end of the twelfth century the relations between the power of the Crown and the Lords developed in a different direction in England. 'It is here that the two paths noticeably diverge. In England from the twelfth century onward royal justice made itself felt with exceptional force.' In France, on the other hand, 'the evolution of royal justice lagged a good century behind that of England and followed a totally different course.'[40]

There were several areas where the growing divergence from the later twelfth century showed itself. Among these were the following. The 'distinction between high and low justice always remained foreign to the English system.'[41] The allodial estates common on the continent, which prevented the final penetration of feudal tenures to the bottom of society, were totally extinguished in England, where all land was ultimately held of the king and not held in full ownership by any subject. England was exceptional in not having private feuding sanctioned after the Conquest; it therefore avoided that disintegrated anarchy which was characteristic of France.[42] Indeed, English feudalism, we are told 'has something of the value of an object-lesson in social organization', not because it was typical of feudal society but because it shows 'how in the midst of what was in many respects a homogeneous civilization certain creative ideas, taking shape under the influence of a given environment, could result in the creation of a completely original legal system.'[43] It is this 'completely original legal system' which provides the key to the problems which we have been discussing.

At a deeper level, Bloch was saying that, as Maitland had argued, England had moved a long way away from that feudalism through which much of the Continent had passed. Bloch noted the centralization and uniformity of the English political and social system. This was different from his major feature of feudalism, devolution, disintegration and the dissolution of the state. The contrasts come out when he compares England and France.

> In England there was the Great Charter; in France, in 1314–15, the Charters granted to the Normans, to the people of Languedoc, to the Bretons, to the Burgundians, to the Picards, to the people of Champagne, to Auvergne, of the *Basses Marches* of the West, of Berry, and of Nevers. In England there was Parliament; in France, the provincial Estates, always much more frequently convoked and on the whole more active than the States-General. In England there was the common law, almost untouched by regional exceptions; in France the vast medley of regional 'customs'.[44]

Thus England was uniform and centralized, France varied and regionalized. Because 'the public office was not completely identified with the fief', Bloch argued, 'England was a truly unified state much earlier than any continental kingdom.' Furthermore, the English parliamentary system had a 'peculiar quality which distinguished it so sharply from the continental system of "Estates"' which was linked to 'that collaboration of the well-to-do classes in power, so characteristic of the English political structure . . .'[45]

Related to these differences was a peculiar status system. England had no formal blood nobility, while such a nobility did develop in France. It was true that 'England had an aristocracy as powerful as any in Europe – more powerful perhaps . . .' At the top was a narrow group of earls and 'barons', who were in the thirteenth century being endowed with privileges. Yet somehow these privileges took a different shape from those on the Continent. They were 'of an almost exclusively political and honorific nature; and above all, being attached to the *fief de dignité*, to the "honour", they were transmissible only to the eldest son. In short, the class of noblemen in England remained, as a whole, more a "social" than a "legal" class.' Although, of course, power and prestige lay with this group, it was 'too ill-defined not to remain largely open'. Thus 'In the thirteenth century, the possession of landed wealth had been sufficient to authorize the assumption of knighthood, in fact to make it obligatory.'[46] Therefore 'in practice, any family of solid wealth and social distinction' never 'encountered much difficulty' in obtaining permission to use hereditary armorial bearings.[47]

Bloch's story is that there was a confusion of ranks up to the Norman invasion, and during the crucial twelfth and thirteenth centuries England did not move in the continental direction. No nobility based on law and blood, no incipient 'caste' in Tocqueville's sense, emerged. This, as his predecessors had argued, gave the English aristocracy their enduring flexibility and power. 'It was mainly by keeping close to the practical things which give real power over men and avoiding the paralysis that overtakes social classes which are too sharply defined and too dependent on birth that the English aristocracy acquired the dominant position it retained for centuries.'[48] It is not surprising that Bloch should head the section, 'The Exceptional Case of England'. At the level of European feudalism, Bloch had demonstrated that indeed, England, as Tocqueville had much earlier guessed, had not moved from contract (feudalism) to status (caste ranks). It had not reversed Maine's famous dictum that 'the movement of the progressive societies is from status to contract'.

Likewise in the lowest rank, there developed something strikingly unlike the situation in France. It is in the same period, namely the second half of the twelfth century, that another structural difference became visible, the peculiar position of the English villein. Bloch points out 'How often has English villeinage been treated as the equivalent of the French *servage* in the 13th, 14th and 15th centuries ... But this is a superficial analogy ... Villeinage is in fact a specifically English institution.' This was a result of 'the very special political circumstances in which it was born', namely that 'As early as the second half of the 12th century ... the kings of England succeeded in getting the authority of their courts of justice recognized over the whole country.'[49] The differences grew wider and wider so that 'The French serf of the 14th century and the English serf or villein of the same period belonged to two totally dissimilar classes.'[50] Elsewhere he elaborates on how, 'in this remarkably centralized country', the royal authority could recapture runaway serfs.[51] This was because under the influence of the Normans and Angevins, 'the judicial powers of the crown had developed to an extraordinary degree.'[52] He confirms Maitland's view that in the 'England of the Norman Kings there were no peasant allods' while these were present in France.[53]

All of these structural differences set England on a very different path to much of continental Europe. Bloch even linked these differences to a growing divergence in relation to liberty and property. In his essay 'A Contribution Towards a Comparative History of European Societies', originally published in 1928, Bloch elaborated the effects of some of these differences. English agriculture became 'individualistic' while French agriculture remained 'communal'. A 'new notion of liberty' was born in England where 'no man, not even the King, may come between him [the serf] and his lord. But there was nothing like this in France. There, royal justice was much slower in developing, and its progress took a quite different course. There was no great legislative enactments like those of Henry II of England.'[54] Thus although England and France were 'neighbouring and contemporary societies' the 'progress and results' of their individual development 'reveal such profound differences of degree that they are almost equivalent to a difference of kind . . .'[55]

Thus we see in Bloch, as in Maitland, a narrative which basically fills out the guesses of earlier theorists. Some of the roots of our peculiar modern world lie in the Anglo-Saxon period. For a century or a little more England and the continent converged. Then, from the twelfth century, law and social and political structures diverged. Much of the continent moved towards Tocqueville's caste and absolutism. For particular reasons one island retains a balance of forces and a dynamic tension between parts of the institutional structure. This would provide shelter for the inventions and ideas of its larger European neighbours.

*

F.W. Maitland's work has tended to be set within too small a frame. Most of those who write about him are historians of England or English lawyers, specialists who are technically equipped to follow parts of his argument. They do not often set him within a European frame or a great tradition of intellectual endeavour. They do not see his real interest in the questions of political economy stemming from his early training and fellowship dissertation; they do not consider his extended temporal frame, a metahistory of England from the seventh to the nineteenth centuries. They are too close to him.

When we step back, as we now can do since he is quite distant from us, we can see, as K.B. McFarlane put it in his metaphor, that he is indeed a mountain rising far above the technical history of medieval English law, and far more than merely a great editor of English documents, though he is both of those things as well. His central problems concerning the origins of liberty and equality are the same as those of Montesquieu, Tocqueville and, as we shall shortly see, Fukuzawa. And his answers, though limited to one country, make up for geographical width by their time-depth and their deep erudition.

Maitland was not a believer in inevitable progress. He was not a 'Whig' historian. Yet he believed in growth, change with continuity, the deep roots of English liberty. He was not an English chauvinist, yet he was proud of English law and saw its virtues despite, or perhaps partly because of, its muddle and empiricism. He was not a vulgar positivist; he realized that historical work depended critically on intuition, hunches, guesswork. Yet he equally realized that careful research into contemporary documents was necessary to prove and correct the intuitions. He moved with ease between theory and data, between minute and accurate detail and grand overviews. He was both one of the best of local historians and also a thinker on an international scale. As Schuyler wrote, the 'combination of broad views and minute investigations, of what Macaulay called landscape painting and map making in the writing of history, is one of his marked characteristics'.[56]

Driven on by the sense of an impending early death Maitland tried to solve within a period of some 20 years the same riddle as earlier thinkers. How had the strange modern world, with its glimpses of liberty, equality and wealth, been made? Why had it found its expression in a certain part of the world and in its earliest and definitive form in England? What precisely were the constituents of this peculiar civilization? His solutions, much more deeply based on documents, were in substance the same as those put forward by Montesquieu, Adam Smith and Tocqueville. The essence of modernity lay in the separation of spheres, the tensions between religion, politics, kinship and economy. Out of these contradictions emerged certain liberties and a dynamic energy. Maintaining the balance between them was extraordinarily difficult. What the others had guessed was that the origins must lie somewhere in the period of the Germanic invasions. What Maitland showed was that while the trail did indeed run into darkness there, it was possible to move back and forth along the trail since that time.

If one did so, one could see that maintaining the balance was a gigantic accident. A whole set of factors, from the general (the nature of islandhood, the accident of the Norman Conquest, the absence of Cathar heresies and the Inquisition), to the individual (the personality of Henry II or Edward I) played their part. What happened on one small island both reflected what happened on its neighbouring continent, but also transformed it. Like some new species of finch on the Galapagos, there developed a new kind of civilization. This would then be magnified and taken to its extreme through other accidents, the development of America, the expansion of the British Empire and the first industrial revolution and so to the modern world. With Maitland we have a developed theory which puts forward a believable answer to one part of the question of how the modern world has been made.

Part II

Yukichi Fukuzawa: The Nature and Effects of the Modern World

Preface to a Study of Yukichi Fukuzawa

This second part of the book cannot properly be understood without an explanation of how I came to be interested in the work of the great Japanese social theorist Yukichi Fukuzawa. For many years now, as an historian and anthropologist, I have been struggling to understand how and why the peculiar modern world in which we live has emerged. Compared to what anthropologists found in other tribes and civilizations, and historians described for *ancien régime* Europe, what has become established over much of the world very recently is strange.

I had for some time sensed that useful clues to an answer to these broad questions might be found in the similarities and differences between two ex-feudal islands at opposite ends of the world, namely England and Japan. So I was delighted to be invited as a British Council visiting scholar to the University of Hokkaido in 1990. When I arrived, like most outsiders I imagine, I had never heard of Fukuzawa. While every Japanese from their school days has studied Montesquieu or Adam Smith, Fukuzawa is almost totally unknown in the West. So I was completely ignorant about his life and role in setting up the Japan I saw around me. The enthusiasm of Professor Toshiko Nakamura, one of my two chief hosts, encouraged me to start to learn about him, and she suggested I start with his most famous book, *A Theory of Civilization.*

I soon realized that Fukuzawa was not just a thinker of local importance. He had addressed the fundamental question of what characterized modern civilization. In other words, he was on the same quest as that on which I am engaged. Furthermore, his answer seemed to coincide very well with that which I was coming to see from other sources seemed to be the quintessence of the difference between past and present civilizations. This was the separation of different spheres, religious, political, social and economic, and then their maintenance in a dynamic set of contradictions and tensions. This is what Fukuzawa also saw as the heart of what seemed most strange and significant about the western world.

I had never before encountered any thinker outside the European intellectual tradition who had seen this and I was deeply impressed. So I decided to learn more about him, both for his own sake but also because, standing between Japan and the West, he acted as a superb introduction to the Japanese world which I was starting to try to understand. Like any really good mediator of cultures or anthropological informant he knew enough about both worlds to be able to act as a shortcut into a distant culture and also a revealing mirror of my own.

I soon wondered how Fukuzawa had managed to place himself in this position as a bridge between cultures. I found that he had written an autobiography at the end of his life and that this had been translated by Eiichi Kiyooka as *The Autobiography of Yukichi Fukuzawa* (New York, 1972). I read this and was entranced. Although it was clearly to a certain extent a sanitized, 'after-the-event' account, it also provided a very lively and fascinating picture of an extraordinary life. I began to appreciate that Fukuzawa was not merely an unusual intellectual, but that his practical contribution to the institutional structure of modern Japan was of considerable importance. I understood why, in the crucial years after the Meiji Restoration, 'all works about the West came to be popularly known as *Fukuzawabon*'.[1] His continuing influence and popularity within Japan I discovered is reflected in the currency. There are only two banknotes in Japan. The 5,000 yen carries a portrait of one of the great modern writers of Japan, Natsume Soseki. The 10,000 yen note has Fukuzawa's portrait, a fitting tribute to a man who did more than any other to make Japan a land of liberty, wealth and equality.

When I decided to approach the history of the great transformation of the world through examining the intellectual biographies of great thinkers, I decided to include him as the only non-European thinker I could find to stand on the same level as the others I had chosen.[2] So I wrote a draft of some chapters on his life and thought. I showed these to Dr Carmen Blacker, the leading western expert on Fukuzawa, and she was extremely supportive and encouraged me to proceed further.

Talking to a number of Japanese academics and giving several lectures on Fukuzawa at Japanese universities brought home to me how highly Fukuzawa is still regarded. It is therefore a considerable responsibility to find oneself introducing him to an English-speaking audience.[3] This is made the heavier by the linguistic difficulty. I do not speak or read Japanese. Only a small part of the more than 100 volumes of Fukuzawa's writings have been translated. I have therefore relied very heavily on my friends and colleagues who are experts, as stated in the acknowledgements. It should be stressed that this is only a preliminary introduction to this great thinker and man of action. It is hoped that it will encourage a wider audience to develop an understanding of Fukuzawa and of the Japan which he shaped. For a Japanese audience I hope it will be received as a tribute to a great man, and perhaps open their eyes to sides of his work and character which are new and unexpected when seen from an outside viewpoint and in a broad comparative framework.

Finally, it should be stressed that this account represents a further shift of focus in my argument. In my earlier book on *The Riddle of the Modern World* and in the preceding chapters on Maitland I have constantly stressed that the important divide was between continental Europe and England (and America). Looking through the eyes of Fukuzawa, we now move to a more distant focus in which the contrast is between Japan on the one hand and a largely undifferentiated 'West' on the other. This is partly a result of Fukuzawa's own knowledge and experiences. He spent too little time in the West, and did not read enough, to know about or be interested in the fundamental, if subtle, differences between English and continental history. Furthermore, it is a reflection of the period he is concerned with. By the second half of the nineteenth century much of mainland western Europe was undergoing an industrial revolution and other changes which were lessening the differences between continental nations and Anglo-American civilization. For Fukuzawa's purposes the 'West' could be treated as a lump, a sort of simple 'Occidentalism'. This does not matter, for the point in introducing his work is not, as it was with Maitland, to help us solve the questions of the origins or early making of the modern world. Fukuzawa's importance lies both in the way in which he saw the basic structural features of what had emerged in 'the West', and in how he tried to promote and construct, literally 'make', a modern world in Japan.

10
Yukichi Fukuzawa and the Making of the Modern World

This study of Fukuzawa was originally written as an integral part of the book which has been separately published as *The Riddle of the Modern World*. The section on Fukuzawa came after a detailed account of the ideas of Montesquieu, Smith and Tocqueville. It is not possible to understand the particular angle I have taken in the following chapters without being aware of the conclusions of those studies. For those readers who have not seen that work, I here include part of the concluding chapter, in order to set the scene for the study of Fukuzawa.[1]

Montesquieu, Adam Smith and Tocqueville were united in their specification of what the central problem of history is. They agree that human beings are creative, inventive, curious, often motivated by strong drives to better their position. In appropriate conditions they will tend to increase their manipulation of the natural world so that their standard of living rapidly improves. They have the potential for cumulative or non-linear growth in their ability to produce resources. Indeed, for short periods in their histories, many regions or civilizations have seen such a growth.

On the other hand, experience showed them that the majority of such periods of growth came to an end quickly and that long periods of stasis or even decline were the norm. Growth was exceptional, stasis was the usual condition. Thus there must be a set of very powerful, negative forces which crush man's natural abilities and desires. Their concern was to specify these constraints or traps and to show how they had operated and sometimes been avoided for limited periods.

They were well aware that as the potential for rapid growth became greater, through higher levels of knowledge and technology, so likewise the negative pressures grew at an equal or greater pace. As each form of civilization succeeded the previous one it faced new and more significant problems. This can be seen if we look at the extremes. To move from hunter-gatherer to tribal societies required a relatively minor shift – domestication of plants and animals. The checks on this were relatively light, though starting at a subsistence level with practically no technological support, the transition was immensely difficult. The push was weak, and the counter-push was also quite weak. The two were well enough balanced to prevent any change in most of the world for over 500 generations of human existence. In Australia, over 300 generations of hunter-gathering never led to anything different before the arrival of white colonists.

At the other extreme, if one took a great empire like China, it was possible to see how both the potentials for transformation and the negative pressures were huge, and again just about balanced each other. The technological, intellectual, cultural and social sophistication of China by the fourteenth century was immense, far ahead of Europe. It had developed a knowledge of almost all the techniques necessary for industrialization, it had a very sophisticated and literate ruling group; it was peaceful and orderly. People were generally hard-working and profit-oriented. Yet 400 years later, apart from the undoubted success in feeding a much larger population, it had made no noticeable technological, scientific or social 'progress' and was now 'falling behind' Europe.

Nearer at home, the greatness of the Roman Empire, heir to all of Greek science and with its own developed organizational technologies, had collapsed, and more recently the promise of the Hapsburg Empire, of Renaissance Italy and southern Germany or even *ancien régime* France, had faded away or reached a plateau.

The potential of all these civilizations for rapid cumulative transformation was immense. Millions of hard-working, ambitious, inventive citizens surrounded by a wealth of practical, reliable knowledge of how to manipulate the natural world to their own uses should have gained in opulence from generation to generation. The fact that they did not do so shows the strength of the negative pressures.

Much of their thought is concerned with these negative pressures and how, occasionally, they were overcome. Their central understanding was that as productive technologies grew in power, they were more than counterbalanced by predatory tendencies, which began to halt productive growth. Within these predatory tendencies they included not only obvious external predation, warfare and raiding of others, which often checked a civilization, but equally important, internal predation, that is to say the predation of priests, lords, kings, and even over-powerful merchant guilds. This internal predation usually took the form of increasingly sharp stratification – castes and estates – and increasingly absolutist religion and government and hence the destruction of personal liberty of action and thought.

The process within agrarian societies was a circular one. As productive technology produced greater surpluses, these almost automatically increased predation by increasing temptations. Success created envy and smaller states or cities were destroyed by neighbours. Even huge civilizations such as China or India or eastern Europe were devastated by predating Mongols. A perpetual levelling took place. Likewise the growing wealth led to the temptation to expand and conquer, and the centre was finally ruined by the burden of imperial dreams, as had happened in Rome, the Hapsburgs or Louis XIV's France. Almost automatically surpluses generated aggressive behaviour. And such militaristic activities directly led to the twin forms of internal predation – higher taxes, rents and social stratification, and increasingly absolutist power and political predation.

This was the central trap, supplemented powerfully by the Malthusian tendency for rapid increases in population to outstrip all growth in production and hence to add famine and disease to war and internal predation as checks on sustained growth. This was the agrarian trap, and every great civilization up to the seventeenth century had finally become entangled in it and either collapsed or, like China and Japan, become immobile.

The riddle to which these three thinkers addressed themselves was how one escaped this apparently inevitable fate. During their lifetimes they speculated on the growing realization that against all the apparent predictions and laws, an escape to something else was indeed happening.

All three looked at the process from the edges of the system, though not nearly as far away as Fukuzawa. From France or Scotland they increasingly focused on a new world which seemed to be emerging first in England and then in America. The natural tendency towards cumulative growth inherent in man's intelligence and nature had always previously been checked by the iron laws of population and predation, which had finally crushed productive increases. This was the first contradiction. Something was happening, and towards the time that Tocqueville wrote, had clearly happened, in England and America, which showed that the iron laws were not laws at all, but just powerful tendencies which could, apparently, be avoided. The difficulty of avoiding them was immense, as the history of all previous civilizations showed, yet a set of peculiar balances might be achieved for long enough to do so. How these mechanisms occurred and worked was the riddle which they sought to answer.

There seems to be a consensus among all our informants that an answer to the riddle must lie in the balance of forces. They were all aware that a structural solution, that is to say one which focused on the *relations* between the parts, rather than the parts themselves, was necessary. The key to the mystery lay in the difference between the normal tendency, which was towards a certain set of interlocked and rigid institutions, and the exceptions, where the parts remained independent, antagonistic even, and hence flexible.

Putting this more explicitly, they suggested that the normal tendency was as follows. In tribal societies, almost everything was encompassed within kinship – political power, religion, economy were all embedded within this. Hence economic or political development was severely constrained. To change one element was to attack them all. The development of civilization depended, to a certain extent, on the weakening of kinship (status) and the growth of the power of other institutions – the economy and technology, the political structure (state systems) and religion (universalistic religions of the book). This was the huge leap and it allowed a freeing of energies and growth in all forms of production.

Yet there seemed a powerful tendency in agrarian civilizations for the structure to solidify again, this time into a new form of overlapping and dominating structure usually based on an alliance of priests and rulers. As productive wealth increased, the tools of power, both military and ideological, increased proportionately. The history of almost all civilizations, or periods within ancient civilizations such as China, was for a period of anarchy and confusion, where productivity was low but flexibility high, to settle down into higher productivity, but declining flexibility. A clear example of this lay, they thought, in the history of western Europe, as most of the continent moved from a lightly populated, technologically backward, but mobile, flexible and highly contractual feudal world which covered the continent from the sixth to twelfth centuries, into

increasingly rigidified, status-based, politically and religiously absolutist civilizations from the thirteenth to eighteenth centuries.

They argued that as part of the swing from production to predation, there was increasing domination of all life by an increasingly
closed world of politico-religious power which had crushed kinship, or suborned it to its use (as in China) and tried to maximize
short-term and even immediate benefit (as in war) from the productive labours in the economy. As the gaps, tensions and balance
between institutions were closed, the space for technological and
productive growth was increasingly reduced. Indeed, any advance
in the wealth of producers – whether craftsmen and manufacturers,
or merchants, or even peasants – was a distinct threat, as well as
an opportunity for predation, and hence quickly crushed. Likewise,
any growth in intellectual production outside the central circle of
power was potentially undermining and quickly put down as heresy.

In a sense we can see the development as a tendency towards
centralization and inequality, of concentric rings of power and status, in which all countervailing forces or relatively independent
centres of production of artifacts or ideas were crushed. Uniformity, homogeneity, a rigid and level landscape emanating from the
centre, where all forms of activity were again made interdependent, as in the Confucian parallel between religious, political and
kinship loyalties, this was the growing tendency. The weight of the
fruit of increased production increasingly brought down the tree.
Or, to use a mechanical analogy, a negative feedback loop was in
operation.

That this was a natural tendency was not surprising. All were
agreed that alongside sexual and intellectual drives, the desire to
dominate and exert power over others was a basic human instinct.
Indeed, much of human progress had arisen from the energy which
this desire prompted. But the desire was ultimately selfish. Each
individual would try to maximize his or her own power, and perhaps that of his small co-ordered group, whether family or caste.
With this powerful aim, and with increased wealth and technologies of domination, predation founded on an alliance of the rulers
and the thinkers, kings and priests, subjecting the rest (the workers
and 'producers') to increasing pressure, was an obvious strategy.

Indeed it was a strategy which could even, plausibly, be argued
to be in the general interest. In a world where three-quarters of
the Eurasian continent was subject to periodic devastation from
the nomadic tribes of central Asia, or more locally from neighbouring

powerful states, it made sense to put a great deal of productive wealth into predation and counter-predation. The philosophy of Machiavelli epitomizes this world where offence was the best form of defence, where those who aspired to virtue, peace, equality and liberty, were soon devastated. Even Christianity, founded on a gospel of turning the other cheek, witnessed the Crusades, the Inquisition and the final defeat of the Islamic threat at Lepanto.

Yet desperate though the ravages of war could be, there were recognizably equal dangers in too much peace. This again was best shown by the history of China and Japan. Long centuries of peace, in both civilizations, when military expenditure was relatively small and there was fairly light taxation, and even a powerful control of disorder, led only to the stagnation of technology and economy. Of course, this could partly be explained by the Malthusian tendency towards rapidly increased population. Or it could be explained by the encouragement of stratification and labour rather than capital and technologically-intensive agriculture partly caused by the peculiarities of rice cultivation. In a sense these countries were a warning of the dangers of too much success. The climate and agriculture produced huge surpluses, there was little to struggle against and the system rigidified. It was a phenomenon which Montesquieu and Smith also noticed in contrasting the early fertility and abundance of Mediterranean Europe with the need to struggle and produce in the Protestant north.

*

All 'advances' are costly to someone – for example, the labour-saving technologies which were the foundation of the industrial revolution were made at the short-term expense of millions of workers. The move to the new sources of agricultural (horses, windmills, watermills) or military (longbows, guns), or ideological (printing) power were all equally a threat to vested interests. Most civilizations were inhibited by such interests, or partially incorporated them as a new means of control. They only tend to be accepted because to fail to do so would mean that the competition from elsewhere would crush one – a sort of intellectual, technological and cultural arms race.

As they pointed out, this appeared to be the great difference between Europe and China or Japan. The plurality of small states in Europe, autonomous but linked by a common history, religion and elite language, almost incessantly at war and when not at war, in fierce cultural and social competition was the ideal context for rapid productive and ideological evolution. There was enough in common for ideas and inventions to travel swiftly, there was enough variation for separate centres of innovation to cross-fertilize. Europe was, to use Gerry Martin's phrase, a large system comprising a network of 'bounded but leaky', autonomous yet competing, states, and it had been so for about 1,000 years before the industrial revolution. The tendency to form a vast homogeneous empire, the dream of Charles V, Louis XIV, Napoleon or Hitler, was never realized. The political and actual geography and the level of communications, military and ideological technology made it impossible. Huge diversities of religion, kinship systems, culture, farming practices and craft production continued to exist and were encouraged by large geographical and climatic differences over a small area.

China, of course, also varied considerably geographically, and even culturally. But it spread politically over a vast area and came to hold a mass of individuals within one system of thought and organization. The geographical differences were not supported by the religious and political differences, which would have encouraged and protected competition. At first this made technological development very rapid. The economies of scale and massive demand set China on a course which put her far ahead of Europe. But it seems as if by the fourteenth century the variability had been largely exhausted. Thereafter a conscious decision to shut out the undermining influences from abroad by ceasing sea or land exploration was completely the opposite of the outward expansion created by the competition of European states.

In western Europe it became obvious that external predation through voyages of discovery and conquest, incorporating new ideas and technologies and peoples, was the way to wealth, as the Venetians, Portuguese, Spaniards, Dutch and finally the British discovered. So the internal variation and competition that had stimulated the first burst of productive creativity and had allowed the explorations to be effective, was supplemented by the enormously varied information from the civilizations of America, Africa, India and eastern Asia. European states absorbed the wealth of their conquests, wrestled with the new knowledge and adapted and evolved their hybrid solutions very quickly. China and Japan closed their frontiers, for five centuries in the case of China, three centuries in the case of Japan, and suddenly discovered that their once superior, but now antiquated technology, was no match for that of America and the European powers.

Thus it appeared clear that if we are to find a solution to the riddle we must look to the relationships between political, ideological, social and economic power or, as they might have put it, the relations between liberty (political and religious), equality and wealth. All of them saw the key to the mystery in a peculiar association between these, manifest in England, which ran against the current that had increasingly led to a growth of rigid uniformity in most civilizations.

Furthermore they knew that the solution must face and answer two further problems. The first was how to avoid the previous law that increasing wealth inevitably brought nemesis, either through internal weakening and hence predation by outsiders, or through the urge to conquer others. Put in another way, how was it possible to achieve that mysterious balance which clearly the Dutch and English had achieved by the seventeenth century where it was possible to be both virtuous (liberal, relatively egalitarian, non-absolutist), highly productive (using almost all one's energy in devising improvements in knowledge and technology) and at the same time militarily powerful. That virtue was not just its own reward, but brought other rewards, was the amazing new fact. Look after the Kingdom of God, aspire to resource expansion, create a balanced polity and a not too uniform legal or social system, and all else would follow. This was decidedly not the experience, except for short periods, of previous civilizations. How could Holland and particularly England and America do something which had eluded the Hanseatic League or the northern Italian city-states?

The second puzzle was how it was possible to overcome the contradiction between the nature of man which was based on 'private vice', and the obvious fact that increasingly complex societies have to be based on a vast amount of trust, cooperation, altruism, generosity. How, in Pope's phrase, could 'self-love and social be the same', become fused into Mandeville's 'private vice, public benefit'. All previous civilizations had seen the contradiction as leading, finally, to destructive and aggressive confrontations, or, where, as in Confucianism, self-love was banned, to apparent stagnation. European society tried to harbour and even encourage self-assertion, individual self-love, yet to temper it so that it gave strength to the whole, rather than shattering it.

Fukuzawa is an heir to their problems and approaches as we shall see. As for them, these were not just theoretical interests. Just as Montesquieu helped lay the foundations for the French and American revolutions and modern liberty, Adam Smith for the modern competitive capitalist system which has provided great wealth, and Tocqueville the world of associations and balance which lies behind modern democracy, so Fukuzawa hoped to unite all of these in his native country. In one generation rather than the three or four it had taken in the West to create 'modern' civilization, he set out to move from one world to another. His life and work are, in a sense, a concentrated version of these three thinkers. Whereas it requires the whole span from 1700 to 1850 to see the various revolutions transform western Europe, Fukuzawa, as he noted, saw the whole process occur within his single life. He lived before, during and after the great transformation in an experience which no European thinker could match. He also lived, at the start, right outside the system, and could hence feel the full strength and strangeness of its assumptions. He visited its heartland in America and England, just like Tocqueville, but his sense of shock was even greater. Furthermore he tried, even more than the other thinkers, to effect practical changes which would save Japan from becoming a mere colony of the increasingly powerful West. Thus he provides a fascinating, outside view on the 'Enlightenment Project'. So who was he and what did he say and do?

11
Early Experience and Character

Yukichi Fukuzawa (1835–1901) is arguably the greatest Japanese social thinker of the last three centuries, yet he is little known outside his native country, except to experts. Contemporaries, on the other hand, recognized his eminence and influence.

The American zoologist Edward Morse wrote: 'I received an invitation to lecture before Mr. Fukuzawa's famous school. Among the many distinguished men I have met in Japan, Mr. Fukuzawa impressed me as one of the sturdiest in activity and intellect.'[1] William Griffis, another perceptive visitor, described him as 'A student first of Dutch in the early fifties, and one of the first to cross oceans and see America and Europe, he wrote a book on the "Manners and Customs in the Western World", which was eagerly read by millions of his hermit countrymen and served powerfully to sway Japan in the path of Western civilization.'[2] Griffis 'knew Fukuzawa well, and was, with him, a member of the Mei-Roku Sha, a club which, as its name imports, was founded in the sixth year of Meiji (1873).'[3] He described how 'As a pioneer and champion of Western civilization, and the writer of books which had reached the total sale of four million copies, he was described by the natives as "the greatest motive force of Japanese civilization," and by Professor Chamberlain as "the intellectual father of half the young men who fill the middle and lower posts in the government of Japan."'[4]

As Basil Hall Chamberlain wrote, 'In our own day, a new light arose in the person of Fukuzawa Yukichi, the "Sage of Mita" thus called from the district of Tokyo in which he latterly resided. So wide-spread is the influence exercised by this remarkable man that no account of Japan, however brief, would be complete without some reference to his life and opinions.'[5] He likened him to Benjamin

Franklin and noted that 'Like the French encyclopaedists, he laboured for universal enlightenment and social reform'.[6] At about the same time Alice Bacon wrote that 'In the whole list of publications on the woman question, nothing has ever come out in Japan that compares for outspokenness and radical sentiments with a book published within a year or two by Mr. Fukuzawa, the most influential teacher that Japan has seen in this era of enlightenment.'[7]

As a recent historian has written, 'Whereas other Japanese became caught up in the small facets of Western civilization, Fukuzawa sought to integrate these facets and observe the overall organization that made this civilization function ... In short, he tried to grasp not only the technology but also the social aspects of Western civilization.'[8] His published works fill 22 volumes and 'cover a variety of subjects ranging from philosophy to women's rights'.[9] As well as this he founded Keio University, a national newspaper and introduced the art of public speaking and debate in Japan.

Of course, he is not the only important Japanese thinker, writer and reformer during the second half of the nineteenth century. Blacker has described some of the other 'Japanese Enlightenment' thinkers with whom he worked and argued.[10] Beasley has surveyed some of the other well-known Japanese who went on voyages to America and England and brought back information about the West.[11] Sukehiro presents a general account of a whole set of reformers and thinkers working to understand how Japan and the West could be integrated.[12] In the next generation there were notable writers and thinkers such as Mori Ogai.[13] A sense of the lively debates, in which Fukuzawa was the most famous and distinguished, but only one among many, is given by the 'Journal of the Japanese Enlightenment', *Meiroku Zasshi*, the first 43 issues of which (1874–5) have been published and which discuss many of the topics to which Fukuzawa addressed himself.[14] Like all great thinkers, it is false to isolate Fukuzawa. He was part of a network. Yet by general consent he is the greatest of them all and as long as we bear in mind that many of his ideas were matters of widespread discussion and excitement, it seems reasonable to focus on his work. If we do so we can learn a great deal.

Fukuzawa pursued Bacon's *New Atlantis*, encouraging learning, debate, controversy and investigation. His influence was immense and we can now read his work as a revealing mirror of capitalist civilization as it penetrated into eastern Asia and was reflected back by a part of the world which has now taken many of its lessons to heart. When he died in 1901 his funeral reflected the austerity and dedication of his life. The *Japan Weekly Mail* wrote that 'No style of funeral could have been better suited to the unostentatious simplicity that marked the life of the great philosopher.'[15] His greatest successor, Maruyama Masao, in the black days of 1943, began an essay on him '"Fukuzawa Yukichi was a Meiji thinker, but at the same time he is a thinker of the present day".'[16] Like Montesquieu, Smith and Tocqueville he has become immortal.

The dialogue with Fukuzawa has a somewhat different purpose from that with earlier thinkers of the western Enlightenment treated in my previous work. The work of Montesquieu, Smith and Tocqueville, when combined, set out a set of conjectures as to how mankind could and perhaps did 'escape' from the normal tendencies of agrarian civilization. Since Fukuzawa (1835–1901) was writing later, and at a great distance from the original 'escape', it is unlikely that he will be able to contribute much that is original to the analysis of this problem. For that we have already considered Maitland's impressive solution. On the other hand, Fukuzawa provides an interesting test case for the utility of their theories. If their model is plausible and seems to have explanatory power, it should be attractive to a thinker whose aim, as we shall see, is to grasp the essence of the first transition from agrarian to industrial civilization so that he can help his own Japanese civilization achieve a similar break-through. If he selects and approves the same central essence as Montesquieu, Smith, Tocqueville and Maitland, their insights would appear to have cross-cultural validity.

An even more stringent test is the degree of success in the material world. In other words, did the recipe work? If an outsider to Europe not only repeated the central theories of those who addressed the riddle of the origins of the modern world, but then applied these to a distant civilization and helped to effect a similar 'escape' in entirely different circumstances, this would be as good a confirmation of the validity of the theory as one could hope for.

The task is made more worthwhile because, despite his eminence and interest, there has only been one book about him in English, and that was also about other thinkers in the Japanese Enlightenment.[17] There have been one or two articles also, but there is no recent intellectual biography of a man who had an enormous impact on Japanese civilization and whose ideas are such a wonderful mirror of western thought and colonial expansion.

Early life

Yukichi Fukuzawa's life and writing are more intimately linked than almost any of the four thinkers I have previously discussed. He underwent in his life from 1835 to 1901 a greater social and personal transformation than any of them. And he travelled more widely than any other of our subjects. It is therefore particularly fortunate that he was also keenly interested in documenting his own experiences from very early on so that we can watch, in an unusually intimate way, the evolution of his thought and life. As he wrote in the *Autobiography*, which he dictated two years before his death, 'Any person is interested in knowing, later on in life, something of the facts and nature of his early existence. I am not sure if everybody is as curious as I am, but since this is my feeling, I have been keeping a record of my children – the manner of their births and the exact time to the minute; the condition of their health in infancy; their nature and habits in childhood.'[18] He likewise applied this curiosity, in so far as he was able, to his own life.

Fukuzawa was born in January 1835 in Osaka, in the same year that Tocqueville's *Democracy in America* (volume I) was published. He wrote: 'My father, Fukuzawa Hyakusuke, was a samurai belonging to the Okudaira Clan of Nakatsu on the island of Kyushu. My mother, called O-Jun as her given name, was the eldest daughter of Hashimoto Hamaemon, another samurai of the same clan.'[19] One of the shaping events of his life occurred when 'A year and a half later, in June, my father died. At that time, my brother was only eleven, and I was a mere infant, so the only course for our mother to follow was to take her children back with her to her original feudal province of Nakatsu, which she did.'[20] Thus Fukuzawa 'never knew my own father and there is preserved no likeness of his features'.[21] All that he really seems to have known of him was that he was a scholarly man and that he was unusually sympathetic to those of an inferior rank to himself. Both were characteristics which Fukuzawa tried to live up to.

The scholarly and educational side of his father's interests and then his sudden death at the age of 44 had a double effect. On the one hand he was aware of his 'father's large collection of books . . . There were over fifteen hundred volumes in the collection, among them some very rare ones. For instance, there were Chinese law books of the Ming dynasty . . .'[22] He heard that his father had expressed an interest in his becoming trained to be a monk and this seems to have given Fukuzawa impetus to study.[23] On the other hand, the normal Chinese, neo-Confucian education which he would have been subjected to, in all probability, if his father had lived was denied him. 'There were no funds to send him to school until he was 14, almost ten years after the usual age for starting school.'[24] Fukuzawa himself noted one of the consequences. 'First of all, I lacked someone to look after my education and I grew up without learning calligraphy very well. I might have studied it later in life, but then I had already gone into Western sciences, and was regarding all Chinese culture as a mortal enemy.'[25] He lamented the loss of the artistic skill. 'This peculiar whim of mine was a great mistake. Indeed, my father and my brother were both cultured men. Especially my brother was a fine calligrapher, and something of a painter and sealcutter, too. But I fear I have none of those qualities. When it comes to antiques, curios, and other branches of the fine arts, I am hopelessly out of it.'[26] Yet it is perhaps not too speculative to suggest that it was the absence of a formal education of the old style which partly set him on an original course for life.

When Fukuzawa's mother moved back from Osaka to the remote Kyushu domain of her husband's clan she kept the memory of her dead husband alive, in particular because of her isolation with her children:

> My father's ideas survived him in his family. All five of us children lived with few friends to visit us, and since we had no one to influence us but our mother who lived only in her memory of her husband, it was as if father himself were living with us. So in Nakatsu, with our strange habits and apparel, we unconsciously formed a group apart, and although we never revealed it in words, we looked upon the neighbors around us as less refined than ourselves.[27]

The isolation and independence of the returned family with their city ways and costumes early created several key features of Fukuzawa's personality and is perceptively described by him as follows:

> Moreover, my mother, although she was a native of Nakatsu, had accustomed herself to the life of Osaka, then the most prosperous city in Japan, and so the way she dressed us and arranged our hair made us seem queer in the eyes of these people in a

secluded town on the coast of Kyushu. And having nothing else to wear but what we had brought from Osaka, we naturally felt more comfortable to stay at home and play among ourselves.[28]

The effects of isolation gave Fukuzawa's mother especial power and it is clear that not only was she an out of the ordinary woman, but that many of Fukuzawa's central interests in life, including the position of women in society, stemmed from her personality and attitudes. He described how 'My mother was an unusual woman who thought individually on certain matters. In religion she did not seem to have a belief like that of other old women of the time. Her family belonged to the Shin sect of Buddhism, yet she would never go to hear a sermon as was expected of everyone in that sect.'[29] Equally important was her egalitarian attitude, a continuation of that of her late husband:

> My mother was fond of doing kindnesses to all people, especially of making friends among the classes beneath her own, the merchants and farmers. She had no objection even to admitting beggars, or even the outcast *eta* (the slaughterers of cattle and dealers in leather who were a separate class by themselves). My mother never showed any sign of slighting them and her way of speaking to them was very respectful. Here is an instance of my mother's charity, which I remember with both affection and distaste.[30]

Fukuzawa claimed that he early learnt to treat those who were theoretically inferior with respect. 'So I believe my feeling of respect for all people was bred in me by the custom of my parents. In Nakatsu I never made a show of my rank in my mingling with any persons, even with the merchants of the town or the farmers outside.'[31] Thus he lived as a happy, but somewhat isolated little boy, playing with his four siblings but cut off from others. 'I still remember that I was always a lively happy child, fond of talk and romping about, but I was never good at climbing trees and I never learned to swim. This was perhaps because I did not play with the neighbourhood children.'[32]

Life in the clan

Much of Fukuzawa's work can be understood only when we realize the clan background into which he moved, and from which he sought to escape. The world of rigid social hierarchy which he so vividly describes, and which provided the shock of contrast with the West and the emerging new world of Japan after the Meiji Restoration of 1868, fixed him initially as a member of an *ancien régime*. It was a hierarchical civilization which he partially rejected and which crumbled away around him in a revolution as dramatic, if less bloody, than that through which France went after 1789.

In his work on *Civilization* Fukuzawa gave a brief autobiographical account of the world of his youth:

> I was born into a family of minor retainers in the service of a weak *fudai* [hereditary house] daimyo during the time of the Tokugawa shogunate. When within the *han* [domain] I met some illustrious high retainer or samurai, I was always treated with contempt; even as a child I could not help but feel resentment . . . Again, when I travelled outside the *han* confines I would run into Court nobles, officials of the Bakufu, or retainers of the three branch families of the Tokugawa house. At post towns they would monopolize the palanquins, at river crossings they would be ferried over first; since high and low were not permitted to stay at the same time in the same lodging house, there were times when I was suddenly turned out in the middle of the night.[33]

Now, writing in the 1870s, 'the circumstances of those days seem ridiculous', but 'it is still possible to imagine the rage felt at the time those things happened'.[34] In a fascinating autobiographical article he fills in some of the details of those early status-dominated days.

He first described the structure of his clan.

> The samurai of the old Okudaira clan of Nakatsu, from the Chief Minister down to the very lowest of those who were permitted to wear a sword, numbered about 1500 persons. They were divided broadly into two classes, though in all there were as many as a hundred different minute distinctions between their social positions and official duties. The upper of the two broad classes comprised all samurai from the Chief Minister down to the Confucian scholars, physicians and the members of the *koshôgumi*, while the lower class included all those from the calligraphers, *nakakoshô*, *tomokoshô* and *koyakunin*, down to the *ashigaru* [foot soldier]. The upper class was about one third the size of the lower.[35]

Fukuzawa's father was a member of the lower two-thirds and a 'lower samurai, whatever his merit or talents, could never rise above an upper samurai'.[36] Thus, 'A lower samurai might therefore aspire to promotion within his own class, but he would no more hope to enter the ranks of the upper samurai than would a four-legged beast hope to fly like a bird.'[37] There was an absolute bar between lower and upper and a rule forbidding marriage. 'Under no circumstances was marriage permitted between those of the rank of *kyunin* and those of the rank of *kachi*. Such alliances were forbidden both by clan law and by custom. Even in cases of adultery, both parties nearly always came from the same class. It was extremely rare to find men and women from different classes forming illicit unions.'[38]

The status difference between upper and lower samurai was fixed by birth and marriage and affected every aspect of life. The lowest rank of lower samurai, the *ashigaru*, 'always had to prostrate himself on the ground in the presence of an upper samurai. If he should encounter an upper samurai on the road in the rain, he had to take off his *geta* [shoes] and prostrate himself by the roadside.'[39] 'Upper samurai rode on horseback; lower samurai went on foot. Upper samurai possessed the privileges of hunting wild boar and fishing; lower samurai had no such privileges. Sometimes it even happened that a lower samurai was refused formal permission to go to another province to study, on the score that learning was not considered proper to his station.'[40] The upper samurai always showed their status by their dress and attendants. 'When they went out of doors they always wore *hakama* [formal trousers] and two swords, and whenever they went out at night they were always accompanied by lanterns. Some even went so far as to have lanterns on bright moonlight nights.'[41] Written and spoken language reflected the differences. 'In letters too there were various rigid and strictly differentiated modes of address, the character *sama* being written differently according to the rank of the person to whom the letter was addressed. In spoken forms of address all upper samurai, regardless of age, addressed lower samurai as "Kisama", while lower samurai addressed upper samurai as "Anata".'[42] Indeed, 'There were innumerable other differences in speech besides these . . . Thus if one heard a conversation the other side of a wall, one would know immediately if those talking were upper samurai, lower samurai, merchants or farmers.'[43]

There were many other differences; 'the upper samurai differed from the lower in rights, kinship, income, education, household economy, manners and customs. It was therefore only natural that their standards of honour and fields of interest should also differ.'[44] There were equal differences between the lower samurai and the other orders of peasants, artisans, merchants and 'outcastes'. The feeling of sullen resentment this created, certainly in Fukuzawa's memory, is palpable. 'The spirit of the times, however, insisted on a strict observance of one's station in life and on preserving a fixed and immovable order in everything, and this spirit forbade the lower samurai to express outwardly the doubt and anger which they constantly harboured.'[45]

All of this was part of the structure which had evolved in the form of 'centralized feudalism' which had already existed for over 200 years of unprecedented peace under the Tokugawa Shogunate by Fukuzawa's birth. Officially, the role of the samurai was to provide the middle level of the military and civilian bureaucracy. Hence each clan was given a corporate existence and corporate estate with a fixed rice rent of a certain amount in order to perform its functions. In theory, the samurai, upper and lower, were meant to be a military and literate elite, who kept themselves away from all mundane tasks such as business, trade, manufacturing, and so on. In practice, however, for some time past, the lower samurai had been experiencing an economic crisis which made it impossible for them to avoid becoming engaged in practical activities. Fukuzawa gives a fascinating account of their predicament.

'The lower samurai ... received stipends of fifteen *koku* plus rations for three, thirteen *koku* plus rations for two, or ten *koku* plus rations for one. Some received a money stipend of even less than this. Those of middle rank and above received a net income no higher than from seven to ten *koku*. At this rate a man and his wife living alone might manage without hardship, but if there were four or five children or old people in the family, this income was not sufficient to cover even the necessities of life such as food and clothing.'[46] The situation forced the lower samurai into a calculative and entrepreneurial mode unknown by the upper strata. 'The lower samurai had to work with both income and expenditure in mind, and hence had to plan their household economy with a minuteness never dreamt of by the upper samurai.'[47]

The only solution was to abandon the principle that samurai did not work with their hands. Thus everyone in the family capable of work, both men and women alike, eked out a poor livelihood by odd jobs such as spinning and handicrafts. These jobs might in theory be mere sidework, but in fact the samurai came to regard them as their main occupation, relegating their official clan duties to the position of sidework. These men were therefore not true samurai. It would be more correct to say that they were a kind of workmen. Thus harassed by the task of making a mere living for themselves, they had no time in which to give a thought to their children's education. The lower samurai were thus very ill versed in literature and other high forms of learning, and not unnaturally came to have the bearing and deportment of humble workmen.[48]

Fukuzawa further described that this had been a growing tendency since

for twenty or thirty years the sidework of the lower samurai had been steadily increasing. At first they did little more than joinery work in wood, making boxes and low tables, or twisting paper cords for binding hair. Gradually however their jobs increased in variety. Some made wooden clogs and umbrellas; some covered paper lanterns; some would do carpentry work in plain wood and then add to its quality by painting it with lacquer; some were so skilful in making doors and sliding screens that they could even vie with professional carpenters. Recently some began to combine handicrafts with commerce. They would build boats, lay in stock and ship it to Osaka, some travelling in the boats themselves.[49]

One consequence was that they had to neglect their official military and literary training. 'Many of them practised the military arts in such little time as they could spare from their sidework, but in literature they would get no further than the Four Books and the Five Classics, and, at a little more advanced stage, one or two books of Meng Ch'iu and the *Tso Chuan*.'[50] Another was that they had to forgo the supposed taboos on becoming involved in handling money, or carrying objects.

Just as it was considered low and vulgar to go out and to make purchases, so it was thought shameful to carry things. Hence apart from fishing rods and the appurtenances of swordsmanship, no upper samurai ever carried anything in his hands, even the smallest *furoshiki* bundle. The lower samurai did not employ servants unless they happened to hold a good post or have a particularly large family. Few of them would go into the towns in daylight to make purchases, but at night it was quite customary for both men and women to go.[51]

Fukuzawa provides glimpses of his own upbringing in this ambivalent world and his family's struggle with relative poverty. 'Originally I was a country samurai, living on wheat meal and pumpkin soup, wearing out-grown homespun clothes.'[52] He recalled that 'Ever since early childhood, my brother and sisters and I had known all the hardships of poverty. And none of us could ever forget what struggles our mother had been obliged to make in the meagre household. Despite this constant hardship there were many instances of the quiet influence that mother's sincere spirit had upon us.'[53] In fact, he came to relish the physical, not to say spartan, side of life.

I was born in a poor family and I had to do much bodily work whether I liked it or not. This became my habit and I have been exercising my body a great deal ever since. In winter time, working out of doors constantly, I often had badly chapped hands. Sometimes they cracked open and bled. Then I would take needle and thread, and sew the edges of the opening together and apply a few drops of hot oil. This was our homely way of curing chapped skin back in Nakatsu.[54]

The absence of freedom and equality in the clan

Much of Fukuzawa's greatest work would be devoted to examining how it would be possible to change Japan from this group-based and hierarchical society, to an individualistic and egalitarian one. In this work he relived his own experiences and used them to explain how he had himself escaped from such a world and how others could do so.

The clan had the right to take an individual and place him in another family, with another set of relatives, through the process of adoption. Of course, this has happened to a certain extent to countless women through arranged marriage, but usually they remain part of their original family as well. In Japan it was much more extreme, and the adopted person severed links and took on the new family as his or her own. This happened twice to Fukuzawa and he even found that at one point 'I had legally become a son to my brother'.[55] It is indeed a wise son who knows his own father in such a situation and it is not surprising that individuals might feel subordinate to the group.

The lack of personal identity was mirrored in the naming system. In most western civilizations a person had one name at birth and kept it – though women often lost it at marriage. In Japan, a name was attached to a position, so if a person moved into another role, his name would change. One part of this is noted by Fukuzawa in relation to the absence of the notion of the individual: 'there is another point in which we can see the warriors of Japan lacked this individualistic spirit. That is the matter of names. Essentially, a man's name is something given him by his parents.'[56] If they wished to change his name, they could do so – as could the clan.

Of course, the degree of freedom depended on one's place in the clan system. Thus 'While my brother was living, I could go anywhere at any time with only his sanction, but now that I had become the head of the family with certain duties to the lord, I had to obtain a permit for going "abroad".'[57] Thus one had elements of that autocratic Confucian system found in China. The senior male was relatively powerful, sons, younger brothers and all women were largely without individual rights, subservient to the clan or household head.

Absence of individuality was symbolized and carried to its furthest extreme in the avoidance of the use of personal pronouns in Japanese. As Fukuzawa noted, 'Another problem which requires explanation is the fact that the personal pronouns, "I", "you", "we", and "us" appear frequently in my translation; whereas, in most cases, the corresponding words are omitted in the original text.'[58] In such a situation, individual opinions and rights, and independent thought do indeed meet a barrier.

The second general feature of Fukuzawa's early situation was the basic assumption of inequality. Fukuzawa was later to describe what he perceived to be the rigid and hierarchical social system of Tokugawa Japan, where men were born unequal. He described how 'In relations between men and women, the man has preponderance of power over the woman. In relations between parents and children the parent has preponderance of power over the child. In relations between elder and younger brother, and between young and old in general, the same principle holds good. Outside the family circle we find exactly the same thing.'[59] He described how 'Back in those childhood days, I lived under the iron-bound feudal system. Everywhere people clung to the ancient custom by which the rank of every member of a clan was inalterably fixed by his birth. So from father to son and grandson the samurai of high rank would retain their rank. In the same way those of lower rank would forever remain in their low position. Neither intelligence nor ability could prevent the scorn of their superiors.'[60]

Thus what was to be found in the family and clan was to be found everywhere:

> Wherever there are social relationships there you will find this imbalance of power. Even within the government itself the imbalance can be extremely great, depending on the position and grade of the officials. When we see a minor official brandishing his authority over one commoner we might think he is a very powerful person. But let this same official meet someone higher in the bureaucracy and he will be subjected to even worse oppression from his superior than he dealt out to the commoner.[61]

It was a system of innate inequalities, which afflicted every relationship. 'Now let me discuss this imbalance as it exists in reality. You will find this imbalance in all relations between man and woman, between parents and children, between brothers, and between young and old. Turn from the family circle to society, and relations there will be no different. Teacher and student, lord and retainer, rich and poor, noble and base-born, newcomers and oldtimers, main family and branch families – between all of these there exists an imbalance of power.'[62] The whole social structure seemed fixed, almost caste-like, and was transmitted over the generations: 'sons of high officials following their father in office, sons of foot-soldiers always becoming foot-soldiers, and those of the families in between having the same lot for centuries without change. For my father, there had been no hope of rising in society whatever effort he might make.'[63]

All this was, of course, bound up with the innate premise of superior and inferior in all relations built into Confucian thought. 'In China and Japan the ruler–subject relationship was considered inherent in human nature, so that the relationship between ruler and subject was conceived as analogous to the relationships between husband and wife and parent and child. The respective roles of ruler and subject were even thought of as predestined from a previous life. Even a man like Confucius was unable to free himself from this obsession.'[64] Oppression and servility were built deep into the system:

> Thus, even in the period of violent warfare between the samurai, this principle of social relationships could not be broken. At the head of one family was a general, and under him household elders; then came the knights, the foot-soldiers, and lastly the *ashigaru* and *chugen*. The duties of upper and lower were clearcut, and equally clear were the rights that went with these duties. Every man submitted to overbearance from those above and required subservience from those below. Every man was both unreasonably oppressed and unreasonably oppressive.[65]

Fukuzawa's rejection of this premise of basic inequality, of subservience to those above and arrogance to those below, seems to have partly stemmed from his parents. He described how 'This respect for people of lower rank was not original with me. It had been handed down from both my parents.'[66] He described a specific example of their more open attitude. 'Nakamura was an able scholar, but he was the son of a dyer who had lived in Nakatsu. Therefore nobody in our clan would befriend this "mere merchant's son". My father, however, admired his personality and, disregarding all social precedents, took him into our house in Osaka and, having introduced him to many people, brought it about finally that Nakamura was made a household scholar in the Minakuchi clan.'[67] More generally, the attitude was that 'the farmers and merchants – the ruled – were totally separated from the rulers, forming an entirely different world. Their attitudes and customs differed.'[68] All of this made Fukuzawa increasingly uncomfortable. He described how in his early days 'The thing that made me most unhappy in Nakatsu was the restriction of rank and position. Not only on official occasions, but in private intercourse, and even among children, the distinctions between high and low were clearly defined.'[69] His growing unease was brought to a head with the overthrow of the Tokugawa Shogunate in 1868 at the Meiji Restoration.

There must have been many boys in Fukuzawa's position, yet only one of them turned into a man who shaped the destiny of his country. Two principal factors were important in selecting him rather than others. One was a particularly stubborn and determined character, the other was chance. Let us look at his personality first.

The character of the growing boy

Fukuzawa's early life as a poor Samurai developed his character in various ways. Not only did he take unusual physical exercise, pounding rice and wood chopping, but he developed a keen interest in practical, do-it-yourself activities of a humble kind. He described how 'As I grew older, I began to do a greater variety of things, such as mending the wooden clogs and sandals – I mended them for all my family – and fixing broken doors and leaks in the roof.'[70] Poverty and pride combined to make him a practical and versatile workman, a Japanese Benjamin Franklin, which later stood him in great stead when he came to study western technology and science. 'When something fell in the well, I contrived some means to fish it out. When the lock of a drawer failed to open, I bent a nail in many ways, and poking into the mechanism, somehow opened it. These were my proud moments. I was good at pasting new paper on the inner doors of the house, which are called *shoji*. Every so often when the old lining of the *shoji* turned gray with dust, it had to be taken off and new white paper pasted on the frame.'[71]

He recalled that he early learnt that 'knowledge' consisted not only of reading books but of doing things – and not just sword play and the calligraphy he had missed. He wrote that 'My own particular talent seems to be in doing all kinds of humble work. While I was in Yamamoto's house, I did all kinds of work in his household. I do not recall ever saying, "I cannot do this", or "I don't want to do that."'[72] He loved tinkering with his hands. 'Thus ever since my childhood, besides my love of books, I have been accustomed to working with my hands. And even yet, in my old age, I find myself handling planes and chisels, and making and mending things.'[73] All this helped to remind him that it was not enough merely to learn, to understand, but vital also to put that learning to use. 'It is not necessary to reiterate here that learning does not consist only in the reading of books. The essence of learning lies rather in its practical application, without which learning is still ignorance.'[74]

Above all, he seems to have developed a huge, practical, curiosity and an openness of mind and scepticism about received wisdom which marks him out as unusual for his own time and again indicates his 'Enlightenment' status. One aspect of this can be seen in his attitude to the supernatural. He was brought up in a world where Shinto, Buddhist and folk superstitions mingled to fill the environment with prohibitions and danger, yet his mother's rationalism and his own curiosity led him to doubt whether there was really truth in them. He decided therefore to carry out some experiments. Two of these are worth recounting. In the first, when he was twelve or thirteen, he accidentally stepped on a document naming his clan lord. His brother told him off, and though he apologised he felt angry and

> Then I went on, reasoning in my childish mind that if it was so wicked to step on a man's name, it would be very much more wicked to step on a god's name; and I determined to test the truth. So I stole one of the charms, the thin paper slips, bearing sacred names, which are kept in many households for avoiding bad luck. And I deliberately trampled on it when nobody was looking. But no heavenly vengeance came. 'Very well,' I thought to myself. 'I will go a step further and try it in the worst place.' I took it to the *chōzu-ba* (the privy) and put it in the filth. This time I was a little afraid, thinking I was going a little too far. But nothing happened. 'It is just as I thought!' I said to myself. 'What right did my brother have to scold me?' I felt that I had made a great discovery! But this I could not tell anybody, not even my mother or sisters.[75]

His scepticism grew until he tried a further test which put paid to all his supernatural fears.

> When I grew older by a few years, I became more reckless, and decided that all the talk about divine punishment which old men use in scolding children was a lie. Then I conceived the idea of finding out what the god of Inari really was. There was an Inari shrine in the corner of my uncle's garden, as in many other households. I opened the shrine and found only a stone there. I threw it away and put in another stone which I picked up on the road. Then I went on to explore the Inari shrine of our neighbor, Shimomura. Here the token of the god was a wooden tablet. I threw it away too and waited for what might happen. When the season of the Inari festival came, many people gathered to put up flags, beat drums, and make offerings of the sacred

rice-wine. During all the round of festival services I was chuck-
ling to myself: "There they are – worshipping my stones, the
fools!" Thus from my childhood I have never had any fear of
gods or Buddha. Nor have I ever had any faith in augury and
magic, or in the fox and badger which, people say, have power
to deceive men. I was a happy child, and my mind was never
clouded by unreasonable fears.[76]

From then on he sought for explanations in this-worldly forces,
and moved along the paths which Montesquieu, Smith and
Tocqueville had all trod.

One major consequence of this was that he applied the method
of doubt and scepticism to all things. Later he was to proclaim the
ideology which has been enshrined from Francis Bacon to Karl Popper.
'Even today the reason that the great persons of the West lead
people on the path to higher civilization is that their purpose is
entirely to refute the once firm and irrefutable theories of the an-
cients, and to entertain doubts concerning practices about which
common sense had never doubted before.'[77] It was the application
of curiosity and methodical doubt to the world which had created
modern science and technology he believed. 'If we seek the essence of Western civilization, it lies in the fact that they scrutinize
whatever they experience with the five senses, in order to discover
its essence and its functions. They go on to seek the causes of its
functions, and anything they find beneficial they make use of, while
whatever they find harmful they discard. The range of power of
modern man is endless. He controls the energies in water and fire
to power the steam engines by which he crosses the vast Pacific.'[78]
His own childhood world had been different for 'the spirit of learning
differs between East and West. The countries of the West stress the
idea of experiment; we in Japan dote on the theories of Confucius
and Mencius.'[79] Yet he had increasingly come to challenge that world,
both at the social and the cosmological level.

There were disadvantages to his agnosticism. For instance, he found
it more or less impossible to understand the obvious force and nature
of religion in western civilization. Like Tocqueville, for example,
he could see from his visits to America and Europe that Christianity played an enormously important part as a social glue and as a
system of meaning. Indeed, like Tocqueville, he believed that whatever
his own scepticism, it was necessary, perhaps essential, for religion
to be encouraged, in a modest way. Summarizing his wishes for

the future at the end of his life he wrote: 'I should like to encourage a religion – Buddhism or Christianity – to give peaceful influence on a large number of our people.'[80] He developed this idea more fully, while expressing forcefully his own agnosticism, when he stated that

> it goes without saying that the maintenance of peace and security in society requires a religion. For this purpose any religion will do. I lack a religious nature, and have never believed in any religion. I am thus open to the charge that I am advising others to be religious, when I am not so. Yet my conscience does not permit me to clothe myself with religion, when I have it not at heart. Of religions, there are several kinds. Buddhism, Christianity and what not. Yet, from my standpoint, there is no more difference between these than between green tea and black tea. It makes little difference whether you drink one or the other.[81]

Basically, like Rousseau, Hume and others, he saw religion as perhaps a marginal social necessity, but often a superstitious nonsense that was used as a prop by the powerful: a very Enlightened and rationalist view. Yet the rationalism also made it difficult for him to understand some of the difference of East and West, 'But still I am not sure I have grasped the real causes of the great differences between the religions of the East and West.'[82]

His admission of bafflement as to causes, is, in fact, one of the reasons for our continuing interest in him. What we admire him for most of all, is his unflagging curiosity and open-mindedness. Considering the pressures upon him from his youth, he had an amazingly rational and independent mind. In his *Autobiography* he wrote of the 'irresistible fascination of our new knowledge'.[83] In his characteristically entitled *Encouragement of Learning* he stressed the need for doubt and questioning. He described to his audience how 'The progress of civilization lies in seeking the truth both in the area of physical facts and in the spiritual affairs of man. The reason for the West's present high level of civilization is that in every instance they proceeded from some point of doubt.'[84] His book had a heading, 'Methodic doubt and selective judgment' and explained that 'There is much that is false in the world of belief, and much that is true in the world of doubt.'[85] He cited famous, perhaps apocryphal, instances. 'Watt (1736–1819) entertained doubts concerning the properties of steam when he was experimenting with a boiling kettle. In all these cases they attained to the truth by following the road of doubt.'[86] All he could note was that 'In the countries of the West religion flourishes not only among monks in monasteries but also in secular society ... and this attracts men's hearts and preserves virtuous ways. But in our Japan religion lacks this efficacy in society at large: it is solely a matter of sermons in temples.'[87]

What else can we learn about the character of the young man growing up in the remote province of a southern Japanese island in the early 1830s? One obvious characteristic was his loneliness and inner strength. Using the heading 'No-one is admitted to my inner thoughts', he described how

> From my early days in Nakatsu I have not been able to achieve what I might call a heart-to-heart fellowship with any of my friends, nor even with a relative. It was not that I was peculiar and people did not care to associate with me. Indeed, I was very talkative and quite congenial with both men and women. But my sociability did not go to the extent of opening myself completely to the confidence of others, or sharing with them the inner thoughts of my heart. I was never envious of anyone, never wished to become like someone else; never afraid of blame, nor anxious for praise. I was simply independent.[88]

That is not to say that he did not have friends; but he kept his own counsel. 'I am of a very sociable nature; I have numerous acquaintances, and among them I count a number of trusted friends. But even in these relations I do not forget my doctrine of preparing for the extreme – for a friend can change his mind.'[89]

The reserve, iron will and self reliance obviously related to his samurai *bushido* ethic and the traditions of *zen* was consciously cultivated. 'One day while reading a Chinese book, I came upon these ancient words: "Never show joy or anger in the face." These words brought a thrill of relief as if I had learned a new philosophy of life.'[90] He became a working model of Kipling's *If*, treating the 'impostors' of praise and blame in the same way. 'Since then I have always remembered these golden words, and have trained myself to receive both applause and disparagement politely, but never to allow myself to be moved by either. As a result, I have never been truly angry in my life, nor have my hands ever touched a person in anger, nor has a man touched me in a quarrel, ever since my youth to this old age.'[91]

He always expected the worst. 'It has been a habit of mine to be prepared for the extreme in all situations; that is, to anticipate the worst possible result of any event so that I should not be confounded when the worst did come.'[92] He combined activity and acceptance of fate in a way that reminds one forcefully of Weber's puritan ethic. 'I have worked with energy, planned my life, made friends, endeavored to treat all men alike, encouraged friends in their need, and sought the cooperation of others as most men do. But believing as I do that the final outcome of all human affairs is in the hands of Heaven, whenever my endeavors failed, I refrained from imploring sympathy and resigned myself to necessity. In short, my basic principle is never to depend upon the whims of other people.'[93] He gave all he could to whatever activity he was engaged in, but accepted the outcome, in the end, was largely determined by forces outside his control. Speaking later of his attempts to set up the first Japanese university of Keio, he wrote: 'Although I give the best of my ability to the management of the institution and put all my heart into it for its future and its improvement, yet I never forget that all my personal worries and immediate concerns are but a part of the "games" of this "floating world", our entire lives but an aspect of some higher consciousness.'[94]

Two other features may be noticed. One was his immensely hard work, physical and intellectual. As a student, in particular, he worked prodigiously hard to learn Dutch and then English. He described how as a student 'I had been studying without regard to day or night. I would be reading all day and when night came I did not think of going to bed. When tired, I would lean over on my little desk, or stretch out on the floor resting my head on the raised alcove (*tokonoma*) of the room. I had gone through the year without ever spreading my pallet and covers and sleeping on the pillow.'[95] We shall see his prodigious energy and hard work manifested in an extraordinarily productive life.

A second feature was his desire to be independent of others. This manifested itself in his refusal to be sucked into any political job, as would have been natural. He later wrote that 'To speak very honestly, the first reason for my avoiding a government post is my dislike of the arrogance of all officials. It might be argued that they need to put on dignity in their office. But in reality they enjoy the bullying.'[96] But added to this was his desire to remain independent. 'All in all, I am determined to live independent of man or thing. I cannot think of government office while I hold this principle.'[97] He thought of himself as an independent spirit. 'As long as I remain in private life, I can watch and laugh. But joining the government would draw me into the practice of those ridiculous pretensions which I cannot allow myself to do.'[98] He saw himself as an analyst of politics, but not a politician or bureaucrat. 'All in all, my activities with politics have been that of a "diagnostician". I have no idea of curing the nation's "disease" with my own hands nor have I ever thought of politics in connection with my personal interest.'[99] This was not through lack of interest, but a desire to keep at arm's length. 'Not that I am wholly uninterested in that field, for I frequently discuss the subject and have written upon it, but for the daily wear and tear of its practice I have no taste. I am like the diagnostician in the medical field who can judge a disease but cannot care for a sick man. So people are not to take my diagnosis of politics as any evidence of personal ambition.'[100]

His independence also showed itself in a terror of being financially involved, or at the mercy of others. Later in his life 'as if for the first time, I came to realize that I had never borrowed any money in my life. That had always seemed natural to me, but it appears it was rather unusual in other people's eyes.'[101] At the end of his life, aged 65, he noted that 'since I left home in Nakatsu at twenty-one, I have been managing my own affairs; and since my brother's death when I was twenty-three, I have assumed the care of my mother and niece. At twenty-eight I was married, had children, and took all the responsibilities of a family on myself.'[102]

Fukuzawa clearly took pleasure in 'going against the grain', however difficult it was. 'In anything, large or small, it is difficult to be the pioneer. It requires an unusual recklessness. But on the other hand, when the innovation becomes generally accepted, its originator gets the utmost pleasure as if it were the attainment of his inner desires.'[103] Thus when he made his studies of Dutch and then English language, with its enormous difficulties, when he made the enormous effort to visit and document America and European civilization, he was finding a model for himself, a world where individual freedom was taken for granted as the premise of life, rather than being seen as largely selfish and destabilizing. He believed passionately that both for himself and for Japan, this was the only way to go. He himself had discovered this in relation to his clan. At the wider level 'The independence of a nation springs from the independent spirit of its citizens. Our nation cannot hold its own if the old slavish spirit is so manifest among the people.'[104]

Much of the tension and interest in Fukuzawa's work comes out of his rebellious nature. He describes himself as a stubborn and individualistic person by character. 'I was always concerned with the way of society, and it was my inborn nature to act always in my own way.'[105] He speaks of 'my principle of independence and self-help'[106] and of 'My general determination was to be independent, to earn my own way and not to beg, borrow or covet other men's property.'[107]

All this hard work, financial and political independence, planning and ambition makes Fukuzawa sound a dry, two-dimensional person. Indeed he realized himself that his *Autobiography* tended to give this impression. 'It may thus appear that I am a queer bigoted person, but in reality I am quite sociable with all people. Rich or poor, noble or commoner, scholar or illiterate – all are my friends. I have no particular feeling in meeting a *geisha* or any other woman.'[108] Yet even here another vice, philandering lust, is dismissed. Was he perfect, then?

To round out the picture we can note three weaknesses. A small one was a certain absentmindedness which reminds us of Adam Smith. Fukuzawa related that 'One day when I was suddenly called out on business, I thought of changing my dress. My wife being out at the moment, I opened the chest of drawers and took out a garment that happened to be lying on top. When I returned, my wife looked curiously at me and said I was wearing an undergarment. She had one more cause for laughing at me. In this case, of course, my unconcern for dress went a little too near the limit.'[109] The implication is that he was also oblivious to social conventions – a sort of Japanese eccentric.

Nor can we strongly condemn what he himself found an ambivalent attitude to money. While he was full of probity in general, he found that when it came to the assets of his clan, he felt no moral necessity to be strictly honest. 'In the narrative so far I may appear to be a highly upright person in matters of money. But I must admit here that I was not always so. I was quite otherwise when it came to money belonging to my clan.'[110] He proceeded to give a few examples of a different attitude to the joint property of an institution which he already resented strongly.

It was in his leisure activities that we find the one real chink in his puritan character. This was not his fondness for Japanese music, which was not taken to excess. He wrote that 'I have always been fond of music, so much so that I am having all my daughters and granddaughters learn both *koto* and *shamisen* and also, partly for exercise, dancing. To sit and listen to them at their lessons is the chief pleasure of my old age.'[111] His chief weakness, and one which he finally successfully overcame, was drink.

Quite early in his *Autobiography* he wrote as follows. 'To begin with the shortcomings, my greatest weakness lay in drinking, even from my childhood. And by the time I was grown enough to realize its dangers, the habit had become a part of my own self and I could not restrain it. I shall not hold back anything, for however disagreeable it may be to bring out my old faults, I must tell the truth to make a true story. So I shall give, in passing, a history of my drinking from its very beginning.'[112] Towards the end of the same book he returned to the same subject, when he wrote:

> I must admit I have had a very bad and shameful habit of drinking. Moreover, my drinking was something out of the ordinary. There is a kind of drinker who does not really like the wine, and does not think of drinking until he sees the wine brought before him. But I was of the kind who liked it, and wanted much of it, and moreover wanted good, expensive wine. At one time when it cost seven or eight *yen* a barrel, my expert taste could tell the better wine from the less expensive if there was a difference of even fifty *sen*. I used to drink a lot of this good wine, eat plenty of nice food with it and continue devouring bowl after bowl of rice, leaving nothing on the table. Indeed, I was 'drinking like a cow and eating like a horse.'[113]

At about the age of 33 he began to realize that this heavy drinking would shorten his life. He remembered an earlier attempt suddenly to give up all drinking and decided to wean himself slowly. 'It was as hard a struggle as a Chinaman giving up his opium. First I gave up my morning wine, then my noon wine. But I always excused myself to take a few cups when there was a guest. Gradually I was able to offer the cup to the guest only and keep myself from touching it. So far I managed somehow, but the next step of giving up the evening wine was the hardest of all my efforts.'[114] It took him about three years to give up the habit entirely, but in this, as in other things, we notice the force of his will and reason.

Yet his ability to curb his body and his emotions does not mean that he was a dry or emotionless man. Again and again in his writing his strong feelings flash out, and we see a man driven by anger, shame or admiration. For instance, when describing the sexual behaviour of many of his countrymen he wrote 'For a man, especially one who has been abroad, to fall into such loose behaviour is too much for me to bear.'[115] Or again, the treatment of women, and the way this treatment was viewed by westerners, made him deeply upset. 'I am stunned beyond words at the brazen shamelessness of our people.'[116] It was not that he did not feel, it was more that he channelled this feeling through his writing and practical activities. As he put it, 'the human body and mind are like an iron kettle. If they are not used, they rust.'[117]

With a preliminary impression of Fukuzawa's character, let us now take up again the story of his life and see how his already unusually independent and inquisitive nature developed under the impact of the most shattering changes that had ever occurred in the long history of Japan.

12
Travels and Comparisons

As he reached the age of fourteen or fifteen Fukuzawa grew increasingly frustrated in the provincial atmosphere of Nakatsu. 'Outwardly I was living peacefully enough, but always in my heart I was praying for an opportunity to get away. And I was willing to go anywhere and to go through any hardship if only I could leave this uncomfortable Nakatsu. Happily, a chance sent me to Nagasaki.'[1] He wrote that a particular event confirmed him in his decision to leave. Fukuzawa's brother had written a letter to the clan's chief minister for which he was reprimanded because it was not properly addressed. 'Seeing this I cried to myself, "how foolish it is to stay here and submit to this arrogance!" And I was determined then to run away from this narrow cooped-up Nakatsu.'[2]

Fukuzawa's chance to escape was one of the many effects of the first shock of the imminent revolution in Japan. In 1854 Commodore Perry had appeared with the American warships off the coast of Japan and this 'had made its impression on every remote town in Japan'.[3] Thus 'the problem of national defense and the modern gunnery had become the foremost interest of all the samurai'.[4] In order to study western gunnery one had to be able to read Dutch, so Fukuzawa volunteered to do that and, in 1854, at the age of nineteen was taken to Nagasaki to learn Dutch and gunnery. 'The true reason why I went there was nothing more than to get away from Nakatsu. . . . This was a happy day for me. I turned at the end of the town's street, spat on the ground, and walked quickly away.'[5]

He set himself hard to work. 'My chief concern was, after all, the Dutch language. I often went to the interpreter's house, and sometimes to the house of the special physicians who practiced

"Dutch medicine". And little by little, after fifty or a hundred days, I came to understand something of the Dutch language.'[6] Because of jealousies within the clan,[7] it became difficult to stay in Nagasaki and the following February (1855) he left and ended up a month later as a student at the school of Koan Ogata in Osaka. Ogata was one of the foremost experts on the Dutch learning in Japan.

Fukuzawa gives a delightful and lengthy account of his life as a student with Ogata. Like many of his young contemporaries he became fascinated with western science and technology. For instance, he describes how

> Of course at that time there were no examples of industrial machinery. A steam engine could not be seen anywhere in the whole of Japan. Nor was there any kind of apparatus for chemical experiments. However, learning something of the theories of chemistry and machinery in our books, we of the Ogata household [school] spent much effort in trying out what we had learned, or trying to make a thing that was illustrated in the books.[8]

Learning about the new science was not easy. For instance, there was no good work on electricity. 'All that we knew about electricity then had been gleaned from fragmentary mention of it in the Dutch readers.'[9] One day Ogata returned with a Dutch volume borrowed from his clan lord. 'I took in the book with devouring eyes ... here in this new book from Europe was a full explanation based on the recent discoveries of the great English physicist, Faraday, even with the diagram of an electric cell. My heart was carried away with it at first sight.'[10] He and his fellow students proceeded to work day and night to copy out the whole long chapter on electricity before returning it. 'This event quite changed the whole approach to the subject of electricity in the Ogata household. I do not hesitate to say that my fellow students became the best informed men on the new science in the entire country.'[11]

Fukuzawa learnt the basics of western chemistry and physics during the years 1856–60. This partly explains his increasing dislike of Chinese Knowledge. 'The only subject that bore our constant attack was Chinese medicine. And by hating Chinese medicine so thoroughly, we came to dislike everything that had any connection with Chinese culture. Our general opinion was that we should rid our country of the influences of the Chinese altogether.'[12] He came, as he explained later, to see Chinese misinformation as a block to knowledge and advance. 'The true reason of my opposing the Chinese teaching with such vigour is my belief that in this age of transition, if this retrogressive doctrine remains at all in our young men's minds, the new civilization cannot give its full benefit to this country.'[13] In his old age he wrote in his *Old Man Fukuzawa's Tales*: 'I am not one who studies western learning and tries to combine it with Chinese learning. I wish to tear up traditional teaching by the roots and open the way to the new culture. In other words I wish to use one learning to destroy the other and these two things have been my lifelong concerns.'[14]

He worked with huge concentration but great uncertainty. There was no obvious job ahead and much anti-foreign feeling in the country. Like others at Ogata's school, 'most of us were then actually putting all our energy into our studies without any definite assurance of the future. Yet this lack of future hope was indeed fortunate for us, for it made us better students than those in Yedo.'[15]

Then in October 1858 the clan needed a Dutch scholar to open a school in Yedo (Tokyo). He moved there and continued his studies. Yet he was in for a sudden shock. He visited Yokohama in 1859 and noted: 'I had been striving with all my powers for many years to learn the Dutch language. And now when I had reason to believe myself one of the best in the country, I found that I could not even read the signs of merchants who had come to trade with us from foreign lands. It was a bitter disappointment, but I knew it was no time to be downhearted.'[16] The language of the world was English, not Dutch. So 'On the very next day after returning from Yokohama, I took up a new aim in life and determined to begin the study of English.'[17] He managed to find a two volume Dutch-English dictionary, and 'Once with these at my command, I felt there was hope for my endeavour. I made firm my determination to learn the new language by my own efforts. So day and night I plodded along with the new books for sole companions. Sometimes I tried to make out the English sentences by translating each word into Dutch; sometimes I tried forming an English sentence from the Dutch vocabulary. My sole interest then was to accustom myself to the English language.'[18] He progressed well and the following year published his first book *Kaei Tsugo* (English Vocabulary and Idioms). 'This was not exactly a translation; my work was limited to adding *kana* (Japanese syllabary) to indicate the pronunciation of the English words, a very simple task.'[19]

Cometh the man, cometh the moment. 'The year after I was settled in Yedo – the sixth year of Ansei (1859) – the government of the Shogun made a great decision to send a ship-of-war to the United States, an enterprise never before attempted since the foundation of the empire. On this ship I was to have the good fortune of visiting America.'[20] In January 1860 Fukuzawa and others started from Uraga on the ship *Kanrin-maru*, reaching San Francisco on 26 February (27 March by the western calendar). He stayed in America itself for about three weeks and returned by way of Hawaii, to arrive back to the publication of his English dictionary in August.

America was quite literally a new and strange world for him. In his *Autobiography* he gives a few examples of the things that shocked and surprised him. Coming from a neat bamboo and paper culture where nothing was wasted, he was amazed by the wealth and profligacy: 'there seemed to be an enormous waste of iron everywhere. In garbage piles, on the sea-shores – everywhere – I found lying old oil tins, empty cans, and broken tools. This was remarkable for us, for in Yedo, after a fire, there would appear a swarm of people looking for nails in the ashes.'[21] Likewise the furnishings and concepts of cleanliness were entirely different. 'Here the carpet was laid over an entire room – something quite astounding – and upon this costly fabric walked our hosts wearing the shoes with which they had come in from the streets! We followed them in our hemp sandals.'[22] The relative expense of this affluent culture was a shock. 'Then too, I was surprised at the high cost of daily commodities in California. We had to pay a half-dollar for a bottle of oysters, and there were only twenty or thirty in the bottle at that. In Japan the price of so many would be only a cent or two.'[23]

Due to his earlier efforts to understand western science and technology, steam, electricity, physics and chemistry, he was not particularly surprised or impressed by American technology. 'As for scientific inventions and industrial machinery, there was no great novelty in them for me. It was rather in matters of life and social custom and ways of thinking that I found myself at a loss in America.'[24] He was puzzled by the relations between the sexes. A small example was western dancing. Going to a ball he found that the 'ladies and gentlemen seemed to be hopping about the room together. As funny as it was, we knew it would be rude to laugh, and we controlled our expressions with difficulty as the dancing went on.'[25]

Also surprising was the absence of interest in kinship and descendants.

One day, on a sudden thought, I asked a gentleman where the descendants of George Washington might be. He replied, 'I think there is a woman who is directly descended from Washington. I don't know where she is now, but I think I have heard she is married.' His answer was so very casual that it shocked me. Of course, I knew that America was a republic with a new president every four years, but I could not help feeling that the family of Washington would be revered above all other families. My reasoning was based on the reverence in Japan for the founders of the great lines of rulers – like that for Ieyasu of the Tokugawa family of Shoguns, really deified in the popular mind. So I remember the astonishment I felt at receiving this indifferent answer about the Washington family.[26]

Fukuzawa left America puzzled and intrigued. He had clearly had a good time and made the most of his opportunities. For instance, to the great envy of his companions, he managed not only to have his photograph taken but persuade the fifteen-year-old daughter of the photographer to pose with him. 'As I was going to sit, I saw the girl in the studio. I said suddenly, "Let us have our picture taken together." She immediately said, "All right", being an American girl and thinking nothing of it. So she came and stood by me.'[27] He had learnt a little of the customs of the natives, but after only three weeks 'Things social, political, and economic proved most inexplicable.'[28] Other than the photograph of himself, his most significant acquisition was a copy of Webster's dictionary, which 'is deemed to have been Fukuzawa's intellectual weapon in understanding modern civilization'.[29]

In 1861, the year after he returned, Fukuzawa was married in traditional Japanese manner, with a go-between, to Toki Kin. She bore him nine children, four sons and five daughters, all of whom grew to adulthood, though twin babies had been born dead. He described how, 'For the next two or three years, I was more occupied with my struggles in studying English than in teaching. Then, in the second year of Bunkyu (1862), a happy opportunity came my way, and I was able to make a visit to Europe with the envoys sent by our government.'[30]

*

This second voyage took him away from Japan for almost a year, and involved months spent in several European countries. His own summary of the trip is as follows.

> We sailed in December, still the first year of Bunkyu (1861) on an English war vessel, the *Odin*, sent over for the purpose of conveying our envoy. We called at Hongkong, Singapore and other ports in the Indian Ocean. Then through the Red Sea to Suez where we landed for the railway journey to Cairo in Egypt. After about two days there, we went by boat again across the Mediterranean to Marseilles. From there we continued by the French railways to Paris, stopping a day at Lyons on our way. We were in Paris for about twenty days while our envoys completed negotiations between France and Japan. Next we crossed to England; then to Holland; from Holland to Berlin, the Prussian capital, and then to St. Petersburg in Russia. The return journey was made through France and Portugal, then retracing our course through the Mediterranean and the Indian Ocean, at length we reached Japan after nearly a year of travelling. It was almost the end of the second year of Bunkyu (1862) when we returned.[31]

In fact, according to western chronology, the journey started in January 1862 and Fukuzawa returned in the December of the same year.

The Japanese authorities who sent out this large fact-finding expedition were caught in a dilemma. They wanted the delegation to gather as much information as possible on all aspects of western 'civilization' so that Japan could prepare itself for development. On the other hand, several hundred years of isolation made these same authorities nervous about the possible effects of this new knowledge on members of the expedition. Thus Fukuzawa noted that 'One ridiculous idea held by our embassy was that its members should not meet the foreigners or see the country any more than they had to. We were under the seclusion theory even when we were travelling in a foreign country.' A member of the expedition was to keep a watchful eye and 'This particularly applied to us three translators.'[32] Thus they were accompanied whenever they went out. 'In spite of all these restrictions, however, we were able to see or hear pretty much everything that we wished.'[33]

An amazing new world revealed itself to Fukuzawa's intensely curious eyes. 'Throughout this tour, new and surprising to us were all the things and institutions of civilization. Everywhere we stayed, we had the opportunity of meeting many people and learning much from them.'[34] Again, he was neither particularly impressed with, puzzled by nor interested in pursuing matters scientific and technological, about which he could and had read books.

> All the information dealing with the sciences, engineering, electricity, steam, printing, or the processes of industry and manufacture, contained in my book, I did not really have to acquire in Europe. I was not a specialist in any of those technical fields, and even if I had inquired particularly into them, I could have got only a general idea which could more readily be obtained in text books. So in Europe I gave my chief attention to other more immediately interesting things.[35]

This proved embarrassing at times, for his hosts were under the impression that the Japanese mission, including Fukuzawa, would be most interested in precisely these technological and scientific advances. This had been a problem in America where his kind hosts directed him to the new marvels.

> But on the contrary, there was really nothing new, at least to me. I knew the principle of the telegraphy even if I had not seen the actual machine before; I knew that sugar was bleached by straining the solution with bone-black, and that in boiling down the solution, the vacuum was used to better effect than heat. I had been studying nothing else but such scientific principles ever since I had entered Ogata's school.[36]

Time was short and Fukuzawa was clear both as to what he did not want to spend his time on, and what was important. 'During this mission in Europe I tried to learn some of the most commonplace details of foreign culture' and the 'common matters of daily life directly from the people, because the Europeans would not describe them in books as being too obvious. Yet to us those common matters were the most difficult to comprehend.'[37] He realized that his interests must have been puzzling to his hosts. 'It was embarrassing on both sides and I regretted it, but somehow I managed to escape to other persons whom I had recognized as likely persons to answer my questions on things I had not found in the dictionaries. All my questions were so commonplace, these gentlemen must have felt the conversation to be wasting of time, but to me, the questions were vital and most puzzling.'[38]

He was particularly interested in the working of institutions and associations and in democratic politics. In terms of institutions, he was fascinated but deeply puzzled by things such as hospitals, the postal services, the police. 'For instance, when I saw a hospital, I wanted to know how it was run – who paid the running expenses; when I visited a bank, I wished to learn how the money was deposited and paid out. By similar first-hand queries, I learned something of the postal system and the military conscription then in force in France but not in England.'[39]

He crammed in an enormous amount, mixing observation with continuous questioning and social contacts.

> Then I was given opportunities to visit the headquarters and buildings of the naval and military posts, factories, both governmental and private, banks, business offices, religious edifices, educational institutions, club houses, hospitals – including even the actual performances of surgical operations. We were often invited to dinners in the homes of important personages, and to dancing parties; we were treated to a continual hospitality until at times we returned exhausted to our lodgings.[40]

Blacker describes how during the six weeks in London, the delegation 'attended the Ball of the Civil Service Volunteers in Willis's Rooms, and the Grand Ball given by the Duchess of Northumberland. They paid frequent visits to the International Exhibition. They inspected Woolwich Arsenal and garrison, the Zoo, the Houses of Parliament, Buchanan's Archery Warehouse, the Crystal Palace, King's College Hospital, and the boiler factories of Messrs John Penn and Son at Blackheath.' They were also 'taken to the Derby, down a Newcastle coalmine, and over Portsmouth dockyard.'[41]

Other experiences were equally interesting and Fukuzawa's enthusiasm and curiosity are apparent; 'the hospitals, poor houses, schools for the blind and the deaf, institutions for the insane, museums and the expositions, were all new to look at and as I learned their origins and their contributions, every detail of them filled me with admiration and fascination.'[42]

Just as Tocqueville found the alien political forms in America and England both the most intriguing and difficult to understand, likewise Fukuzawa, coming from an even greater distance, found the political systems in Europe puzzling, yet he sensed their importance. Under a heading 'The people and politics of Europe', he wrote that 'Of political situations of that time, I tried to learn as much as I could from various persons that I met in London and Paris, though it was often difficult to understand things clearly as I was yet so unfamiliar with the history of Europe.'[43]

He noted that 'A perplexing institution was representative government'[44] and gave a vignette of his bewilderment in England when he saw the system in action.

> When I asked a gentleman what the 'election law' was and what kind of bureau the Parliament really was, he simply replied with a smile, meaning I suppose that no intelligent person was expected to ask such a question. But these were the things most difficult of all for me to understand. In this connection, I learned that there were bands of men called political parties – the Liberals and the Conservatives – who were always fighting against each other in the government. For some time it was beyond my comprehension to understand what they were fighting for, and what was meant, anyway, by 'fighting' in peace time. 'This man and that man are enemies in the House,' they would tell me. But these 'enemies' were to be seen at the same table, eating and drinking with each other. I felt as if I could not make much of this. It took me a long time, with some tedious thinking, before I could gather a general notion of these separate mysterious facts. In some of the more complicated matters, I might achieve an understanding five or ten days after they were explained to me. But all in all, I learned much from this initial tour of Europe.[45]

The vast amount of new information he gathered, and the sight of a new world, would provide the foundation for his life's work.

He put down all his observations and summaries of his conversations in a notebook. 'So, whenever I met a person whom I thought to be of some consequence, I would ask him questions and would put down all he said in a notebook ... After reaching home, I based my ideas on these random notes, doing the necessary research in the books which I had brought back, and thus had the material for my book, Seiyo Jijo (Things Western).'[46] We are told that 'One of his notebooks has been preserved. It is crammed with information in Japanese, English and Dutch on such varied subjects as the cost per mile of building a railway, the number of students in King's College, London, and the correct process for hardening wood.'[47]

The comparative perspective

Fukuzawa's three foreign visits and his knowledge of Dutch and English gave him a unique vantage point both in relation to his own civilization and understanding the West. As he realized, he had the basis for a double comparison: the *'ancien régime'* past of his clan youth, and the post-revolutionary world that was opening up, and the comparison of Japan and the West. In relation to this he summarized his experiences at the end of his life thus:

> My life begun in the restricted conventions of the small Nakatsu clan was like being packed tightly in a lunch box. When once the toothpick of clan politics was punched into the corner of the box, a boy was caught on its end, and before he himself knew what was happening, he had jumped out of the old home. Not only did he abandon his native province but he even renounced the teaching of the Chinese culture in which he had been educated. Reading strange books, associating with new kinds of people, working with all the freedom never dreamed of before, travelling abroad two or three times, finally he came to find even the empire of Japan too narrow for his domain. What a merry life this has been, and what great changes![48]

The experience of rapidly expanding intellectual horizons, where 300 years of western thought suddenly became available, is beautifully captured in the following reminiscence.

> When we read history, we realise that Nakatsu was but one of three hundred clans which existed during the Tokugawa period, and that the Tokugawa were merely persons who happened to have seized power in the single island of Japan. We see that beyond Japan lie the almost innumerable countries of Asia and the west, whose histories leave evidence of heroes and great men. When we contemplate the works of Napoleon and Alexander, or imagine the erudition of Newton, Watt or Adam Smith, we realise that there are Hideyoshis beyond the seas and that Butsu Sorai was but a small man of learning from the East. When we read even the bare elements of geography and history, our minds must

needs be lifted from their old ways of thought. Into what lofty
realms will they rise therefore when we look into the theories of
the great thinkers of the west, analysing and comparing inquiring into the cause and effects of all things from the organic laws
of the physical world to the formless affairs of men. As we pon-
der deeply on what we read, we experience a state of rapture as
though we were transported into a different world. When, from
this position, we look back on the world and its phases, governments seem like small compartments of men's affairs, and wars
like the games of children.[49]

The changes within Japan itself were immense. 'The opening of
the country and the restoration of Imperial rule caused a great revolution never before experienced in our history. It even affected all
our customs, education, and industry, and even such details as clothing, food and housing.'[50] Everything was confusion. 'Japanese met
Westerners for the first time since the founding of the Japanese
islands. It was a sudden leap from the silent depths of night into
broad daylight. Everything they saw stupefied their minds; they
had no categories for understanding anything.'[51] Everything was
questioned.

> The fall of the Tokugawa regime of three hundred years' stand-
> ing gave me the cue, and for the first time I realized that my
> lord was as human as I, and that it was shameful to treat him as
> I had. I was not the least surprised to see myself undergoing the
> transition, refusing even the stipend that the clan had willingly
> offered me. I did not stop to reason this out at the time, but I
> am convinced now that the fall of the feudal government was
> what saved me from my slavish attitude.[52]

In contrast with the might and sophistication of Europe and
America, the first temptation was to lose faith in one's culture, or
at least to recognize realistically that it had 'fallen behind'.

> As a result of our recent ties with foreigners we have begun to
> contrast our civilization with theirs. Our inferiority to them on
> the external technological level is obvious, but our mentality
> also differs from theirs. Westerners are intellectually vital, are
> personally well-disciplined, and have patterned and orderly social
> relations. In our present state, from the economy of the nation

down to the activities of single households or individuals, we are no match for them. On the whole, it has been only recently that we have realized Western countries are civilized while we as yet are not, and there is no one who in his heart does not admit this fact.[53]

Japan had been sheltered from all this by the formidable bulk of China, but now China had been humiliated.

The only trouble with us is that we have had too long a period of peace with no intercourse with outside. In the meanwhile, other countries, stimulated by occasional wars, have invented many new things such as steam trains, steam ships, big guns and small hand-guns etc. We did not know all that, for we did not see anything beyond our borders, the only studies we have had being Chinese books, and the only military arts fencing with swords and spears. Naturally we are finding ourselves very much behind times and fearful of the foreign countries.[54]

The vast scale of the changes required were indeed daunting after the long period of seclusion.

True, we have often been shaken by the changing fortunes of history in our two and a half millennia. But as a force which has shaken the very depths of men's minds, the recent relations with foreigners have been the most powerful single set of events since Confucianism and Buddhism were introduced from China in the distant past. Furthermore, Buddhist and Confucian teachings transmitted Asian ideas and practices. They were different only in degree from Japanese institutions, so they may have been novel, but they were not so very strange to our ancestors. The same cannot be said of relations with foreigners in recent history. We have suddenly been thrust into close contact with countries whose indigenous civilizations differ in terms of geographical location and cultural elements, in the evolution of those cultural elements, and in the degree of their evolution. They are not only novel and exotic for us Japanese; everything we see and hear about those cultures is strange and mysterious. If I may use a simile, a blazing brand has suddenly been thrust into ice-cold water. Not only are ripples and swells ruffling the surface of men's minds, but a massive upheaval is being stirred up at the very depths of their souls.[55]

The difficulty was increased by the speed at which Japan would have to adapt if it were not to follow the path of India and China and Africa and become European colonies.

What are, then, the alarming factors that confront the Japanese people in the Meiji Era? The foreign relations are what they are. In commerce, the foreigners are rich and clever; the Japanese are poor and unused to the business. In courts of law, it so often happens that the Japanese people are condemned while the foreigners get around the law. In learning, we are obliged to learn from them. In finances, we must borrow capital from them. We would prefer to open our society to foreigners in gradual stages and move toward civilization at our own pace, but they insist on the principle of free trade and urge us to let them come into our island at once. In all things, in all projects, they take the lead and we are on the defensive. There hardly ever is an equal give and take.[56]

The enormous gap in every aspect became more and more apparent and the bitterness at the way in which Chinese knowledge had provided such a feeble bulwark is evident in another passage.

If we compare the levels of intelligence of Japanese and Westerners, in literature, the arts, commerce, or industry, from the biggest things to the least, in a thousand cases or in one, there is not a single area in which the other side is not superior to us. We can compete with the West in nothing, and no one even thinks about competing with the West. Only the most ignorant thinks that Japan's learning, arts, commerce, or industry is on a par with that of the West. Who would compare a man-drawn cart with a steam engine, or a Japanese sword with a rifle? While we are expounding on *yin* and *yang* and the Five Elements, they are discovering the sixty-element atomic chart. While we are divining lucky and unlucky days by astrology, they have charted the courses of comets and are studying the constitution of the sun and the moon. While we think that we live on a flat, immobile earth, they know that it is round and in motion. While we regard Japan as the sacrosanct islands of the gods, they have raced around the world, discovering new lands and founding new nations. Many of their political, commercial, and legal institutions are more admirable than anything we have. In all these things there is nothing about our present situation that we can be proud of before them.[57]

So far Fukuzawa was only reflecting what a number of his friends were saying. What makes him great is that he applied his intelligence effectively to doing something about the situation. One thing he did was to move beyond the first realistic assessment of western superiority to a more sober assessment of the weaknesses of that system. He combined enthusiasm for the new world of liberty and democracy, with a knowledge that it was far from perfect. He appeared at times to be advocating a total abandonment of Japanese traditions, writing 'If we are to open our country to the world, we must open it all the way and bring in everything of the West. This is what I have always advocated.'[58] Yet on the very same page he urged selectivity: 'Not every product of the West will be good or useful. But if there is something clearly inferior or bad on our side, then we must without a moment's delay correct it.'[59]

He found the new civilization, especially in America, over-obsessed with material wealth. Although producing many things,

the results of attaining the benefit of the best and the most beautiful have been disappointing. Their men spend their lives in the feverish pursuit of money. The only function of their women is feverishly to breed male heirs to carry on the economic struggle. Can this be called the ideal society? I hardly think so. This observation of Mill suffices to give us some ideas of at least one undesirable aspect of the American character.[60]

He also noted that although proclaiming equality, the *de facto* situation was not, perhaps, as good as it was in Japan. 'The civilization of the West is of course to be admired. It has been only recently since we have begun to do so. But it would be better not to believe at all than to do so superficially. The West's wealth and power must truly be envied, but we must not go so far as to imitate the unequal distribution of wealth among her peoples as well.'[61] Likewise, while western nations proclaimed the sovereignty of nations, the rule of international law, etc., they behaved with predatory unscrupulousness in their massive imperial expansion into Asia and elsewhere. Individually, many westerners were loutish, aggressive and unpleasant in their dealings with the Japanese. Or again, he noted that 'The taxes of Japan are not light, but if we consider the suffering of the poor people of England because of oppression by the landlord class, we should rather celebrate the happy condition of Japan's farmers. The custom of honouring women in the West is among the finest in the world. But if a wicked wife dominates and plagues her husband, or a disobedient daughter scorns her parents and gives free reign to disgraceful conduct, let us not be intoxicated over the custom.'[62] In summary, the West was far ahead in its material life, its political and social institutions and scientific knowledge, but its ethical foundations were less laudable. 'When I observe the ethical behaviour of Japanese men and compare it with that of men in other civilized countries, I do not find Japanese men inferior.'[63]

Fukuzawa saw his task as combining western science, technology, and political institutions and a market economy, with the traditional 'spirit' or ethic of historical Japan. That Japan is today such a curious blend of 'West' and 'East' is in no small part due to his clear vision of the problem, for 'the superiority of Western over Japanese civilization is certainly very great, but Western civilization is hardly perfect'.[64]

Fukuzawa's greatness also arises from the fact that he saw himself as a spectator looking at two worlds, both from the outside. In relation to his own Japanese upbringing and world, he had become a sympathetic outsider, participant and then observer.

A man goes through life as if sailing on the sea in a boat. The men in the boat naturally move with the boat, but they may well be unaware of how fast and in what direction the boat is moving. Only those who watch from the shore can know these things with any accuracy. The samurai of the old Nakatsu clan moved with the clan, but they may have been unaware of how they were moving, and may not realise just how they came to arrive at their present state. I alone have stood, as it were, on the shore of the clan, and, as a spectator, may have had a more accurate view of the samurai within the clan. Hence I have committed my spectator's view to writing.[65]

Equally interesting is the fact that he could look at western civilization as it reached its greatest period of expansion and technological superiority, from the outside. While people like Mill and Buckle and others could only conjecture what a pre-industrial, *ancien régime* world was like, Fukuzawa could relive in his own lifetime the experience of 150 years of dramatic change. Compressed into his single life was the most massive shift which has occurred in human history in the last 10,000 years.

He saw very clearly that this gave him an advantage, the shock of surprise and amazement which is the basis of deep discovery.

We also have the advantage of being able directly to contrast our own personal pre-Meiji experience with Western civilization. Here we have an advantage over our Western counterparts, who, locked within an already matured civilization, have to make conjectures about conditions in other countries, while we can attest to the changes of history through the more reliable witness of personal experience. This actual experience of pre-Meiji Japan is the accidental windfall we scholars of the present day enjoy. Since this kind of living memory of our generation will never be repeated again, we have an especially important opportunity to make our mark. Consider how all of today's scholars of Western Learning were, but a few years back, scholars of Chinese Learning, or of Shinto or Buddhism. We were all either from feudal samurai families or were feudal subjects. We have lived two lives, as it were; we unite in ourselves two completely different patterns of experience.[66]

He believed that this would give him a peculiarly valid set of insights.

What kind of insights shall we not be able to offer when we compare and contrast what we experienced in our earlier days with what we experience of Western civilization? What we have to say is sure to be trustworthy. For this reason, despite my personal inadequacies, I have endeavoured in this humble work to put to use my own limited knowledge of Western Learning... my whole purpose has been to take advantage of the present historically unique opportunity to bequeath my personal impressions to later generations.[67]

13
The Making of a New Japan

For five years after his return from his travels, Fukuzawa mainly worked as a teacher and translator in Edo. This was a time of growing tension and threat to the old order. For instance, on one occasion he moved out of the city fearing a British attack. Because of anti-western sentiments, he avoided certain contacts. But his family grew and he settled into writing. In 1866 he published the first volume of *Seiyo Jijo, Things Western*, which sold, in the end, over a quarter of a million copies. He was made a retainer of the Shogun and continued to work as a teacher. Then in January 1867 he went on his third and last overseas expedition, again to America, and returned six months later. Although he comments less on what he learnt from direct observation, he came back with other treasures.

On my second journey to America, I had received a much larger allowance than on the previous one. With all my expenses being paid by the government, I was able to purchase a good number of books. I bought many dictionaries of different kinds, texts in geography, history, law, economics, mathematics, and every sort I could secure. They were for the most part the first copies to be brought to Japan, and now with this large library I was able to let each of my students use the originals to study. This was certainly an unheard-of convenience – that all students could have the actual books instead of manuscript copies for their use.[1]

This set the trend, he wrote, for the use of American books in Japan over the next ten years.

His innovation here was supplemented by others. In particular he introduced the concept of tuition fees from students, which he had no doubt seen in the West, and this helped him to set up a school, which, when it moved to a new site in April 1868, was the foundation of the first Japanese university, Keio. He continued his teaching and lecturing as the fate of Japan was decided around him, for in 1868 the Tokugawa Shogunate, which had lasted for two and a half centuries, was overthrown by the revived Imperial power, and the Meiji Restoration was effected through a series of pitched battles.

The Emperor partly won because of superior weaponry, and here again Fukuzawa recognized an opportunity. He obtained a copy of a foreign work on rifles which he hoped to translate, but wondered 'Was I not too brazen to think of translating a book on rifles without knowing anything of it?'[2] So with the aid of the book he dismantled and put together a gun, and 'with this experience, I gained much understanding of the rifle and at once took up the translation of the book and published it.' It came out in 1866 and sold many thousands of copies and he later learnt that his translation had helped one of the greatest of Japanese generals, General Murata, who was later to become a world expert on ordnance.

*

The restoration of the Meiji Emperor in 1868 did not, at first sight, look likely to change Japan or Fukuzawa's life very much. The Emperor's supporters had been, if anything, more xenophobic and traditionalist than those of the Shogun. As far as Fukuzawa could see at first, the new government looked like 'a collection of fools from the various clans got together to form another archaic anti-foreign government which would probably drive the country to ruin through its blunders'.[3] Yet there was a swift change and he and others discovered that they were in fact 'a collection of energetic, ambitious young men prepared to build up a new Japan on thoroughly western lines . . .'[4] Fukuzawa and his friends began to feel 'as though they were seeing enacted on the stage a play which they themselves had written'.[5] There was now scope for new work and for the widespread dissemination of the old.

There was also a chance to break finally with his clan. For a while in the 1860s Fukuzawa remained, officially, a member of his clan and drew a stipend and obeyed certain orders. His relations with the clan became more strained over time and he started to question the political views of some of his elders.

Having taken such an attitude, I could hardly enter the politics of the clan, nor seek a career in it. Consequently I lost all thoughts of depending on the favours of other men. Indeed I attached little value on any man or clan.'[6] After the Meiji Restoration he increasingly followed his own inclinations and finally made a stand. 'If this is disagreeable to them, let them dismiss me. I shall obey the order and get out.[7]

Looking back on the events, he remembered how difficult it had been at the time. 'This lack of attachment to the clan may seem quite creditable now, but in the eyes of my fellow-clansmen it was taken as a lack of loyalty and human sympathy.'[8] He was adamant, however: 'I did not consider the right or wrong of the conflict; I simply said it was not the kind of activity that students should take part in.'[9] Finally, 'This argument seemed to dumbfound the officials. My salary was given up, and all official relations between the clan and myself were broken off as I had proposed.'[10] Thus, Fukuzawa was in the odd situation of having created an independent and individual space within a 'small group' society. He used this space to maximum advantage as he launched more fully on his career of writing and teaching.

It is possible to argue that up to about 1870 Fukuzawa had confined his writing mainly to the explanation of technical matters, non-contentious technological and institutional features of the West. For example, the information he collected on his voyages formed the basis of his three volume work titled *Seiyō Jijō* or *Conditions in the West*, published in 1866, 1868 and 1870. The first volume describes in detail a 'number of Western institutions: schools, newspapers, libraries, government bodies, orphanages, museums, steamships, telegraphs'. It then 'gives capsule sketches of the history, government, military systems, and finances of the United States, the Netherlands and Britain'. The second volume contains 'translations from a popular British series, *Chambers' Educational Course*. This had been written by John Hill Burton and published by Robert and William Chambers of Edinburgh. 'In this volume, entitled the *Outside Volume* . . . the "corner-stones and main pillars", the intangible social network constituting civilized society, was discussed.'[11] The third volume 'presents general material by Blackstone on human rights and by Wayland on taxes and then supplies historical and other data on Russia and France'.[12]

This technical work was enormously influential, coming just at the moment when Japan was opening to the West. We are told that 'The work exerted a powerful influence on the Japanese public of the time.' The first volume alone sold 150,000 copies, plus over 100,000 thousand pirated copies. One of the drafters of the CHARTER OATH and the new proto-constitution for the Meiji Restoration wrote that he and his colleagues relied almost exclusively on this work.[13] Fukuzawa was thus not boasting when he gave an account of its impact on his contemporaries.

> At that moment, they came across a new publication called *Seiyō Jijō*. When one person read it and recognized it as interesting and appropriate guide to the new civilization, then a thousand others followed. Among the officials and among the private citizens, whoever discussed Western civilization, obtained a copy of *Seiyō Jijō* for daily reference. This book became the sole authority in its field exactly as the proverb says even a bat can dominate the air where no birds live. Indeed, my book became a general guide to the contemporary society of ignorant men, and some of the decrees issued by the new government seem to have had their origins in this book.[14]

It was the right book at the right time. 'Then, how did it happen that this book became a great power and dominated the whole society of Japan? I reason that this book came upon the right time after the opening of the country when the people, high and low, were feeling lost in the new world.'[15] He had started the work before the Meiji Restoration and the three volumes were completed before the outcome was clear. 'Even if they were to win some attention, I had no idea that the contents of the books would ever be applied to our own social conditions. In short, I was writing my books simply as stories of the West or as curious tales of a dreamland.'[16] Yet the 'dreamland' became the avid focus of Japanese attention and Fukuzawa's ambition increased.

He continued to supply popular and useful works for a westernizing Japan. For example, he decided that a rational accounting system was essential for Japan, but first the principles of economics needed to be explained.

> I sat back and thought over the situation, and came upon the idea that the merchants and the men in industry should have been acquainted with the principles of the Western economics

before they took up the Western method of business practices. To jump to the reform of their books without this basic knowledge was against the natural order of things. What one should do now would be to teach a wide circle of young men the general and basic principle of Western economics and wait till they grow up and take over the business. After that, the practical value of the new bookkeeping will be realized. With this idea in my mind what I produced in a textbook style was this *Minkan Keizairoku*.[17]

He then produced the follow-up, the book on accounting, admitting, as he had done with his book on rifles, that it was one thing to explain the principles, another to be able to use them.

In the early years of the Restoration I translated a book on the methods of bookkeeping, and I know that all the correct texts follow the example of my book. So I should know something of the practice, if not enough to be an expert. But apparently the brains of a writer of books and those of a business man are different; I cannot put my bookkeeping into use. I even have great difficulty in understanding the files which other people make.[18]

The early 1870s saw a rapid shift in the level of his work as he recognized that his mission was not merely to explain and help introduce science, technology and institutional structures (for instance, he helped to lay the foundations of a western-style police force),[19] but, much more difficult, to change culture and ideology. He set about trying to introduce the 'spirit' of the West, that is the concepts of liberty, equality and democracy. Thus the 1870s saw the publication of his major philosophical works heavily influenced by Guizot, Mill and Buckle, and hence stemming from the French and Scottish Enlightenment.

In 1872 he started modestly with *A Junior Book of Morals* and then over the next four years wrote the pieces which would constitute one of his major works, the *Encouragement of Learning*. This constituted seventeen pamphlets which came out over the period 1872 to 1876 which, because of their simplicity of style and stringent criticisms of the Tokugawa world, sold enormously well, reaching over 3,400,000 copies.[20] In 1875 he synthesized much of his speculation into an *Outline of Civilization* and the following year published a book close to one of Tocqueville's main themes, *On Decentraliza-tion of Power*. Three years later he wrote a *Popular Discourse on People's Rights* and also *A Popular Discourse on National Rights*. These two last books are at the turning point when, for reasons to be dis-cussed below, Fukuzawa's growing distrust of the imperial ambitions of the West led him into a mood of aggressive nationalism which lasted until the defeat of China in 1895. After 1878, he contrib-uted little more that has been widely influential, apart from his *Autobiography*, written in 1899.

Fukuzawa described his writing (with a brush, Japanese fashion) as only one of his two major weapons. 'Consequently I renewed activities with "tongue and brush", my two cherished instruments. On one side I was teaching in my school and making occasional public speeches, while on the other I was constantly writing on all subjects. And these comprise my books subsequent to Seiyo Jijo. It was a pretty busy life but no more than doing my bit, or "doing the ten thousandth part" as we put it.'[21]

He was also involved in publishing. He founded the daily newspaper *Jiji Shimpō* in which many of his writings appeared after 1882, and from time to time published his own writings. So successful were all his writing and publishing efforts that 'at that time all works about the West came to be popularly known as *Fukuzawa-bon*'.[22]

Yet the teaching and speech-making were equally important. Here also he was a pioneer and had to invent traditions which were taken for granted in the West. For example, the art of speech-mak-ing was something which he had witnessed in the West, but was totally absent in Japan. He gives a graphic account of the back-ground that led up to the publication of his book *Kaigiben* (How to Hold a Conference) in 1873. His account again illustrates his prob-lems and inventiveness when introducing new concepts.

He noted that

> The actuality today is that people hold no wonder over the practice of a man speaking out his own thoughts and communicating them to a group of listeners. Even the technique of shorthand writing has been developed for everyday use. In such a world, some people are liable to feel that the public speaking is a cus-tomary art of many centuries. But the fact is that the public speaking was a new and a strange art only twenty odd years ago, and those who endeavoured at it for the first time experi-enced some untold trials.[23]

Thus he decided to give the history of its introduction into Japan. In 1873 a colleague

> came to my residence with a small book in English and said that in all the countries in the West, the 'speech' was considered a necessary art in all departments of human life; there was no reason why it was not needed in the Japanese society; rather, it was urgently needed, and because we didn't have it, we were sorely deficient in communicating our thoughts from man to man in politics, in learning and in commerce and industry; there was no telling what our losses were from the inevitable lack of understanding between parties; this present book was on the art of speech; how would it be to make the content of this book known to all our countrymen?[24]

So Fukuzawa, who had already seen the practice at work in England and puzzled over confrontational politics, looked into the matter.

> I opened the book and I found it was indeed a book introducing an entirely new subject to us. 'Then, without further ado, let us translate its general content', I said. I completed in a few days a summary translation, and it is this *Kaigiben*. In the translation, I was met with the problem of finding a proper Japanese word for 'speech'. Then an old recollection came to me that in my Nakatsu Clan, there was a custom of presenting a formal communication to the Clan government on one's personal matter or on one's work. It was not a report or a petition but an expression of one's thoughts, and this communication was called *enzetsu* letter. I have no knowledge as to the customs in other Clans. But as I remembered this word clearly from my Nakatsu days, I discussed it with my colleagues and decided on it as the translated word for 'speech'.[25]

The word he invented became incorporated into national life and without word and concept modern democracy could not have developed in Japan. 'At present, the speech has become an important element in the National Diet and in all occasions of our lives even in small villages in the countryside. But this word, *enzetsu*, traces its origin to a custom in Nakatsu Clan of Buzen Province, chosen by the members of Keio Gijuku, and then it spread to the rest of the country. Other words such as "debate" was translated *tōron*, "approve" *kaketsu* and "reject" *hiketsu*.'[26] Fukuzawa had once again thought things through, and a combination of his wide experience and independence of mind had led to a new conclusion. Although all his friends and colleagues said speech-making was impossible in the Japanese language, 'But when I stopped and thought about it, I came to think that there is no reason why it is not possible to make a speech in Japanese. The reason for the difficulty must be that we Japanese people have not been used to making speeches since olden times. But if you don't try it because of the difficulty, it will stay difficult forever.'[27] We are told that 'He himself demonstrated beautifully the art of public speaking in the presence of sceptics and built a public speaking hall at Keio where he, his fellows and students, held many gatherings and speaking contests'.[28] The hall is called the Enzetsukan, and survives in a rebuilt form.

Yet the change that needed to be effected was much deeper than a question of the art of public speaking. Speech itself was much more embedded and socially controlled in Japan than in the West. This made rational, impersonal speeches very difficult. Speech, as well as gestures and postures, altered dramatically depending on whom one was speaking to. Fukuzawa carried out various experiments to show how strong was this absence of personal consistency and stability. For instance, 'it showed that they were merely following the lead of the person speaking to them'.[29] Much of his effort to teach the Japanese the art of public debate and public speech-making tried to deal with this problem. The desire for approval, to fit in, made it very difficult for people to state an absolute opinion as their own, to take a stand, to argue forcefully and consistently. Everything tended to slip towards the social context. The individual and his views did not matter: he or she must submit to group harmony, sacrifice all individual will to the group. This was built into the language, the bowing, the political and kinship system.

Another part of the problem was that people found it impossible to separate their words and their feelings. As we saw, during his travels he was amazed at the way in which politicians in England could attack each other in the House for their ideas, without any personal animus. The art of debate seemed to be a kind of elaborate game, like a legal confrontation, but it made it possible to separate ideas from their social context and, in other words, allowed 'reason' to prevail.

More generally, the very concept of allowing political parties to express their dissent, or even exist, was alien to the Japanese tradition. Thus 'in political practices in Japan, a group of more than three to make agreements among themselves privately was called "conspiracy", and the *kōsatsu* (the official bulletin board on the street for announcing government decrees) pronounced that conspiracy was an offence, and indeed it was one of the gravest of offences.'[30] Yet he saw something very puzzlingly different on his visit to Europe. There 'in England I heard that there were what they called "political parties" and they openly and legally made games of fighting for the supremacy.' When he first encountered this he wondered: 'Did that mean that in England, people were permitted to argue and to make attacks on the government decrees and they were not punished?' How could such a system not lead to anarchy? 'Under such untidy condition, it was a wonder that England preserved her internal peace and order.' But he persisted in his observations and questions until 'I felt I was grasping the basis of the English Parliament, the relation between the Royalty and the Parliament, the power of popular opinion and the customs of Cabinet changes – or, did I really grasp them? All the human affairs were baffling.'[31] In his writings he worked through the system of democracy and explained it to himself and his Japanese audience.

Another part of the problem in Japan was that there were no rules of procedure for meetings. 'From the earliest times in Japan, whenever people have assembled to discuss some problem, nothing could be settled because of the lack of any set rules for discussion. This has always been true of disputes among scholars, of business conferences, and of municipal meetings.'[32] All this has to be learnt from a civilization in western Europe which has developed on the basis of Greek philosophy and Western jurisprudence, a complex set of procedures to make decisions and sift out the best arguments.

Even if all these things could be changed, there were other practical problems. There were not even places in which conferences, speeches or lectures could take place. So Fukuzawa set about physically building the first lecture hall in Japan. Speaking of what would become Keio University, he wrote: 'I returned to my school and at once commenced on the plan for introducing the new art to the whole country. The first necessity, we decided, was an auditorium, and that became our first undertaking.'[33] The experiment was a success. Here again he brought in an institution which had been absent in Japan for at least 1,000 years. He recognized that western invention and success did not come out of the blue. Selecting the

University of Glasgow in the later eighteenth century as his model, he reminded his audience that 'When Watt invented the steam engine and Adam Smith first formulated the laws of economics, they did not sit alone in the dark and experience an instantaneous enlightenment. It was because of long years of studying physical sciences that they were able to achieve their results.'[34] He himself had escaped from his Nakatsu background through the educational path and much of his later life was devoted to the Baconian project of the 'Advancement', or as Fukuzawa put it, the 'Encouragement' of Learning.

Indeed, it is clear that a part of Fukuzawa's enthusiasm for western-style education lay in his belief that it was a very powerful force in the fight against inequality. He shows this in particular in his account of the history of his Nakatsu clan after the Meiji Restoration. He describes the fortuitous coming together of events as follows:

It was owing to this entirely fortuitous stroke of good luck that the Nakatsu clan was able to escape the disasters which fell upon most of the other clans at the time of the Restoration. Later something happened to consolidate this stroke of fortune: namely the establishment of the Municipal School. About the time of the abolition of the clans in 1871 the men who had held official positions in the old clan conferred with the staff of Keiogijuku in Tokyo and decided to divide up the hereditary stipend of the old clan governor and amalgamate it with the savings of the old clan to form a capital fund for promoting Western studies. They then built a school in the old castle town which they called the Municipal School. The rules of the School stipulated that all pupils were to be treated alike, irrespective of their birth or rank – a policy which was not only proclaimed in theory but also carried out in practice. This principle held good from the very day the School was founded, so that it was just as if a new world of equal rights for all people had appeared in the midst of the fading dream of feudal privilege. Many of the staff of Keiogijuku had been samurai of the old Nakatsu clan but they had never interfered in any way with the clan administration, and through all the various disturbances which the clan had undergone had merely looked on with calm hostility.[35]

The school exercised a magical effect. 'As soon as they really put their hearts into the School they lost all their old notions of birth and rank.'[36] Thus future generations would avoid the bitter memories of his own childhood. 'Whether it be due to mere luck or to a recognisable cause, it is certainly clear that today one sees no trace of resentment or ill-feeling between the clan samurai.'[37] Independence of mind, curiosity and the treating of all mankind (including women) as born equal, these were the values which Fukuzawa saw as the foundations of his educational work.

Combining western science and eastern spirit

Fukuzawa's work was centrally concerned with the question of how it would be possible to make Japan rapidly as wealthy and militarily strong as possible. His concern with wealth lay in the growing confrontation between Europe and America on the one hand, and Asia on the other. The tiny island of England had humiliated the mighty Chinese Empire in the Opium Wars in 1839–42. Then in 1853 and 1854 the 'black ships' of America had sailed into a Japanese harbour and shown up the hollow weakness of the Japanese Empire. He lamented the fact that 'In general, we Japanese seem to lack the kind of motivation that ought to be standard equipment in human nature. We have sunk to the depths of stagnation.'[38]

Fukuzawa became increasingly aware of the menace of European expansion. He noted that 'In China, for instance, the land is so vast that the interior has as yet to be penetrated by the white man, and he has left his traces only along the coast. However, if future developments can be conjectured, China too will certainly become nothing but a garden for Europeans.'[39] This had already happened in the once mighty civilization of India, and Fukuzawa feared that if India and soon China became provinces of Europe, then Japan would go the same way. The effects would be disastrous. 'Wherever the Europeans touch, the land withers up, as it were; the plants and the trees stop growing. Sometimes even whole populations have been wiped out. As soon as one learns such things and realizes that Japan is also a country in the East, then though we have as yet not been seriously harmed by foreign relations we might well fear the worst is to come.'[40] As the century progressed he felt the increasing menace; if one succumbed, one became a slave; if one competed, one was an outcast. He noted that 'the whole world is dominated by Western civilization today, and anyone who opposes it will be ostracized from the human society; a nation, too, will find itself outside the world circle of nations.'[41]

His aim was to help turn Japan into a country that was as wealthy as the new industrial nations of the West – and out of this wealth as militarily powerful. He wrote that 'The final purpose of all my work was to create in Japan a civilized nation as well equipped in the arts of war and peace as those of the Western world. I acted as if I had become the sole functioning agent for the introduction of Western learning.'[42] Elsewhere Fukuzawa defined the purpose of his work as follows. 'After all, the purpose of my entire work has not only been to gather young men together and give them the benefit of foreign books but to open this "closed" country of ours and bring it wholly into the light of Western civilization. For only thus may Japan become strong in the arts of both war and peace and take a place in the forefront of the progress of the world.'[43]

The essential point was to preserve political independence through economic wealth and military power. He believed that 'foreign relations in our country are a critical problem, from the standpoint both of economics and of power and rights', subservience to foreign powers 'is a deep-seated disease afflicting vital areas of the nation's life'.[44] At times he states that independence is the end, and 'civilization' the means. 'The only reason for making the people in our country today advance toward civilization is to preserve our country's independence. Therefore, our country's independence is the goal, and our people's civilization is the way to that goal.'[45] At other times he saw independence and civilization as synonymous; 'a country's independence equals civilization. Without civilization independence cannot be maintained.'[46]

He realized that Japan and Asia had a long way to go in order to 'catch up'. He found that when he compared 'Occidental and Oriental civilizations' in a 'general way as to wealth, armament, and the greatest happiness for the greatest number, I have to put the Orient below the Occident'.[47] Yet he believed that 'it would not be impossible to form a great nation in this far Orient, which would stand counter to Great Britain of the West, and take an active part in the progress of the whole world.' This was 'my second and greater ambition'.[48]

In these ambitions Fukuzawa was a central figure in the wider Japanese 'Enlightenment', which sought to make Japan both more powerful and more content. Thus he was a founder member of the school of historiography which was 'known as *bummeishiron* (history of civilisation) – so called because its chief purpose was to discover from the past the answers pertaining to the nature of civilisation:

what exactly was civilisation and how did it come to be what it is?'[49] Part of his immense popularity and influence arose out of his realization that he was reflecting a national mood. The 'arrival of the Americans in the 1850s has, as it were, kindled a fire in our people's hearts. Now that it is ablaze, it can never be extinguished.' Combined with the later overthrow of the Shogunate and Meiji Restoration of 1868, events 'have become spurs prodding the people of the nation forward. They have caused dissatisfaction with our civilization and aroused enthusiasm for Western civilization. As a result, men's sights are now being reset on the goal of elevating Japanese civilization to parity with the West, or even of surpassing it.'[50]

In order to do this, it was not enough to introduce isolated bits of western technology, to follow China in buying weapons from the West, for instance. It was essential that Japan learnt the principles or spirit behind the technology and created the appropriate institutional structures. 'The idea seems to be that, if England has one thousand warships, and we too have one thousand warships, then we can stand against them.' This was not enough. It was 'the thinking of men who are ignorant of the proportions of things'. Much more was needed. 'If there are one thousand warships, there have to be at least ten thousand merchant ships, which in turn require at least one hundred thousand navigators; and to create navigators there must be naval science.' Even more than this was required. 'Only when there are many professors and many merchants, when laws are in order and trade prospers, when social conditions are ripe – when, that is, you have all the prerequisites for a thousand warships – only then can there be a thousand warships.'[51]

Fukuzawa was particularly proud that the Japanese seemed to have the ability to assimilate amazingly quickly the art of making and using things, not just buying them:

it was only in the second year of Ansei (1855) that we began to study navigation from the Dutch in Nagasaki; by 1860, the science was sufficiently understood to enable us to sail a ship across the Pacific. This means that about seven years after the first sight of a steamship, after only about five years of practice, the Japanese people made a trans-Pacific crossing without help from foreign experts.[52]

Yet even this was not enough. He wrote that the

civilization of a country should not be evaluated in terms of its external forms. Schools, industry, army and navy, are merely external forms of civilization. It is not difficult to create these forms, which can all be purchased with money. But there is additionally a spiritual component, which cannot be seen or heard, bought or sold, lent or borrowed. Yet its influence on the nation is very great. Without it, the schools, industries, and military capabilities lose their meaning. It is indeed the all-important value, i.e. the spirit of civilization, which in turn is the spirit of independence of a people.'[53]

It was essential to change institutions and ideology first, and then the material forms would follow. 'The cornerstone of modern civilization will be laid only when national sentiment has thus been revolutionized, and government institutions with it. When that is done, the foundations of civilization will be laid, and the outward forms of material civilization will follow in accord with a natural process without special effort on our part, will come without our asking, will be acquired without our seeking.'[54] This 'spirit' of civilization had to be understood and then transferred to Japan. This was an immensely difficult task, but one to which he devoted his life.

What he wanted to bring in were not just the *techniques* of the West, but the 'civilization' of the West. He defined this central concept as follows. 'What, then, does civilization mean? I say that it refers to the attainment of *both* material well-being *and* the elevation of the human spirit.'[55] As he began to learn more about the West, first through his book learning, then from his visits to America and Europe, he realized how very different the 'civilization' of Asia and the West were and it was this that puzzled and intrigued him. 'With regard to a nation as a whole, it may be called "a nation's ways" or "national opinion". These things are what is meant by the spirit of civilization. And it is this spirit of civilization that differentiates the manners and customs of Asia and Europe.'[56]

Fukuzawa's writings were part of a general 'Enlightenment' movement known as *Keimō*, meaning literally 'enlightening the darkness of the masses'. It was based on a proposition which linked it directly to the European Enlightenment. This was that there was a strong and necessary association between three things: wealth, liberty and equality. We are told that there was agreement among Japanese scholars of the West in the nineteenth century that 'the spiritual secret of the strength and wealth of the western nations lay in the fact that their people were equal and therefore free. It was because the western peoples enjoyed freedom and equal rights and were hence imbued with the spirit of enterprise, initiative and responsibility that the western nations had succeeded in becoming strong, rich and united.'[57] For example, 'In the preface to his translation of Smiles' *Self-Help*, published in 1871, Nakamura Keiu stated boldly that the reason why the western nations were strong was not that they possessed armies, but that they possessed the spirit of liberty.'[58] What the Japanese nation needed to learn was the 'spirit of independence, initiative and responsibility such as characterised a people enjoying freedom and equal rights...'[59]

Thus the key questions for Fukuzawa became those of liberty and equality and how they were to be encouraged. His personal experience in pre-Meiji Japan gave him especial insights into the vast change required, and it is fascinating to see the way in which all of his work is in a sense an autobiography, an externalization of his own struggle to move from lack of freedom to liberty, and from hierarchy to equality.

*

The shift towards a more nationalistic and chauvinistic attitude between about 1875 and 1895 is obvious. Carmen Blacker describes his shifting views in some detail. She quotes him as writing in 1878 that '"International law and treaties of friendship have high-sounding names, it is true, but they are nothing more than external, nominal forms. In fact international relations are based on nothing more than quarrels over power and profit... A few cannons are worth more than a hundred volumes of international law. A case of ammunition is of more use than innumerable treaties of friendship."'[60] There is much more to this effect and in the following year he wrote: '"A nation does not come out on top because it is in the right. It is right because it has come out on top."'[61] He saw the senselessness of it all, but what was one to do? '"All this may be useless and stupid, but when others treat one stupidly one can only do the same back to them. When others use violence, we must be violent too. When others use deceitful trickery we must do likewise."'[62] He asked: '"Have the European countries really respected the rights and interests and integrity of the countries with which they have come into contact? What about Persia? And India? And Siam? And Luzon and Hawaii?... Wherever the Europeans come, the land ceases to be productive, and trees and plants cease to grow. Worse still, the human race sometimes dies out.'"[63] Japan should 'join' the West and behave as western countries did. In an article in 1885 he wrote: 'Our immediate policy, therefore, should be to lose no time in waiting for the enlightenment of our neighbouring countries (Korea and China) in order to join them in developing Asia, but rather to depart from their rank and cast our lot with the civilized countries of the West... We should deal with them exactly as the Westerners do.'[64]

Fukuzawa also noted the arrogance of foreigners in Japan. '"They eat and drink, and then leave without paying. They ride in *rikishas* without paying. They accept payment in advance for a contract, and then fail to deliver the goods... Not only are they grasping about money; they often break laws and offend against propriety."'[65] Blacker notes that his earlier praise of democratic and balanced polities, and of individual rights, was almost abandoned for a few years as he became an autocratic nationalist and quasi-imperialist. She quotes him as writing in 1882 that the '"one object of my life is to extend Japan's national power... Even if the government be autocratic in name and form, I shall be satisfied with it if it is strong enough to strengthen the country."'[66] This, of course, ran right against many of his liberal statements, for instance that 'For true human beings to be treated like instruments is an insult, for the honour and dignity of human beings is disregarded and makes death preferable to life.'[67] Yet it is clear that he had indeed switched. 'If Fukuzawa's sudden neglect of people's rights in favour of national strength at this period might appear illiberal, the policy he recommended Japan to adopt towards the other Asiatic countries was frankly imperialistic.'[68] It was Japan's duty to become the leader of Eastern Asia and, if necessary, invasion of neighbouring states was justified. His 'nationalistic sentiments reached their climax during the Sino-Japanese War', which he vigorously supported.[69]

Albert Craig argues even more strongly that Fukuzawa lost his faith in the law of nations and natural rights for a considerable period. Thus 'By 1881 Fukuzawa's disillusionment with the morality of natural law had become even more profound. He retained the ideal of civilization as a noble concept, but he denied it any real grounding in nature.'[70] Craig quotes extensively from some of his writings. '"Laws are made for evil men, as medicine is for the diseased. *Millions* of years hereafter, when disease has vanished and all men are good, laws and medicine may be abandoned. In the meantime it is useless to speak of popular rights based on nature (*tennen no minkenron*); they are not worth discussing."'[71] He became increasingly cynical. In 1881 he asked:

> Do nations . . . honour treaties? We can find not the slightest evidence that they do . . . When countries break treaties . . . there are no courts to judge them. Therefore, whether a treaty is honoured or not . . . depends solely on the financial and military powers of the countries involved . . . *Money and soldiers are not for the protection of existing principles they are the instruments for the creation of principles where none exist*. . . . in my opinion the Western nations . . . are growing ever stronger in the skills of war. In recent years every country devises strange new weapons. Day by day they increase their standing armies. This is truly useless, truly stupid. Yet if others work at being stupid, then I must respond in kind. If others are violent, then I must become violent . . . Those of my persuasion follow the way of force.[72]

Like Blacker, Craig believes that in this period, 'much of the liberal content of his earlier thought slowly seeped away'.[73] He argues that in this period, 'there was nothing other to turn to than the spiritual power of the emperor or the residues of irrational samurai morality.'[74] Although Fukuzawa still 'favoured cultural diversity and political pluralism', for a time he felt that 'Japan, at its stage of civilization, could not handle these things without grave internal disturbances. Fukuzawa foresaw that instant constitutional government in a developing nation could lead to violent rifts in the national consensus, which in turn might destroy constitutional government and bring dictatorship.' Thus for a time, 'he stressed the emperor, who alone could make Japan strong and united while advancing toward full constitutional government.' At this period, 'Fukuzawa spoke more of duties and less of rights, more of science and less of freedom.'[75]

It is not difficult to see how the world must have looked to someone on the edge of the rapid advance of western imperialism and capitalism as it swept across Asia. On his visit to Europe he had seen 'the miserable conditions of the native people living under western colonialism during stopovers in British Ceylon and Hong Kong. He realized that advanced western countries ruled the poor nations of Asia under the principal of "might is right".'[76] For a while the ability of Japan to withstand colonialization hung in the balance. Proof that it could do so was afforded by the victory of the Japanese over the Chinese in 1895. As Fukuzawa wrote,

> The Sino-Japanese War is the victory of a united government and people. There are no words that can express my pleasure and thankfulness: to experience such an event is what life is for... In truth the Sino-Japanese War does not amount to much; it is but a prelude to Japan's future diplomacy, and is no occasion for such rejoicing. Yet I am so overcome by emotions that I enter a dreamlike state... The strength, wealth, and civilization of the new Japan are all due to the virtues of those who went before.[77]

Craig comments that 'Victory in war removed the load of Japan from Fukuzawa's shoulders. No longer was it necessary for him to talk up the national spirit or warn the people of present perils... he began again to talk of the larger philosophical issues of ethics and cosmology that had occupied his attentions during the early 1870's.'[78]

It is clear that 'civilization' and political independence were always inextricably linked in Fukuzawa's thought. If he became cynical about the motivations of the western powers and came to believe that all their preaching of natural rights and the dignity of man conflicted with their predatory behaviour, he had good cause to be alarmed. It is indeed part of his interest that he reflected on those very issues of trying to combine democratic and liberal ideals with *realpolitik* which face many developing nations today.

*

Fukuzawa's life spanned the period from the first great work of Tocqueville in 1835, to the middle of the career of Max Weber in 1901. He had witnessed two great discontinuities. Through his travels he had seen the huge gap that had developed between East and West by the 1850s. In the 1860s and 1870s he had seen a revolution from the *ancien régime* of the Tokugawa to the new Meiji world, a change greater even than that witnessed by Tocqueville. Developments which had taken over 200 years in the West occurred in a decade in Japan. He recognized the central revolution which had taken place, and he realized that in many ways his task was to understand the implications of that change for Japan – namely the scientific, industrial, economic and political revolutions of early modern Europe. Thus, he wrote, 'Take the history of any Western country and read about it from its beginning up to the 1600s. Then skip the next two hundred years, and pick up the story again from around 1800. So astonishing will have been the leap forward in that country's progress that we can hardly believe it is the official history of the same country.'[79] Yet he also stressed continuity. 'Inquiring further into the cause of its progress, we will find that it has been due to the legacy and gifts of those who went before them.'[80] This was vitally important for Japan. Not all that had existed in its great civilization of 1,000 years or more was useless. The new world should also build on the legacy of the past, including the Imperial tradition and the ethic of his samurai antecedents.

So, at the end of his life, when Fukuzawa looked back, his far-off youth, and his travels to America and Europe, felt very distant. The changes had been immense. 'Sixty-odd years is the length of life I have now come through. It is often the part of an old man to say that life on looking back seems like a dream. But for me it has been a very merry dream, full of changes and surprises.'[81] He felt he had 'nothing to complain of on looking backward, nothing but full satisfaction and delight'.[82] We can share that satisfaction in another way by looking at the method and theories which he developed during his life.

14

The Essence of the Modern World

Methods in the study of a new civilization

It is one thing to have seen a new world and to wish to bring its best features to an old one. It is quite another to explain what one has seen in terms that make it comprehensible and attractive. Here we find another part of Fukuzawa's genius. Like all the great thinkers I have considered, he devoted special attention to style and rhetoric. Montesquieu wrote and rewrote everything with great care, Adam Smith attempted a very clear and simple style, as did Tocqueville, trying out all his writing on close friends. It was important for them to be widely understood. It is thus interesting to find the same preoccupation with style and writing in Fukuzawa. Again in his case there is perhaps even more attention to the matter for he faced problems which were much greater than his European mentors, as we shall see.

In his early days Fukuzawa was given very good advice by his teacher Ogata.

At that time, I was engaged in translation of a book on fortification by a Dutch man named C.M.H. Pel. One day, Ogata Sensei gave me a kind advice, saying: 'The book you are translating is for the use of the *samurai*. If *samurais* are to be your target, be careful in the use of the Chinese characters. Never use any difficult character or words, because most of them are poor in scholarship and for them high-flown words are tabu. Take the average of the *samurais* you know, you would find yourself high above the average though you are still young and not a scholar of Chinese classics. And so, your effort in decorating your translation with high-sounding words will simply add to the difficulties for the reader. Use only those words and characters you know.

Never look in a dictionary for grander words. Such dictionaries as *"Gyokuhen"* and *"Zatsuki Ruihen"* you should never keep near your desk.'[1]

Fukuzawa took this to heart. 'While writing, whenever a rare word began to appear at my pen point, I reminded myself of the master's admonition and made a special effort in looking for an easier word.'[2]

So he began to develop his own simple and direct style which would break down the barrier between the old Chinese-influenced *literati* and the mass of a well-educated but basically Japanese-speaking public.

And here I came to the conclusion that I must change the whole style, or concept, of expression in order to reach a wider public. However much *kana* (Japanese syllabary) one might use between the Chinese characters, if the basic style was Chinese, the result would stay difficult. On the contrary, suppose one used the plebeian Japanese for basic style, even when some Chinese characters were mixed in for convenience, it would stay plebeian and easy to read. And so, I mixed the popular Japanese and the graceful Chinese together in one sentence, desecrating the sacred domain of the classical, so to say, but all for the convenience of reaching a wide circle with the new thoughts of the modern civilization.[3]

His freedom to experiment and to avoid over-elaboration was increased by his conscious decision not to show his work to highbrow readers before it was published. 'All of my books were done entirely on my own initiative without orders from or consultation with others. I never showed the manuscripts to any of my friends, to say nothing of asking prominent scholars for prefaces and inscriptions.'[4] On the other hand, he did want to make sure that they could be understood by ordinary readers. And so, just as Tocqueville had every word read by his father and brother, Fukuzawa showed his work to ordinary members of the household. 'At that time, I used to tell my friends that I would not be satisfied unless these books could be understood by uneducated farmers and merchants, or even a serving woman just out of the countryside when read to her through the paper door. And so, I did not once show my manuscript to a scholar of Chinese for criticism and correction. Rather, I let women folks and children in my house read it for rewriting those portions which they had difficulty in

understanding.'[5] He believed, correctly, that this attention to simplicity of style was one of the major reasons why his books reached
millions of ordinary Japanese readers; 'the style of my writing is
generally plain and easy to read. That has been recognized by the
public and I too fully believe it is.'[6] Nishikawa comments that
'Fukuzawa's style in *An Encouragement of Learning*, and in other text-
books and manuals was completely new in Japan.'[7]

As well as overcoming the much greater gap in vocabulary,
Fukuzawa faced problems which were far greater than that of his
Enlightenment predecessors. One of these was the intricacy and
ambiguity of even the ordinary Japanese language. He gave the
following example of its notorious ambiguity. 'Since the first line
may signify either "gourd" or "warfare", the second has the idea of
"the beginning", and the last may equally be taken for "cold" or
"rocket", the whole verse may be read in two ways: 1) The first
drink from the gourd, we take it cold. 2) The first shot of the war,
we do it with the rocket.'[8]

Another difficulty lay at the heart of his enterprise. He was trying to introduce a whole new world from the West, full of alien
concepts. Many of these had no Japanese equivalents. He therefore
had to invent a new language to deal with such topics as profit,
rights of man, and so on. Thinking about this, 'I was led finally to
determine that I should make myself a pioneer in creating new
words and characters for the Japanese language. Indeed, I created a
number of new words. For instance, the English word "steam" had
traditionally been translated *joki*, but I wanted to shorten it.'[9] In
this process he was faced with innumerable difficulties. The very
things which he had been most interested in and were distinctively western, small details of everyday life, important institutional
features, were the most difficult to translate. 'Therefore, what gave
me the most difficulty was the common words which were too
common in the native land to call for explanation in a dictionary.'[10]
And it was equally difficult to move out of his Japanese categories
to understand what he was to translate. 'Another reminiscence is
of "direct tax" and "indirect tax" which I came upon in an English
book. Direct means "straight reaching", and with the negating "in"
it will indicate "deviating". So far, quite clear. But then, in taxes
how could there be "straight" and "deviating" taxes?'[11]

Given all this, it is not surprising that his translations contain
numerous cases where he has shifted the meaning somewhat. Often
this was deliberate. In the original account of how the western

family worked, Fukuzawa read that the primary relationship was between husband and wife. When he translated this, he deliberately changed this to read so that the primary relationship was between parents and children.[12] Another example is as follows. The original work upon which the 'translation' comes is: '"From these few examples, it is perceived that political economy is not an artificial system, but an explanation of the operation of certain natural laws. In explaining this system, the teacher is not more infallible than the teacher of geology or medicine."'[13] This was translated as follows: 'Economics is in its essentials clearly not a man-made law. "Since the purpose of economics is to explain natural laws (*tennen no teisoku*) that arise spontaneously in the world, the explanation of its principles is [to trade or commerce] like making clear the relation of geology to descriptive physical geography or of pathology to medicine."'[14] There are several subtle shifts here which change the meaning quite considerably. A great deal could be learnt about Japanese mentality by studying the way Fukuzawa refracted western concepts through the lens of his mind.

As for his actual method of working, his writings contain a few hints. It is clear that he worked at great speed. In one record case, 'There was no pausing for the master nor the employees before the thirty-seventh day when all the work was done and several hundred copies of the two volumes of *Eikoku Gijiin Dan* were ready. This thirty-seven days from the day the author took up his writing till the publication was a record speed in the days of woodblock printing.'[15] Or again, we are told that 'Fukuzawa Sensei commenced writing "A Critique of 'The Greater Learning for Women'" and "The New Greater Learning for Women" last year in the middle of August. Writing one or two or three instalments a day, he finished the whole on September 26 . . . The actual time he spent on the work was some thirty-odd days.'[16] On the other hand, his *Outline of a Theory of Civilization* 'took an exceptional amount of time and toil . . . The manuscipts, which are preserved today, show that they were revised again and again.'[17]

This speed was partly due to the fact that the final writing was often merely putting together thoughts which had occurred to him over a long period and which he had jotted down, like Montesquieu or Tocqueville, mulled over and then turned into prose.

In his busy schedule, he would, every now and then, take out a copy of *The Greater Learning for Women* by Kaibara Ekken, and for future reference, he would jot down comments in it. Sometimes he would misplace the book and buy a new copy. It is said that there were two or three copies that were lost and replaced, proof that Sensei's interest in the present problem endured over a very long period in time.[18]

In fact, much of his work reads more like a conversation between Fukuzawa and his readers. It flows directly out of his life and experiences and is almost autobiographical. In this, again, it is very reminiscent of Tocqueville or Montesquieu's style. Of them, also, it could be written, as it is of Fukuzawa, that 'these thoughts are simply an organized expression of his everyday words and deeds, or a study of his actual life.'[19] Yet, unlike Montesquieu and Adam Smith, it seems to have been important for him to write himself, rather than dictate his work to an amanuensis. It is true that in an illness shortly before his death he did dictate his *Autobiography*, but after that when 'he found some spare time and tried dictating some of his criticisms of *The Greater Learning for Women* . . . he found that dictation was unfit for the purpose, and he took to seriously writing his views . . .'[20]

As for his speculations on those deeper problems of logic and causation to which Montesquieu, Smith and Tocqueville devoted so much attention, I have not been able to find anything particularly novel or original in his translated work. He was perfectly familiar with the current logic of scientific and social explanation and as a great admirer of J.S. Mill expounded these ideas to his audience. 'Every action has a cause. We can subdivide this into proximate and remote causes. The proximate are more readily visible than the remote causes. There are more of the former than of the latter. Proximate causes are apt to mislead people by their complexity, whereas remote causes, once discovered, are certain and unchanging. Therefore, the process of tracing a chain of causality is to begin from proximate causes and work back to the remote causes. The farther back the process is traced, the more the number of causes decreases, and several actions can be explained by one cause.'[21] He illustrated this with two examples. In one he showed how, by tracing back along links of a chain, the proximate causes of water boiling was burning wood, but if one moved back along further one found oxygen – the same cause that made humans breath.[22]

Likewise, as a student of Buckle and others, he was perfectly familiar with the idea of the statistical tendencies which lie behind everyday life, made famous later in Durkheim's study of suicide. 'If we chart the figures for land area and population, the prices of commodities and wage rates, and the number of the married, the living, the sick, and those who die, the general conditions of a society will become clear at a glance, even things one ordinarily cannot calculate. For example, I have read that the number of marriages in England every year follows fluctuations in the price of grain. When grain prices go up, marriages decline, and vice versa. The ratio can be predicted . . .' Thus, while the proximate cause of marriage 'were the desires of the couple, the wishes of their parents, the advice of the matchmaker, and so forth' these were not 'sufficient to explain the matter'. 'Only when we go beyond them to look for the remote cause, and come up with the factor of the price of rice, do we unerringly obtain the real cause controlling the frequency of marriages in the country.'[23] He was thus competent in a wide area of sociological and scientific method.

*

In order to see where Japan fitted into the scheme of things and how it could develop further into a higher 'civilization', Fukuzawa made use of a 'stage theory' of progress. He believed that 'civilization is not a dead thing; it is something vital and moving.' Therefore, 'it must pass through sequences and stages; primitive people advance to semi-developed forms, the semi-developed advance to civilization, and civilization itself is even now in the process of advancing forward.' He reminded his readers that 'Europe also had to pass through these phases in its evolution to its present level'.[24] His 'stages' of civilization are very similar to those of Adam Smith, Kames, Ferguson and other Scottish Enlightenment thinkers, which then became absorbed as the foundations for anthropology in the following century.

We are told that 'As early as 1869 Fukuzawa had described humanity as divided into four "kinds". Of the lowest kind, *konton*, the aborigines of Australia and New Guinea were examples; the second lowest kind, *banya*, was represented by the nomads of Mongolia and Arabia; the third lowest, *mikai*, by the peoples of Asiatic countries such as China, Turkey and Persia; while the highest kind, *kaika-bummei*, was exemplified by western nations such as America, England, France and Germany.'[25] This, of course, more or less exactly parallels the normal anthropological division into hunter-gatherers, tribesmen, peasants and urban-industrial societies, although they would replace value-laden words like 'lower' and 'higher'.

A few years later he tried a three-fold model. We are told that he 'had already read the stage theory in J.H. Burton's *Political Economy* (pp. 6–7), in which three stages are called "barbarous and/or primitive", "half civilized" and "civilized".'[26] In 1876 he distinguished between *Yaban* – illiterate savages; *Hankai* – peoples such as Chinese and Japanese 'who, though they might possess flourishing literatures, yet had no curiosity about the natural world, no original ideas for inventing new things, and no ability to criticize and improve on accepted customs and conveniences; and *Bummei* – civilized people who had all these qualities.'[27] Or again, he wrote that 'present-day China has to be called semi-developed in comparison with Western countries. But if we compare China with countries of South Africa, or, to take an example more at hand, if we compare the Japanese people with the Ezo [Ainu] then both China and Japan can be called civilized.'[28] These 'stage' models, so popular after Darwin, were combined with a view of the inevitable *progress* from one to another which is another of the features which he shared with many European thinkers.

Carmen Blacker describes his general belief in the inevitability of progress as follows. 'Simply, Fukuzawa believed, because progress was a "natural law". Man's nature was such that he was bound and destined to progress, and hence would naturally, even unconsciously, fulfil the conditions which would lead to progress. The process could, certainly, be arrested artificially for a certain time, but ultimately it would prove to be like a tide which would sweep all obstacles out of its way.'[29] Hence his reference, as we have seen, to the surge of individual rights and liberty. And hence his belief in the inevitability of growing freedom. He followed Tocqueville in believing that '"Careful study of politics will show us that there is an unceasing force causing autocracy to change to freedom, just as water always flows towards the low ground. There may certainly be reversals of this tendency, but they are only temporary fluctuations. The facts show indisputably that the long-term trend stretching over tens of thousands of years is for monarchy to give way to democracy, and for tyranny to give way to liberalism."'[30] Like Tocqueville, he had visited America and seen the future – and there could be little doubt in his mind that the future lay in wealth, equality and liberty.

Hence his interest in those historians in the west who most

fully endorsed the strong 'Whig' view of history, the march of civilization and progress. We are told that 'Buckle's *History of Civilization in England* and Guizot's *General History of Civilization in England* were examples of the supremely optimistic school of positivist historical writing which grew up in Western Europe during the second half of the nineteenth century... Both... were translated early into Japanese and became the guiding scriptures of the *keimō* school of historiography known as *bummeishiron* (history of civilisation)...'[31]

Despite the belief that history was, in the long term, on his side, Fukuzawa recognized that there could be hiccups – like the 250 years of Tokugawa rule. He also had periods of doubt. As Albert Craig argues, we can detect three main phases in his thought. During the 1860s and first half of the 1870s he believed that rapid progress was possible. Then the 'year 1875 is a transitional point in Fukuzawa's thought. He has become uncertain. He has become a moderate relativist. Utopian civilization has receded several thousand years into the future.'[32] After some twenty years or so of doubt, he returned to his greater optimism and 'In some respects this was a revival of Fukuzawa's earlier "enlightenment" belief in a beneficent natural order, for once again he saw progress toward an ideal society as possible within a finite period of time.'[33] The period from roughly 1875 to 1895 exactly coincides with the nationalistic and aggressive phase of his thought.

Yet whether the highest level of civilization was close or far, Fukuzawa's main task was to analyse its constituent elements and to understand how a country like Japan could adopt it. This took him to his deepest analysis of what was special about the West. Having located the mystery roughly in the area of liberty and equality, he was still faced with the problems of the institutional mechanisms needed to encourage these nebulous virtues. It was not a simple matter of setting up schools, newspapers, universities, and so on. All this would help, but there was a deeper essence to be grasped. In attempting to penetrate to the 'spirit' of the West, Fukuzawa provides a number of insightful passages on the mystery of the unusual civilization which he saw and read about on his trip to America and Europe.

The essence of modernity: the separation of spheres

Fukuzawa based his ideas on the work of Guizot and Mill. This led him to believe, like Montesquieu, that there must be a separation and balance of powers. If there was the Confucian fusion of kinship and politics, there would be hierarchical absolutism. If there was a fusion of politics and religion, there would be despotism. For instance, he commented that in the case of Buddhism, 'its teaching has been entirely absorbed by political authority. What shines throughout the world is not the radiance of Buddha's teachings but the glory of Buddhism's political authority. Hence it is not surprising that there is no independent religious structure within the Buddhist religion.'[34] Or again, if there was a fusion of society and economy there would be stagnation. If there was a fusion of public life and private morality there would be absolutism. The parts needed to be separated and artificially held apart.

Let us look first at a few of his general remarks on the necessity for a dynamic balance, a tense contradiction or separation between spheres. 'To use a simile, if you take metals such as gold, silver, copper and iron, and melt them together, you would not end up with gold, or silver, or copper, or iron, but with a compound mixture that preserves a certain balance between the various elements, and in which each adds strength to the others. This is how Western civilization is.'[35] There must be a never-ending contest, which no part wins.

> The point of difference between Western and other civilizations is that Western society does not have a uniformity of opinions; various opinions exist side by side without fusing into one. For example, there are theories which advocate governmental authority; others argue for the primacy of religious authority. There are proponents of monarchy, theocracy, aristocracy, and democracy. Each goes its own way, each maintains its own position. Although they vie with one another, no single one of them ever completely wins out. Since the contest never is decided, all sides grudgingly are forced to live with the others.[36]

The general openness of the society can only be guaranteed if freedom to dominate is held in check. 'Now in the first place, the freedom of civilization cannot be bought at the expense of some other freedom. It can only exist by not infringing upon other rights and privileges, other opinions and powers, all of which should exist in some balance. It is only possible for freedom to exist when freedom is restricted.'[37] Again we have the idea of the dynamic balance of powers and opinions. Many opinions and many institutions should flourish in healthy competition; this is the essence and secret of western civilization.

> Once they start living side by side, despite their mutual hostility, they each recognize the others' rights and allow them to go their ways. Since no view is able to monopolize the whole situation and must allow the other schools of thought room to function, each makes its own contribution to one area of civilization by being true to its own position, until finally, taken together, the end result is one civilization. This is how autonomy and freedom have developed in the West.[38]

The domination of one sphere, for instance the kinship or political system, is a 'disease'. 'All of this is the result of the imbalance of power, an evil that has arisen from not paying attention to the second step of things. If we do not take cognizance of this evil and get rid of the disease of imbalance, whether the country is at peace or in turmoil no real progress will be made in the level of civilization of the country.'[39]

A particular danger, of course, was for the imbalance to lead to the growth of central political power, political absolutism. 'This I call the curse of imbalance. Those in power must always take stock of themselves.'[40] There must be limits on the powerful. 'Thus, in any area of human affairs, whether it be the government, the people, scholars, or bureaucrats, when there is one who has power, whether it be intellectual or physical, there must be a limit to that power.'[41] As Carmen Blacker summarizes his thought here, 'The reason why it was so important for the government's and people's respective spheres to be kept separate was that in the proper balance between the two lay one of the secrets of progress in civilisation.' Thus, 'It was precisely in her failure to appreciate the importance of this balance, Fukuzawa was convinced, that Japan's greatest weakness lay.'[42] He argued that the government should be strictly limited in its objectives. Like the 'nightwatchman state' advocated by his Scottish Enlightenment predecessors 100 years earlier, he believed that the view that the 'government should not encroach on the private sphere meant that it should have nothing to do with such activities as religion, schools, agriculture or commerce . . .'[43]

In advocating this balance and separation, he realized that he was going against the grain of the Confucian and Chinese legacy in Japan. There was the strong inclination we have already seen to merge kinship and political allegiance which tended towards autocracy in both. 'In the countries of Asia, the ruler has been called the parent of the people, the people have been called his subjects and children. In China, the work of the government has been called the office of shepherd of the masses, and local officials were called the shepherds of such-and-such provinces.'[44] It permeated the whole of the hierarchical structure of deference and arrogance which he had noted in his youth.

> While bowing before one man, he was lording it over another. For example, if there were ten people in A, B, C, order, B in his relation to A expressed subservience and humility, to a point where the humiliation he suffered ought to have been intolerable. But in his relation with C he was able to be regally high-handed. Thus his humiliation in the former case was made up for by the gratification he derived from the latter. Any dissatisfaction evened itself out. C took compensation from D, D demanded the same from E, and so on down the line. It was like dunning the neighbour on one's east for the sum loaned to the neighbour on one's west.[45]

It was thus a disease of imbalance which permeated all relations, not just governmental power but also all social relations. 'According to the above argument, arbitrary use of authority and imbalance of power is not found in the government alone. It is embedded in the spirit of the Japanese people as a whole. This spirit is a conspicuous dividing line between the Western world and Japan, and though we must now turn to seeking its causes, we are faced with an extremely difficult task.'[46]

Japan did have one great advantage over China, however. This was that the crucial separation between ritual and political power had occurred many centuries earlier when the Shogun became the *de facto* political ruler, while the Emperor was the ritual head. Fukuzawa saw this separation, the breaking of what in the West was the tendency towards Caesaro-Papist absolutism, as a point at which freedom could enter. Whereas in China to attempt to challenge any part of the social or intellectual system was simultaneously to commit heresy, treason and filial impiety, in Japan reason could find a chink between the opposing concept of ritual and political power.

Fukuzawa expounded his interesting thoughts on this matter at some length.

> The two concepts of the most sacrosanct and the powerful were so obviously distinct that people could hold in their heads, as it were, the simultaneous existence and functioning of the two ideas. Once they did so, they could not help adding a third, the principle of reason. With the principle of reason added to the idea of reverence for the imperial dignity and the idea of military rule, none of these three concepts was able to predominate. And since no single concept predominated, there naturally followed a spirit of freedom.[47]

'It was truly Japan's great good fortune that the ideas of the most sacrosanct and of the most powerful balanced each other in such a way as to allow room between them for some exercise of intelligence and the play of reason.'[48]

Japan's good fortune could be seen by comparing its situation with that in China, where the normal *ancien régime* blending of religious and political power was at its most extreme with the ancient rule of its God-Emperor. The situation in Japan 'obviously was not the same as in China, where the people looked up to one completely autocratic ruler and with single-minded devotion were slaves to the idea that the most sacrosanct and the most powerful were embodied in the same person. In the realm of political thought, therefore, the Chinese were impoverished and the Japanese were rich.'[49]

Another fusion is between the economy and the society. Anthropologists have written a good deal about how the economy is 'embedded' in the society, that is to say it is impossible to separate economic and social transactions in the majority of societies. Polanyi believed that the 'great transformation' from this situation occurred in eighteenth-century England with the rise of commercial capitalism.[50] Max Weber and Karl Marx believed it occurred in the fifteenth and sixteenth centuries with the rise of capitalism and the separation of the social and economic.[51] Fukuzawa's *Autobiography* provides a delightful instance of an attempt to 'disembed' an economy, as an individual and at a theoretical level.

As a member of a Samurai family, Fukuzawa's *bushi-do* ethic was strongly opposed to purely commercial transactions. This took the form, for instance, of fearing money – that ultimate symbol of the marketplace. He described how there were embarrassing altercations with merchants, who refused to receive payment for their goods, presumably preferring social rewards. 'He wanted to give the money back to me, but I insisted on leaving it, because I remembered what my mother had told me. After some arguing, which was almost like quarreling, I forced the money on the merchant and came home.'[52] Fukuzawa admitted that 'When I went to Osaka and became a student at Ogata school, I was still afraid of money.'[53] He remembered that 'I had no taste or inclination to engage in buying or selling, lending or borrowing. Also the old idea of the samurai that trade was not our proper occupation prevailed in my mind, I suppose.'[54] Thus he organized his life so that 'Our home is like a world apart; the new methods of Western civilization do not enter our household finances.'[55] From this personal experience of the power, alienation and aggressiveness of capitalist, money, transactions, Fukuzawa gained the insight to be able to begin to bridge the gap between the competitive western capitalism he had seen in America, and the embedded world around him.

A key incident was when Fukuzawa started to read the educational course published by William and Robert Chambers. There was a volume explaining in a simple way the principles of western economics. Fukuzawa described how 'I was reading Chamber's book on economics. When I spoke of the book to a certain high official in the treasury bureau one day, he became much interested and wanted me to show him a translation.'[56] So Fukuzawa began to translate the work into Japanese, a translation which formed a part of the second volume of his *Conditions of the West*. As he did so he ran into an illuminating difficulty in translating the central premise of western economic systems. 'I began translating it (it comprised some twenty chapters) when I came upon the word "competition" for which there was no equivalent in Japanese, and I was obliged to use an invention of my own, *kyoso*, literally, "race-fight". When the official saw my translation, he appeared much impressed. Then he said suddenly, "Here is the word 'fight'. What does it mean? It is such an unpeaceful word."'[57] The confrontation between the war of all against all, competitive individualistic behaviour in the marketplace, and the Confucian ethic of harmony and co-operation has seldom been more graphically exposed.[58]

It was now necessary for Fukuzawa to defend and explain his translation. '"That is nothing new", I replied "That is exactly what all Japanese merchants are doing. For instance, if one merchant begins to sell things cheap, his neighbour will try to sell them even cheaper. Or if one merchant improves his merchandise to attract more buyers, another will try to take the trade from him by offering goods of still better quality. Thus all merchants 'race and fight' and this is the way money values are fixed. This process is termed *kyoso* in the science of economics.'"[59] All this was half-true, as he knew. But he was also aware of a basic difference between Japan and the West, and had to insist that the bitter confrontational element in western capitalism had to be swallowed, not merely by merchants, but by everyone. 'I suppose he would rather have seen some such phrase as "men being kind to each other" in a book on economics, or a man's loyalty to his lord, open generosity from a merchant in times of national stress, etc. But I said to him, "If you do not agree to the word 'fight', I am afraid I shall have to erase it entirely. There is no other term that is faithful to the original."'[60]

Fukuzawa noticed a strange paradox, which had also intrigued his Enlightenment predecessors. While western society was driven by narrow, anti-social and, it would seem, self-interested greed, the result was public wealth and a high standard of honesty and private morality. While his Japanese Confucian contemporaries subscribed to a benevolent Confucian desire to promote harmony and kindness, the product was dishonesty and private immorality. He summarized the difference very elegantly. 'Westerners try to expand their business to gain greater profits in the long run. Because they are afraid dishonest dealings will jeopardise long-range profits, they have to be honest. This sincerity does not come from the heart, but from the wallet. To put the same idea in other words, Japanese are greedy on a small scale, foreigners are greedy on a large scale.'[61] While Japanese merchants, like Chinese ones, could not be trusted 'Western merchants, in contrast, are exact and honest in their business dealings. They show a small sample of woven goods, someone buys several thousand times as much of the material, and what is delivered differs in no wise from the sample. The buyer receives the shipment with his mind at peace; he does not even open any of the boxes to check the contents.'[62] It was a strange paradox. Fukuzawa noted that growing affluence seemed to lead to an improvement in private morals. 'In England, France and other countries in the modern world, the people of the middle class progressively amassed wealth; with it they also elevated their own moral conduct.'[63]

What Fukuzawa realized was that in order to increase 'rationality' in economic transactions, such exchanges needed to be separated from the social relationship, just as in order to achieve 'rational' social relations, one had to separate politics and kinship. He also realized that in order to achieve 'rational' science, one had to accept the separation of fact and value, of humanity and nature, of the moral and the physical. This was especially difficult in a neo-Confucian society where the very essence of the system was to blend the human and natural worlds. We are told that Japanese Confucianists 'thought that western science explained everything by physical laws: This was treating nature as dead and mechanical, unrelated to man, and hence destroying the harmony of the universe.'[64] Fukuzawa was indeed taking on a difficult task.

15
Liberty, Equality and Human Relations

As we have seen, Fukuzawa was born into a system which made strenuous efforts to inhibit individual 'selfishness'. The basic element of Japanese social structure at Fukuzawa's level was not the individual, but the clan, the 'house'. He described how 'The Japanese people suffered for many years under the yoke of despotism. Lineage was the basis of power. Even intelligent men were entirely dependent upon houses of high lineage. The whole age was, as it were, under the thumb of lineage. Throughout the land there was no room for human initiative; everything was in a condition of stagnation.'[1] Putting it another way, he described how 'The millions of Japanese at that time were closed up inside millions of individual boxes. They were separated from one another by walls with little room to move around.'[2] In Japan when 'we deal with a person, be he rich or poor, strong or weak, wise or ignorant, capable or incompetent, we either fear him or look down upon him, entirely on the basis of his social position. A spirit of independence has never existed in even the slightest degree.' This feature came out especially when set against what he had seen in America and Europe. 'If we compare the Western attitude of independence with that of us insulated Japanese, we can see how enormous the difference is.'[3]

His reading of Guizot, J.S. Mill and others made him conclude that the differences were of long standing. The individuality and freedom in the west seemed to be rooted in the period of turmoil after the fall of Rome when 'the German barbarians left behind a legacy of autonomy and freedom'.[4] If this were the case one might have expected that 'the Japanese warrior class would also produce its own spirit of independence and autonomy'.[5] Yet, as a member of that class, he knew that this was not so. For 'although the samurai of this time seemed fiercely independent, their spirit sprang neither from a personal, chauvinistic attitude nor from a strong individuality that exulted in the self's freedom from all outside influences. It was always motivated by something outside the person, or at least aided by it.'[6] Thus he argued that 'human relations in Asia have evolved into definite patterns of discrimination and prejudice, and social feelings are lukewarm. As if this were not bad enough, despotic government has also made possible the enactment of laws that prohibit political factions and public discussions.'[7] Much of Fukuzawa's work was concerned with liberating himself and the Japanese people from these fetters, for he believed that 'There are no innate bonds around men. They are born free and unrestricted, and become free adult men and women.'[8]

As a disciple of Mill, and hence in the tradition of Montesquieu and Tocqueville, Fukuzawa advocated private liberty, that right to be free from external pressures which is central to western thought. He argued that 'each man deserves his private liberty. It is not proper, and society does not permit prying into the privacy of an independent man.'[9] And when he said 'man', he was speaking of mankind and not the male gender. He set out his views of the meaning of freedom, directly following Mill, in the following words. A person 'can conduct himself in freedom, as long as he does not infringe upon the rights of others. He can go as he pleases, work or play, engage in some business, study hard or, if that does not agree with him, loaf around the whole day long. Provided these actions do not affect others, there is no reason for men to censure them from the sidelines.'[10]

Like all those who have thought deeply about the matter, Fukuzawa realized that the other side of the coin of liberty was equality; one was not possible without a certain amount of the other. The link between the two can be seen, for example, in the contextual instability of language and behaviour which he noted. In an interesting passage he compared the fixity of the western social structure to the contextual situation in Japan, which was dependent on the power relationship.

> Comparing these social patterns to material objects, power in the West is like iron; it does not readily expand or contract. On the other hand, the power of the Japanese warriors was as flexible as rubber, adapting itself to whatever it came in contact

with. In contact with inferiors, it swelled up immensely; in contact with those above, it shrivelled up and shrank. The sum total of this hierarchy of power constituted that whole known as the prestige of the military houses . . .'[11]

He had found a very different world in America and Europe. He found that 'even in the West not everyone is equal in terms of wealth or prestige. The strong and wealthy often control the weak and poor in a cruel and arrogant manner. The weak and poor, in turn, may fawn on and deceive others. The ugly aspects of human life are certainly no different from what we find among Japanese. Sometimes they are even worse.'[12] Yet the situation, though on the surface just as bad, was different. For 'even with such social injustice there is still a pervading spirit of individuality and nothing hinders the expansion of the human spirit. Cruelty and arrogance are merely by-products of wealth and power; flattery and deception are merely by-products of poverty and weakness. Neither might nor weakness is innate; they can be dealt with by means of human intelligence.'[13]

His distinction between the *de jure* and the *de facto* helped him to explain that changing the laws was only part of the solution. He noted optimistically that 'In one powerful stroke the great upheaval of the Imperial Restoration abolished the class system. Since then, we have enjoyed a society of equality for all peoples: the daimyo, courtiers, samurai, farmers, artisans, and merchants – all became of equal rank and marriages became possible among them. And so, a great man is now able to openly marry the daughter of a petty merchant or a soil-tilling farmer.'[14] Yet the spirit of subservience, the actual attitudes, were slower to change. 'Since the Meiji Restoration, the equality of all peoples has been declared. Farmers and merchants are supposed to be enjoying this privilege, but they are still as subservient as ever, so difficult is it to break away from old ways.'[15]

Thus Fukuzawa explicitly set out in his writing and in his life to challenge the premise of the basic inequality of man. In order to test the inherited system of deference and how much of it was built into the symbolism of gestures and speech, he carried out an experiment as he walked down a high road. 'So I proceeded, accosting everyone who came along. Without any allowance for their appearance, I spoke alternately, now in samurai fashion, now merchant like. In every instance, for about seven miles on my way,

I saw that people would respond according to the manner in which they were addressed – with awe or with indifference.'[16] But even Fukuzawa found limits to his egalitarian spirit. 'I have always used the honorific form of address in my speech generally – not of course to the lowly workmen or grooms or petty merchants in the really casual order of life, but to all other persons including the young students and the children in my household.'[17]

His attack on the premise of inequality, we are told, 'contradicted one of the most fundamental assumptions of the traditional political philosophy. Hitherto it had been commonly believed, not that men were naturally equal, but that society was naturally hierarchical.'[18] Fukuzawa proclaimed the opposite.

Although a poor peasant and a high daimyo 'differ like the clouds above and the mud below, still from the point of view of inherent human rights all men are equal without the least distinction between superior and inferior human beings.'[19] In the very first sentence of his *Advancement of Learning* he made the revolutionary proclamation, like Rousseau, of the natural equality of men. 'It is said that heaven does not create one man above or below another man. This means that when men are born from heaven they are all equal.'[20] He then explained how, 'At the beginning of the first section I said that all men are equal, and that they can live in freedom and independence without hereditary status distinctions. I want to develop that idea further here.'[21] He did this by explaining the difference between inherent, *de jure* equality, and achieved, *de facto*, inequality. 'Therefore, if we inquire into the balance of human relations, we must say that all men are equal. They may not be equal in outward appearances. Equality means equality in essential human rights.'[22] It was really only relative wealth that gave temporary advantage, not birth or occupation. '"Since we are poor we obey the rich, but only as long as we are poor must we submit to them. Our submission will disappear along with our poverty, while their control over us will vanish along with their riches."'[23]

The ideas here were so revolutionary that there was no word for them in Japanese. 'For example, the one principle which was basic to Fukuzawa's entire philosophy was *dokuritsu-jison*, a compound word which he coined. Though other English translations have been made of this, perhaps the best translation is "independence and self-respect."'[24] We are told that 'To a nineteenth-century Japanese, on the other hand, *dokuritsu-jison* was a shockingly revolutionary Western concept designed to undermine the entire Confucian social order which for many centuries had welded Japanese society into a rigidly-stratified yet cohesive unit.'[25]

Human relations in the modern world

Fukuzawa's ideas were particularly revolutionary when they were applied to the Japanese family and especially the relations between men and women. One of Fukuzawa's central interests throughout his life was in the practical effects of equality on the relations of men and women. Like Tocqueville, he realized that gender relations both mirrored and contributed to other forms of social relations. He may have developed both his interest in the subject and his advanced view partly from his own unusual mother, whose independence of mind and egalitarian outlook we encountered in an earlier chapter. That influence may help to explain how he developed such an early interest in the subject, and why it continued literally until his death-bed. We are told that 'Fukuzawa's thoughts on women date back to the days when he first came to Tokyo at the age of twenty-five and was already jotting his critical comments in the margins of his copy of *The Greater Learning for Women*. Toward his end, when he slipped into a coma following a stroke that was to eventually take his life, he was heard mumbling about women's rights.'[26]

This early interest was greatly reinforced by his three visits to the West. To his surprise he found that 'It appears that in the civilized countries of the West, much of the social intercourse is managed by women, and even though they do not run society, they work in harmony among men, and help smooth the situation.'[27] In particular, in America, he thought 'women are high, men are humble'.[28] By Asian standards, indeed, they seemed too free and equal. 'For instance, from the standards of Chinese ethics, the behaviour of Western ladies and gentlemen is barbarous, with no sense of etiquette or propriety, because they talk together, laugh together, and, though they do not go so far as to bathe together, they sit and eat together, and they pass things to each other directly from hand to hand; not only that, they hold hands – and among themselves that is considered good manners.'[29] Indeed even Fukuzawa was a little shocked by the extremes. 'In the West, women's behaviour sometimes goes beyond control; they make light of men; their minds are sharp, but their thoughts may be tarnished and their personal behaviour unchaste; they may neglect their own homes and flutter about society like butterflies. Such behaviour is no model for Japanese women.'[30]

As well as personal observation, Fukuzawa learnt about the dynamics of egalitarian family life from his reading, including the work of J.S. Mill. For example his reading of works on domestic relations in Chambers' *Educational Course* suggests a model of the companionate, affectionate, western family. This he described for his Japanese readers thus.

> Husband and wife, parents and children in one household constitute a family. Family relationships are bound by feeling. There is no fixed ownership of things, no rules for giving and taking. Things lost are not cried over; things gained are no special cause for jubilation. Informality is not upbraided, ineptitude does not cause embarrassment. The contentment of the wife or children becomes the joy of the husband or the parents, and the suffering of the husband and parents pains the wife and children too.[31]

He described how he tried to put this into practice. 'Above all, I believe in love and love only for the relation between parents and children. Even after children are grown, I see no reason for any formality in the relationship. In this my wife and I are perfectly of the same opinion.'[32] Thus he had a strong model of what 'civilized' family life was like and he worked hard to fulfil his wish, which was 'to let the women of Japan grow to be like the women of the West as a first step in their progress.'[33]

In essence, he believed in the innate equality of the genders. 'It is an irrefutable fact that men and women do not differ in their body structures and in the workings of their minds, and that they are equal beings.'[34] This led him to advocate the equal treatment of boy and girl children. 'When a baby girl is born, love her and care for her as much as one would a baby boy; never slacken in vigilance over her because she is a girl. When she grows up, see to her healthy development, first in body and then in mind. In her schooling and other education never discriminate because of her sex.'[35] It also led him to advocate equality in the marriage relationship. 'Not only should women be allowed to share the management of material property, but the affairs of the heart too, whether they are private or public. If a couple always talks things over thoroughly and seriously, then even at the misfortune of the husband's dying early, the household management will not fall entirely into darkness.'[36]

These views were truly revolutionary in late nineteenth century Japan. How unusual they were and how hard Fukuzawa felt he had to work, as well as an impression of his righteous indignation, comes out when we consider his description of the actual position of many Japanese women in his society, set against the ideal model of his hopes and experiences in the West.

Japanese women were without independence. 'They are given no responsibility at all. As in the saying "Women have no home of their own anywhere in the world," when she is born, she is brought up in the house which is her father's; when she is grown and married, she lives in a house which is her husband's; when she is old and is being cared for by her son, the house will be her son's. All the family property is her husband's property; women are only allowed to share in the benefits of that property.'[37] In summary, 'Women of our country have no responsibility either inside or outside their homes and their position is very low.'[38] They existed for men. 'In other words, women exist at the mercy of men and their security and their fate are in the hands of men.'[39] Their life was a continuous waiting on men. 'Women's lives are nothing but series of services, first to parents when young, then to husbands and parents-in-law when married, and when children come, they are busy caring for them and supervising the food and kitchen work.'[40] They were trapped. 'This is the actual condition of our society, and women are being forced into a narrower and narrower confinement, their sphere of social intercourse made smaller and smaller until they are like birds in a cage.'[41]

Fukuzawa quoted the criticism which outsiders, and particularly American women, made of the situation. Quoting one such visitor, he wrote ' "The Japanese women are miserable, their lives are truly not worth living, I am sorry for them. I pity them. We Americans would not tolerate such a situation for even a moment. We would fight even at the risk of our lives. Japan and America are separate countries, but the women of both are sisters of the same human species. We American women must do something to destroy this evil custom." She said this with tears falling and she gritted her teeth.'[42] He clearly felt sympathy for such criticism, noting that 'when the truth becomes known and the ladies of the West see the actual conditions with their own eyes, they are liable to condemn Japan as a hell and inferno for women'.[43]

Given the huge gap between the actual situation as he perceived it, and the ideal 'civilized' state of equality which he hoped to achieve, how was Fukuzawa to proceed? The first thing he did was to put forward an explanation for the low and subservient position of women.

He put forward two major theories to account for the situation. One placed the blame in the medieval period or earlier, where a combination of the feudal political order and the powerful lineage system built up the structural inequality of women. In relation to politics, he wrote that 'In the feudal ages of the past, the whole social system from the government to every aspect of human life was constructed on the idea of authority and compulsion. The relation between men and women naturally also followed this general trend, and men acted like lords and women like vassals.'[44] This political system, Fukuzawa argued, was linked closely to the presence of powerful kinship groups or lineages, which traced descent through the male line and kept property in the hands of men. 'The old custom of the feudal days which valued lineage of a family above all other things and forced the maintenance of the line on the male members of the family, pushing women into a position of virtual nonexistence – that custom, from now on, must be discontinued completely.'[45] The idea of male descent must be rejected. Although 'the strange fact is that since very old times in our society, there has been what is called a family, which has been carried on by male descendants.'[46]

In particular, the exclusive rights of men to lineage property must be surrendered. The present situation, he thought, was that 'No women in Japan possess any property. As the saying goes, a woman has no house of her own anywhere in this world; thus it is a natural consequence that there is no woman with her own property.'[47] Indeed, the absence of 'property', or rights in assets, extended far beyond physical things like a house. 'At home, she owns no property of her own, and in society she cannot hope for a position of any consequence. The house she lives in is a man's house and the children she brings up are her husband's children.'[48] All this must be changed by completely abandoning the lineage system which had existed for hundreds of years, and moving towards the European and American conjugal family model.

Fukuzawa added a second argument, not entirely consistent with his first, which placed most of the blame on Chinese, and particularly neo-Confucianist ideology. In this theory, he played down the feudal and lineage arguments and stressed that Japanese women's position had declined dramatically during the period from the seventeenth century. 'In my own thoughts, I suspect that the restrictions on women's behaviour is something that began in the prolonged peace of the Tokugawa period. When all the armed conflicts in the country ended and the society became settled in the years of Genna [1615–23], Confucianism gradually rose to advocate what it called the great doctrine to clarify the social ranks of high and low, noble and mean.'[49] Or again, he wrote that 'Since the years of Genna [1615–19], when the peace began, most of the samurai youth were brought up under the influence of this Confucianism and its teachings of benevolence, loyalty, etiquette, wisdom, filial piety, brotherly love, loyalty to the master and faithfulness to friends.'[50]

Much of Fukuzawa's work on women is therefore devoted to undoing what he considers to be the harmful effects of neo-Confucian thought, and particularly that work *The Greater Learning for Women* on which he started scribbling critical comments from the age of twenty-five. He described how 'Confucianism characterizes men as *yang* (positive) and women *yin* (negative); that is, men are like the heavens and the sun, and women like the earth and the moon. In other words, one is high and the other is humble, and there are many men who take this idea as the absolute rule of nature. But this *yin–yang* theory is the fantasy of the Confucianists and has no proof or logic.'[51] He wrote with sarcasm how 'In a book called *Onna daigaku* there is enunciated a principle of "triple obedience" for women: a) to obey her parents when young, b) to obey her husband when married, and c) to obey her children when old. It may be natural for a girl to obey her parents when she is young, but in what way is she to obey her husband after marriage?'[52] The book further stated that 'even if the husband is a drunkard or is addicted to sensual pleasures, or abuses and scolds her, and thus goes to the extreme of dissipation and lechery, the wife must still be obedient. She must respect her dissolute husband like heaven, and only protest to him with kind words and soft countenance.'[53]

He was particularly outraged by the last chapter of *The Greater Learning of Women* whose 'attack on women is so severe that it may as well be called a spiteful work of literature full of curses and abuses heaped on women. The author pronounces that most women, seven or eight out of ten, have the five faults of women – indocility and disobedience, discontent and spitefulness, slander, jealousy, and shallow intellect – and, therefore, women are inferior to men.'[54] Yet it was not just neo-Confucianist texts which were to blame. Similarly, 'A Buddhist scripture says that "Women are full of sins". Indeed, from this point of view, women are from birth no other than criminals who have committed great crimes.'[55] He gave a number of examples of 'harm done to women and children through the concept of the moral subordination of inferiors to superiors . . .'[56]

Fukuzawa was not content merely to diagnose some possible pressures on women, but went on to examine each part of the sexual and marital relationship and to advocate changes which would bring Japanese women closer to their emancipated western counterparts.

Starting with childhood and adolescence, he noted that 'The family customs are usually Confucian, which dictates that boys and girls after reaching the age of seven must not be seen together or share anything together.'[57] Consequently, all relations between the sexes were discouraged before marriage. Speaking of the relations between young men and women, he suggested that 'there is practically none at all. If by chance there is such contact between the sexes, it is looked on with suspicion and it certainly will become a target of reprimand from elders.'[58] Consequently, there was no chance for the prolonged courtship which was a necessary prelude for companionate marriage in the West. 'When they grow up to be of marriageable age, the rules of social oppression dictate that it is necessary to separate them further and further. Even to exchange words out of necessity is forbidden to them and the suspecting gazes around them make them hesitate. A glimpse of one another from a distance makes them uncomfortable. The result is their complete separation into entirely different worlds.'[59]

One consequence is that the marriage has to be arranged by others. 'Being brought up in such a restricted environment, when the time comes for the boy to marry, he does not know any girls. He will have to depend on the go-between's recommendation and meet a girl for the first time. This is called *miai*, a trial meeting.[60] All that happens at this 'trial meeting' is that 'the boy and girl manage to steal a glance at each other once, and they are married soon after.'[61] This is very different from the courtship which is essential for forming an equal relationship in the West, for 'according to the Western custom the man and the woman should look for and choose each other on their own, get to know each other, and when they have made up their minds to marry, tell their parents, and, with their consent, hold a marriage ceremony.'[62]

Despite this difference, Fukuzawa did notice that Japanese children did seem to have more power than in many 'arranged marriage' societies. He noted that 'On the surface, it will appear as if marriages are arranged by the parents and the young folks only accept the final decision, but the truth is not so. The parents are only the ones to suggest and not the ones to decide.'[63] He elaborates what happens as follows: 'When the suggestion is made to the young people and if they are not happy with it, the issue cannot be forced. In such a case, the parents abandon their first choice and begin anew on a second search. Foreigners think that the Japanese marriage is arranged by the parents, but this is a false image constructed by ignorant people.'[64] In this one respect, the situation is not as bad as it might be. 'Therefore, aside from extreme cases, women today in general should not have much to complain about in the actual marriage process.'[65]

Although not at the extreme of arranged marriage, the lack of courtship, and other pressures, meant that there was little companionship in most Japanese marriages, Fukuzawa thought. He noted that 'Even after marriage, it is rare that the woman knows anything about her husband's reputation in society or how his colleagues regard him or what his accomplishments are.'[66] Thus, 'For ordinary people, when the husband comes home tired after a day's work, his wife is entirely insensitive to his labors, and she cannot offer proper concern when they talk together.'[67] The woman's main role, and the main purpose of the marriage is not companionship but procreation. 'In our society, the most humiliating expression for women is that a man's purpose in taking a wife is to ensure his posterity. The tone of this expression resembles "The purpose of buying a rice cooker is to cook rice."'[68] Again the kinship system biases the system against the woman. 'From this attitude stems the saying so often heard that the womb is a "borrowed" thing. The meaning of this saying is that a child which is born into this world is its father's child and not its mother's – the rice that grew this year is born from the seed that was sown last year and the soil has no relation to it.'[69]

A particular way in which any companionship of husband and wife was stifled was through the pressure of the husband's parents. Ideally, the eldest son, at least, would live with his parents and his strongest tie would be to them and particularly his mother. The new wife would compete with her mother-in-law and traditionally came a poor second. Fukuzawa rightly gives a good deal of attention to this important structural tension in the Japanese family. He noted the inhibiting effects of the parents. While 'The in-laws who live with the couple . . . will pray for the happy relations between their son and his wife . . . at the same time they pray that the couple will not become too intimate. If a tender sentiment seems to appear between them, the older folks become alarmed.'[70] As just one example, he noted that 'when the husband sets off on a long journey and the wife shows emotion at the parting or when the wife is ill and the husband tries to nurse her, the parents-in-law regard it as unsightly and warn them against it.'[71] The pressures against any show of affection extended outwards to the neighbours as well. Thus when husband and wife set off for a journey, 'the present practice for them is to walk apart for a while and when they reach a predesignated spot, they meet and begin to walk side by side. The reason for this devious device is that they have many acquaintances around their house and it is embarrassing for the couple to be seen together.'[72] Yet the greatest pressure was always the co-resident, or nearby presence, of the parents-in-law.

Fukuzawa realized that this was a structural contradiction, not a matter of individual personalities. 'The mothers-in-law are not all wicked women, nor are the new wives. Without regard to being good or bad in character, the relations between the two are almost always at odds. The reason cannot be in the characters of the par-ties; it must be in the general atmosphere.'[73] Almost always there was a huge tension. 'Only one out of a hundred households made up of several young and old couples living together under the same roof will truly preserve peace and harmony among them. I do not exaggerate in saying that the remaining ninety-nine are what you would call paradise outside and purgatory inside with inmates made up of fake saints and false noble wives.'[74] At other times he put the odds against a harmonious mother and daughter-in-law relation-ship much higher. 'Thus, the relations between in-laws, regardless of the characters of each member of the household, will not be like that of true parents and child, except for a very rare case of one in a thousand or even ten thousand.'[75]

There was only one solution, which was for the generations to live entirely separately, as in the West. He noted that 'There are some families in which the newly married couple live apart from the parents. This I consider a very wise step, most appropriate to human nature.'[76] He believed that 'the ideal way is to have the young couple, as soon as they are married, settle in a new home of their own apart from their parents.'[77] Indeed, it was not just a matter of living apart, but of having as little to do with each other as possible. 'In short, it is important to let the two families have as few points of contact as possible.'[78]

Fukuzawa also believed that the subordination of women was both reflected in and caused by other institutions. One of these was the plurality of marital and sexual relations in Japan. He noted that 'The West is made up of countries, in all of which monogamy – one wife to one husband – is the law, while Japan is a country where one husband may have many wives simultaneously. Could there be any contrast greater and more serious than this?'[79] He noted that 'A man of high rank and of wealth had many concubines, with the result that both the wife and the concubines suffered from small shares in the man's attention. This is a well-known fact.'[80] On the other hand, middling and poorer people resorted to prostitutes. Nor, given the lack of emotion within marriage and the tensions with the in-law relations, could he blame them. 'When one realizes that men are cut off entirely from establishing normal and friendly associations with women, and that they are confined to dull and lifeless relationships, it becomes natural that once they evade the restrictions, they will seek the extremes of freedom, or licentiousness . . .'[81] Whereas in the West, the home was the place to relax and to feel warmth, often in Japan it was necessary to escape from it. 'The fact is that the houses of concubines and the gay quarters are a separate world free from social rules and customs, the only havens where one may escape from social oppression.'[82] All of this was a very old and understandable pattern in Japan, but it must be changed. 'It is true that this Japanese practice of polygamy has a history of some unknown thousands of years. But now that the whole country has advanced into the modern civilization, I had thought that some scholars would turn their attention to this question and endeavour to devise some corrective measures.'[83]

The structural tensions in the family and the very weak position of women was also reflected in the ending of marriage. 'Divorce, which is very common and frequent in this country, must be caused by many factors, but the most important one is the nonexistence of social intercourse between men and women.'[84] There were seven grounds for divorce, according to neo-Confucian thought, the first two which Fukuzawa gave are particularly revealing. 'i) A woman shall be divorced for disobedience to her father-in-law or mother-in-law. ii) A woman shall be divorced if she fail to bear children, the reason for this rule being that women are sought in marriage for the purpose of giving men posterity.'[85] The latter, Fukuzawa commented, 'indeed is a preposterous statement without reason or human sentiment behind it.'[86] If the husband died, the widow was left in a very difficult position for there was a great deal of pressure against remarriage. 'My consistent advice for such a person has been remarriage, but Japanese society is still very unreceptive to such a concept, and even among educated people, there are very few who support it. The general attitude is to recognize widowhood as a beautiful virtue in a woman. Some even say this is an extension of the saying about a virtuous woman never taking two husbands. It is sad to see such advocates placing obstacles in the way of remarriage.'[87]

Fukuzawa's extensive writing on women and family relations partly reflected his desire to introduce selected aspects of the marriage pattern which he had seen and read about in the West to Japan, in particular monogamy. Yet he also wanted to change the emphasis on various features of the western system. We can see this when he wrote: 'the relation between husband and wife should not depend on love alone. Besides love and intimacy, there should be an element of mutual respect.'[88] Mutual support, intimacy and sharing was the perfect form. 'The true meaning of marriage should be for a husband and a wife to share a house, helping and being helped, enjoying the greatest happiness in life.'[89]

Thus the pattern that he advocated was neither the 'traditional' Japanese one, nor the western. Toshiko Nakamura compared his treatment of marriage and the family with my own model of the English marriage system and found significant differences. In England, romantic love was the ideal basis for marriage. Fukuzawa, however, 'expected the feelings based on morality between men and women rather than romantic love' to be the basis of marriage, that is to say 'Respect'. 'Love and Affection' were specifically confined to the parent–child relationship. Second, while Christianity and directly religious symbolism and ritual was a central context of western marriage, religion, as such, was much less important in Japanese marriage. Finally, the western family system was based on strong individualism. Apart from husband and wife, all relationships were based on contracts or rules. In Japan the whole family of parents and children was a moral zone, based on mutual respect and affection and excluding contract. Contractual relations started outside the nuclear family.[90]

Fukuzawa also had a wider aim, for he realized that the inequality of the genders was both a cause and consequence of the wider inequalities which ran through Japanese society. What he really objected to was the link between political and family relations which was explicit in neo-Confucian thought. Above all, Fukuzawa attacked the Confucian assumption of a direct parallel between all the five relations, the ruler–ruled, husband–wife, parent–child, brother–brother, master–servant. He attacked the assertion that the family was a mirror of the polity, and hence any objection to male or parental power was also treason, and he attacked on the other side the assertion that the state relations mirrored the family, and hence to attack a superior was also unfilial, impious, unnatural. On the latter he argued that 'if we consider the facts more deeply, the relation between government and people is not that of flesh and blood. It is in essence an association of strangers.'[91] If this were so, then 'Personal feelings cannot be the guiding principle in an association between strangers. It is necessarily based on the creation of a social contract.'[92] In other words, he was driving a wedge between kinship and politics.

This was truly revolutionary. Most absolutist states, whether China or Louis XIV's France, tried to combine these. Filmer, in seventeenth-century England in his *Patriarcha*, had tried to do the same. But Fukuzawa echoes John Locke almost word for word in arguing that only mutual affection and mutual contract could be the basis for both the relations in the state and the family. Blind obedience, uncritical submissiveness were wrong whether in the state or the family. All people, including women, had natural and inalienable rights. This was an enormous change, but Fukuzawa was confident that it was happening. 'Recently we Japanese have undergone a great transformation. The theory of human rights has flooded the land and has been universally accepted.'[93]

He realized that the implications of changing one part of the social system, gender relations, would change everything. 'People may say that the foregoing argument is all logical, but from a practical point of view, the extension of women's rights today means disturbing the social order and it cannot be approved without reservation. However, it is inevitable that rectifying social evils will entail some readjustments. If one wants to avoid that disturbance, one will have to sit in silence and forbearance.'[94] And indeed, he showed in his own life the immense difficulties of changing the whole family system in one generation. In relation to his own family he found himself caught in contradictions. He noted the difficulty in his *Autobiography*. 'Some moralists are advocating love for all men in the whole world. I would be a beast not to give my own children equal love and privilege. However, I have to remember the position of my eldest son who will take my place and become the center of the family after my death. So I must give him some privileges.'[95] This was privileging the oldest child. He made less explicit his failure to live up to his preaching on the equal education of women. While he wrote that 'Among my family of nine children, we make no distinction at all in affection and position between boys and girls',[96] this is not how one daughter remembers her childhood.

Carmen Blacker describes the following 'personal communication' from Mrs Shidachi, Fukuzawa's only surviving daughter, whose testimony shows that 'Fukuzawa failed entirely to put his precepts into practice in the upbringing of his own daughters.' He left their education entirely to the mother who was '"very conservative" and convinced of the innate inferiority of women.' Consequently, 'Mrs Shidachi was never allowed out alone, never allowed to express her opinion in the presence of her elders, and never allowed to speak to guests when they came to the house ... she was allowed next to no contact with men until her marriage at the age of eighteen, and even then her opinion was not consulted. Her education was, in fact, very little different from other girls 'except in so far as she learned English.'[97] A slightly different interpretation is given by Keiko Fujiwara who describes Fukuzawa's various attempts to educate his daughters, trying schools and then private tutors and commenting that 'Perhaps he was disappointed in school education, for he never did send his two youngest daughters to school. They were taught entirely by tutors at home. In these irregular attempts to educate his daughters, we can see the figure of a father struggling to provide the best education for his daughters.'[98]

This is a reminder that there is a considerable gap between the autobiographical reminiscences of Fukuzawa, dictated in his mid-sixties, and his actual behaviour. Just as Craig shows that he selectively rearranged his political activities in the *Autobiography* to present himself as detached and apolitical,[99] so his self-portrait needs to be treated with caution as an indication of his actual behaviour in other respects.

Yet rather than taking this gap between precept and practice as an indication of hypocrisy or weakness, it is better to see it as evidence of one of the many enormously strong pressures upon

Fukuzawa. He tried to change almost everything in Japan, the political, economic, legal, moral, technological and social systems. All this was to be effected within 20 or 30 years in an old and complex civilization. It is hardly surprising that not everything was achieved and much has, in fact, remained unchanged below the surface. For our purposes here, what is interesting is to see how he perceived the essence of western family systems and their difference from the Japanese tradition.

*

In the account above I have largely followed the conventional interpretation of Fukuzawa by Masao Maruyama and others. This suggests that Fukuzawa renounced his Confucian heritage and absorbed a thoroughly western model of civilization. But it is worth ending by pointing out that future research may well come to challenge this interpretation. It may well turn out that just as in his personal life, where Fukuzawa stressed the traditional costume and food and educational values, so in his thought, his ideas contain much more of his traditional upbringing than even he himself realized. Indeed, his thought, on deeper inspection, may provide clues to the way in which Japan has become a nation which blended a long tradition of neo-Confucian thought and institutions with the new ideas and institutions of the west. This new interpretation is largely based on the work of Professor Toshiko Nakamura.[100]

Fukuzawa had been brought up as a child and young man within the traditional clan and family structure of Tokugawa Japan. He had spent 37 years as a Confucian scholar and although he may have consciously believed that he rejected this period, in fact, it probably continued to influence him deeply for the rest of his life. A close inspection of his works, Professor Nakamura points out, shows many references to Confucian works. Confucian though this was, it is important to remember that the Japanese neo-Confucian version developed during the Tokugawa period was very different from the Chinese version of Confucianism. Furthermore, Fukuzawa took this implicit model and altered it fundamentally.

One example of the fusion of the neo-Confucian heritage and western models into something different from both has already been alluded to in the discussion of his ideas on the family and women's role in society. Although he advocated greater equality between the sexes, he maintained the importance of respect for parents, the primarily arranged marriage, and marriage based not on romantic love but mutual respect. It was not the western conjugal marriage system I have described elsewhere.[101] The 'fusing' of husband and wife which was supposed to occur when man and wife became 'one flesh and one blood' in the marriage service was not to become a feature of Japanese marriage. Husband and wife would remain mutually respectful separate individuals. Yet nor was the system he advocated just a continuation of what had existed previously in Japan. Something new, yet traditional, was created out of the blend, neither 'western' nor 'Tokugawa'.

This was related to a basic tension in Fukuzawa's treatment of the individual. It could be argued that his ideas on the individual are basically neo-Confucian. He uses the Confucian word 'Head of ten thousand things' to describe the individual. The idea is that the individual must become this 'Head' by 'polishing' his reason and virtue and thus deserving the title. There is little of the idea of a bounded, separate individual which is the key idea in western philosophy. His concepts seem to have been based on his early experience and on reading, that is to say samurai and neo-Confucian. It is true that at certain points he thought it would be necessary to change Japan entirely and to imitate the West. Thus in the 1870s he read Guizot, Buckle, Mill and Tocqueville and wrote his *Theory of Civilization* as a way of coming to terms with their very different concepts of the relation between individual and society. Yet he only partially absorbed their ideas.

For Fukuzawa the individual was not the separate entity, only fused with one other person during life, namely in marriage. This western model, which placed the individual in the centre of his or her world, with one deep relationship to a spouse, and then with widening rings of contractual relations, did not appeal to Fukuzawa. Instead, he argued that the whole family of parents and children formed one unit based on respect between husband and wife, and love and affection between parents and children. This was the basic emotional and moral unit. Only outside this, in society, did contractual relations begin. Morality in society more generally was created by an extension of family ethics and trust to the whole society. This is not Chinese Confucianism, where the respect for all ancestors is stressed and the husband–wife relationship is diminished. But nor was it the atomistic system, based on the individual or the dyadic husband–wife relation, which he had seen in England and America and read about in western books.

Another area where there is a fusion of two streams of ideas in order to create something which is neither western nor Tokugawa was in his philosophy of history, which also encompassed his theory of morality. He altered the neo-Confucian theory of time and history in various ways. One change was in moving the focus of the utopia or goal of life. Classic Confucianism placed the golden age in the past. The aim was to live in a way which would return one to the great ways and days of the past. Hence it was a conservative, authoritarian and quite rigid system. It looked down on the present as a deterioration from the past. Fukuzawa held on to the idea of a golden age, but through his reading of Guizot, Buckle and others, he mixed in a sort of 'Whig' or progressivist view of history. This was forward-looking. So the golden age was moved to the future. The idea of Enlightenment progress could be absorbed within his vision. The present was part of a forward movement, better than a barbarous past, but still only some steps along the way to a final, glorious, future. To this extent he accepted the western, nineteenth-century view of progressive evolution. But the nature of the final golden age was not the Whig one of equality, individualism, wealth, democracy and science. It was much closer to the Confucian dream of harmony, right relations, loving care of the weak, virtue, respect, even if it was all tinged with western rationality. It contained a contractual and individual element, but also had many features, particularly in relation to family sentiments and affection, missing in the Whig story. In the golden age ahead human beings would combine the rationality and knowledge of Newton and the morality of Confucius. Thus the historical dynamic is Whig and the goal Confucian.

As Professor Nakamura explains with the help of diagrams, the history of civilization saw the true nature of man gradually expanding from the barbarian state, where it was crushed by the wider society, to its development through the expansion of the family, so that one would end up with a peaceful world civilization based on reason and morality. All relations would have the respectful, affectionate and non-contractual nature of family relations and all disorder, violence and conflict would be eliminated.

Such a fusion of two paradigms had several consequences for Fukuzawa. It turned a conservative programme into a progressive, revolutionary and forward-looking one. It valued the present and gave the Japanese a sense of achievement and success. It set standards by which even the West was lacking and inadequate in terms of morality and order. The West was further along this path than Japan in terms of knowledge and technology, but Japan was heading more accurately in the right direction. And it eliminated the need for any further philosophy of history, whether that of Hegel, Marx, modernization theory or whatever. In the end the dynamism (Whig) and goals (utopian) were adequately represented in the theory. Yet curiously enough, it also paved the way for the late acceptance of Marxism in Japan, for in many ways all that was needed was a substitution of the Marxist Utopia for the Confucian one. And to a large extent they overlapped, seeing the goal of life in a universal human brotherhood based on respect, love and harmony.

Thus Fukuzawa may well be seen in the future as an intellectual in the old Japanese tradition, filtering western ideas, reconstructing them and fitting them into a pre-existing pattern. He did not just abandon the framework within which he was brought up. Instead, he used that set of ideas as a kind of grid into which he placed the new knowledge. Thus the pieces of his picture were mainly taken from the new knowledge derived from the West. The content or vocabulary was western. But the structure or grammar remained heavily influenced by a modified neo-Confucian framework. This blend of two traditions makes him much more appropriately a fore-runner of Japan with its curious blending of apparently contradictory forces.

In many respects his attempt to combine the Japanese and western ways reminds one of Tocqueville's attempt to blend the *ancien régime* with the 'modern' world. In many ways Tocqueville's ambivalence about the new values of equality, individualism and so on remind one of Fukuzawa. Though the gap between French and Anglo-American thought systems was not nearly as great as that between neo-Confucian and western ideas, it was still large. So Tocqueville wrestled with the contradictions and used each to criticize the other, as did Fukuzawa. A difference was that Tocqueville had less of a confidence in progress, though he did at times see a 'spirit of history' in the steady progress of the spirit of equality.

Professor Nakamura's tentative new interpretation of Fukuzawa as a largely implicit neo-Confucianist adds a certain richness to the interpretation. It fits with much recent anthropological study of non-western societies where indigenous peoples have been found to have reinterpreted and fought back against the externally im-posed models of the West. If the theory comes to be accepted it puts into question Fukuzawa's own representation of himself as a wholehearted westernizer. It makes him an even more interesting example of a great man trying to overcome some very deep contradictions between his heart and head, his early experience and his later findings. He stands caught between two civilizations, Japan and the West, which were locked into an increasingly close embrace.

*

In terms of his life and experiences Fukuzawa embodied great contradictions. He moved in one lifetime from one type of world into its almost complete opposite. Furthermore this forced upon him deeper and wider comparisons than any of them. Although he spent less effort on working out a sophisticated methodology than his European counterparts, he concentrated with intense concern on the riddle of the nature of the modern world, and how it could be achieved in Japan.

We can see that his picture was very much like that of his western counterparts. Equality, individualism, liberty and the separation of spheres were the essential underpinnings for wealth and technological success. But there were other things which they took for granted but which he specified, for example, the art of public speaking and discussion, confrontational politics, the relative equality of men and women, individual rights and modern accounting. All these Fukuzawa had to explain and teach to his fellow countrymen. But in essence, for most of his life, he proclaimed the Enlightenment message; wealth and power would follow a rise in equality, liberty and individualism. Technological imports without these changes would be worthless.

What makes Fukuzawa special is that his message coincided with the Meiji Restoration when his ideas suddenly became absorbed into the official policy of Japan. A relatively backward society, caught in many of the traps of the agrarian world – hierarchy, a certain degree of absolutism, technological stagnation – suddenly attempted to 'join the West'. No other Asian country had ever attempted to do this, let alone succeeded in making the massive transformation in just two generations.

The amazing fact is that, partly on the basis of the blueprint, a simplified replica of the best of the Enlightenment, Japan performed the miracle, effected the exit from the agrarian world. Within 50 years it had developed from an isolated and relatively weak Asian polity into one of the great world powers which had defeated China and Russia. The growth of its industrial production, of its exports and of its agriculture was astounding. It had found the secret bridge from the agrarian world. The importation of western science and technology, though an essential part of this transformation, was only a part. The cultural, social and political changes were equally important. The fact that the same technology and science were available to China, South-East Asia and India, yet had little dramatic effect there for some 80 years after the Japanese transformation, shows how much more was involved.

Of course, there were many other necessary preconditions in Japan; the craft skills, ingenuity, hard work, self-discipline, cooperativeness and flexibility of the workforce. Yet all of these had been present for 250 years of peace and increasingly easy taxation and had led nowhere in particular. It could be argued that it was the opening of Japan, and particularly the adoption of the Enlightenment message which tipped the balance from internal predation to internal production. Fukuzawa added little to the theoretical subtlety of the earlier analysis, but he was a highly intelligent thinker who sought to relay its central message, an enormously energetic man who sought to propagate these new views as widely as possible, and a man who was lucky enough to find that the tide was flowing with him.

Thus the miracle of the exit from an agrarian world had been reproduced in a civilization what was in many respects different from its earlier home. Fukuzawa was in the end wiser than Marx, whose blueprint, with its closure of the separations between spheres by merging ideology and polity, taking equality far beyond its productive bounds, and creating the greatest despotisms the world has ever known, was a disaster. That a modern system of industry with some of its underpinning happened in Japan some two generations earlier than anywhere else in Asia is not unconnected to the work of Japan's greatest modernizer and analyst of modernity, Yukichi Fukuzawa. He deserves his place on the highest denomination Japanese banknote.

Synthesis

16
The Making of the Modern World

We can now return to some of the more general issues raised by this study of two theories concerning the making of the modern world. These are general reflections, stimulated by the thoughts of Maitland and Fukuzawa, but also drawing on other work I have undertaken over the last ten years. In particular, the chapter also draws on ideas generated by the two other books which I have written exploring these broad themes of the origins and nature of the modern world.[1]

By the time of Fukuzawa's death in 1901 and that of Maitland in 1906, the mystery of how the modern world has been made had been clearly identified and a set of hypotheses to explain it had been put forward. Yet much of the subsequent work during the more than 90 years since then has buried both the question and any possible answers, so that the earlier work has become increasingly obscured. This book, and its companion on Montesquieu and his successors, has largely been an excavation to unearth something which was once widely known but is now largely forgotten.[2] Before we examine this mystery once more, it is worth speculating briefly on why the very existence of an enormous puzzle has virtually disappeared.

One part of the answer stems from Tocqueville's profound remark that 'great successful revolutions, by effecting the disappearance of the causes which brought them about, by their very success, become themselves incomprehensible.'[3] The transformation of the world during the last few centuries is certainly a 'great successful revolution', and it has largely erased, at least among many western intellectuals, the memories of how difficult that transformation has been and hence any incentive to try to understand it.

Thus the fact that the Enlightenment solution, centring on liberty, wealth and equality, has spread so far and wide and become a part of the air which the world breathes is one of the reasons why it is now so difficult even to see that there was once a mystery at all. A 'modern' citizen of a 'modern' nation, however gifted, finds it hard even to see that there was any doubt about the current triumph of 'modernity'. It is worth briefly summarizing a few of the major changes in order to see how the actual course of events has concealed the mystery.

Part of the argument of all of the great Enlightenment thinkers was that England was a bridge from the *ancien régime* to the modern world. England for a very long time was a receiver of ideas from outside. The artifacts and philosophies from the ancient civilizations and of all the other contemporary world civilizations poured into her over the centuries, were modified and then disseminated again. This transference is equally true of other countries. What makes England special is a set of accidents. At a crucial point, when western Europe was on the ascendant, England took the lead. It was able to do so because through the process of the absorption of ideas, it largely developed a new socio-technical form, the industrial system. At the same time it had accumulated the largest empire the world has ever known, including the vast population of India, and it replicated itself within this empire as well as on the continent of North America which would one day be the dominant power on earth.

This means that the curious set of institutions, funnelled through one small island, spread widely over the world. With the demise of communism and with the creeping capitalism of China, there are now only limited alternatives to the system which evolved over the centuries in England. If we probe below the surface we shall find that now, while England itself has shrunk to a second-rate power, the 'virtual' England spreads very widely. It has lost its Empire, but to a large extent the inner principles which made it so odd in the middle of the eighteenth century are now taken for granted either as a reality or an aspiration through much of the world.

The political trap has been broken, temporarily at least. The absolute sway of a single ruler or small group has been challenged and for all its weaknesses, democracy, the rule of the people by the people, is proclaimed as the only acceptable form of government. As Fukuyama shows, the victory of this form is only very recent.[4] As late as the 1960s the majority of the countries in the world were ruled undemocratically. Now there are only a few exceptions to democratic rule. Such democracy always involves some form of parliament. In this respect a system that has lasted 1,000 years, in essence, in England, has become the basis of the world's political systems.

The central feature of the modern political system is the separation of political power from other forms of activity based on religion, kinship and economics. Although many countries are still struggling to attain or maintain this separation, it is an ideal in almost all. Put in other words, the central hope and message of Montesquieu and Tocqueville that political liberty is paramount has been achieved more widely than they could have hoped, and much of this has passed over the Anglo-American bridge.

Closely related to this is the legal system. The 'Declaration of the Rights of Man' in America, which proclaimed it as a self-evident truth that men were born equal and free, could be conceivable only within a certain legal order which supported individual rights and liberties, contracts and 'fair' trials. Again the exceptional, balanced, jury-based, non-arbitrary legal system that was developed in England from the twelfth century onwards has become absorbed into the legal systems of almost all the world. The basic principle which treats humans as equal at birth and with intrinsic and inalienable rights, irrespective of birth, gender, caste, class or creed, is now very widely accepted, at least as an ideal.

Religious toleration is another Enlightenment ideal which has widely been accepted. In 1700, 'freedom of conscience', the idea that a person's relation to God or whether he or she believed or engaged in religious rituals was their own private business, was present in a very limited part of the world. All through Catholic Europe, Islam, Hinduism and in large areas of Asian Buddhism, conformity to the major opinion was enjoined. The Counter-Reformation had recaptured most of Europe and in Calvinist countries such as Scotland there was intolerance of religious independence. The spread and increasing toleration of sectarianism, that separation of the public and private which Tocqueville documented, this and much else spread from the tiny enclave of Holland and England, through America until it is formally accepted in theory, if not in practice, through much of the world.

Turning to the Enlightenment hopes for greater equality, we again see a massive shift over the last three hundred years. The Enlightenment thinkers were deeply opposed to what Tocqueville termed 'caste', that is extreme, birth-based stratification. In the eighteenth century, only a tiny fragment of the world espoused the idea that all forms of birth-based inequality were wrong – from slavery, to extreme privileges for the nobility. Yet this tiny minority view has now spread over most of the world. Although there are vast differences in *de facto* wealth, *de jure* distinctions are rejected almost everywhere.

Men are born equal – and 'men' includes 'women'. The equalization of the genders, an even more eccentric idea in the eighteenth century, is now a widespread goal. The emancipation of women in many parts of the world has been partially achieved, though inequalities of course remain. Foot-binding and *sutee* have been abolished and though bride-burning and female circumcision and *purdah* still continue, there is little doubt that an appreciable shift has occurred. The proportion of those who would openly subscribe to the view of women as a sinful, inferior creature, born to be the slave of man, has decreased dramatically.

There has also been an opening up and levelling of knowledge. The closed worlds of priesthood and *literati* have begun to wither before mass education, the rapid spread of printing and other communication technologies, the growth of scepticism and tolerance. The ordinary educated citizen may not have specialist knowledge in many fields, but the division of knowledge is no longer between the tiny minority who have keys to all that is known, and the vast majority who are totally excluded.

Many of these changes have been made possible by the third of the Enlightenment forces, wealth. Adam Smith described in his *Wealth of Nations* the peculiar world of English capitalism with its odd disassociation of the economy from society, religion and politics. At that time, such a system existed in only a tiny part of north-western Europe and in America – perhaps 5 per cent of the world population. Now the system of market or consumer capitalism, with its division of spheres, division of labour, its in-built separation of fact and value and combination of private vice and public benefit, is almost universal. We have seen, during the last dozen years of the twentieth century, how two-thirds of the world's population in China, India, eastern Europe and the former Soviet Union, have switched to this system in the hope of those materialist benefits which Smith promised. We are almost all capitalists or Smithians now, just as we are almost all followers of Montesquieu in relation to liberty – and the two, as they showed, are connected.

Related to all these forces, and indeed forming their underpinning, was the technological structure of a post-agrarian world, or what, in short-hand, we call the 'industrial revolution'. By 1700 England, with Holland, had already advanced a long way towards new forms of manufacturing, but most of it was focused on agriculture and its by-products. There were already significant gains in efficiency and productivity. Then in the next century the treasures of the carboniferous mines were unlocked, and with steam and factories, mankind for the first time, as Wrigley powerfully argues, could live off the vast stores of fossil energy accumulated from the sun.[5] The techniques and their embodiment in work practices and behaviour were invented in England. By 1800 industrial civilization covered perhaps 2 per cent of the globe or less, some 10 million people in the countries affected at the most. Two hundred years later the whole world has been transformed and the lives of thousands of millions are dependent on machinery and on non-human forms of energy.

In extending liberty, equality and wealth, some of the hopes and dreams of the Enlightenment thinkers have been partially achieved. That difficult balance of forces whereby religion, economy, polity and society were all restricted and separated, which they saw as only really existing in Holland, England and partly in Switzerland, has, through America, become the almost universal premise of most nations in the world. The vision of our Enlightenment thinkers is far more secure now than it was 300, or even 60, years ago.

*

A second part of the answer to why the question has largely been forgotten lies in the development of theoretical frameworks since Maitland's death. These new historical and sociological paradigms have shaped our questions and our answers and they have been elaborated partly in response to the revolutions which have been described. Basically what happened was that under a number of pressures the 'shape' of the past changed. The Enlightenment account, from Montesquieu to Maitland, was quietly abandoned and a simple model of the past was developed whereby all societies went through a series of 'stages'. In essence, western Europe went through these stages first, and within western Europe, England did so a little earlier, but the rest of the world would inevitably do so. Whether this was seen within a Marxist framework, or an avowedly anti-Marxist one, as with the work of Walt Rostow, it was basically the same story, with images of a runway with societies, like planes, waiting to 'take off' into modernity.[6]

According to a rising orthodoxy, the last 1,000 years of history were reduced to three 'stages'. Up to the fifteenth century, all of western Europe was 'peasant' and 'feudal'. Then there was a period of 'transition', a 'watershed', a century or two of revolutionary change, and then in the eighteenth century the modern capitalist and industrial world emerged. It was a neat and satisfying pattern with its radical oppositions of pre-capitalist/capitalist, pre-industrial/industrial, collective/individualist, and so on.

This three-stage model eliminated the mystery which I have been discussing and hence any chance of finding a solution. It was obvious that since all societies were moving along the runway, to do so was the 'natural' thing. 'Progress' was natural, and the problem was to understand why those few places, perhaps suffering from some variant of the terrible disease of 'Oriental despotism' or the 'Asiatic mode of production' seemed unable to 'take off'. The development of industrial capitalism was no problem. It was bound to happen, being part of the working-out of the spirit of history. The only question was where and when it would happen.

There was, in the Marxist version, an inner instability built into each mode of production, so that it was bound to evolve into the next, 'higher', stage. In a rather curious way, a Whig notion of inevitable 'progress' became mixed up with a Marxist version of the unfolding of history. The Marxist version was the most powerful of many variants since, in relation to recent history, it laid out in detail two basic modes of production in the West, the feudal and the capitalist. The historian's job was to describe how one inevitably led into the other. By the 1960s this was the framework which, despite some local resistance, dominated much of historical research on the last millennium.

Within this framework, the only questions to ask were how the inevitable contradictions within the feudal system occurred, the precise nature of the collapse and transformation to 'modernity', and the nature of the new world that was born. It was no mystery that it happened. It was bound to happen in one place, if not another.[7] Nor was there any problem in it being spread to other parts of the world since, in essence, the agrarian civilization of medieval Europe was basically of the same order as that of China, India or elsewhere. This was the paradigm within which I was increasingly taught in the early 1960s, as I have explained at more length elsewhere.[8] Within the debates of that time, there was hardly a mention of the Enlightenment alternatives sketched out in this book. The past was cut and dried, there was no real mystery or sense of wonder.

Other possible reasons for the loss of the earlier vision of continuity with change is suggested by James Campbell. He argues that attacks on the Stubbs–Maitland picture arise from a fear of appearing anachronistic. He notes that 'historians dread the charge of anachronism', that the 'principal element in the rejection of Stubbs has been a morbid fear of anachronism'. Campbell rejects the re-interpretation of the Anglo-Saxon and medieval history by many recent historians and again suggests that the reasons for their mistakes were 'many', but 'behind them all lies, one may suspect, again the fear of anachronism, reinforcing the belief that somehow or other everything changes in the sixteenth century'. Another reason why 'the study of the early history of England' moved to a situation where people were 'avoiding the largest issues and the most arresting questions' was that 'it had fallen into the hands of trained medievalists', who did not have the wide philosophical backgrounds of men like Maitland.[9]

*

Looked at from the perspective of all of human history and all other human civilizations, what has happened during the last 300 years is extraordinary. A new kind of civilization has emerged which has an unprecedented set of organizational principles. All other civilizations have been based on the principles of an ordering of institutional parts in two ways. There was a strict vertical hierarchy, some form of stratification where orders were integrated through a set of levels, whether castes or otherwise. These were based on birth and indicated to people where they were placed, how to behave, how to live. Yet the overturning of these premises is precisely what has happened in the last three hundred years and anarchy, on the whole, has not ensued. This is part of the tendency towards equality which Tocqueville analysed. That this happened raises two great questions. How did such a strange thing as the breakdown of hierarchy occur, and how could a civilization not based on it work? What could hold equal people together and prevent them either from falling apart into atomistic confusion or, equally dangerously, from surrendering their liberty to some form of absolutist government?

Put in another way, the problem could be seen in terms of the loss of the sovereignty of groups. In the long history of mankind, people had always existed as subordinate to groups, but now, for the first time, a world arose where the individual came before the group. This is often seen as the quintessence of modern liberty. Again this poses the double question of how such a strange situation could have emerged, and, once present, how it could possibly work. Too much atomization would surely lead to the collapse of the social system. This was one of the great quandaries for the anthropology and sociology of the nineteenth century and lay behind many of its best-known theories.

Yet not only did this unprecedented social order work, it worked so well, at least at the material level, that the area where it first developed, Holland, England and then America and western Europe, rapidly became the richest and most powerful areas of the world and hence dominated and spread its system, until, now, it envelops almost the whole world. Likewise, it seems to work extremely well when transferred to parts of Asia, and particularly, in the early period, Japan.

One might put the same story in a slightly different way, following hints from Fukuzawa. Human life can for convenience be divided into four major spheres, the pursuit of power (politics), the pursuit of wealth (economics), the pursuit of salvation and meaning (religion), the pursuit of social and sexual warmth (kinship). In the normal state of affairs these are fused into one totality, a holistic merging based on the dominance of one sphere to which everything else is secondary. Tribal societies provide this dominance or infrastructure through kinship, India and Islam through religion, traditional China through kinship and ethics (Confucianism), *ancien régime* Europe increasingly through kin-based politics. What is peculiar about modernity is that there is no institutional infrastructure, or, if it exists, it is provided by the impersonal, contextual, contractual pressures of the 'free' market economy and the ethic of trust upon which it has to be based.

Again one has to ask how such a state of affairs, where the spheres have become separated and balanced came about and, once dominant, how it can possibly work. People kept together only by the 'invisible hand' would surely soon realize that it was not just invisible, but did not exist. Anyway, how could the predatory tendency of each sphere to dominate the others be restrained and, furthermore, how were the different areas integrated when each was supposedly autonomous and proud of its liberties? For example, how was religion largely kept out of family relations, or kinship out of economics? These are themes discussed by Fukuzawa, Maitland and the Enlightenment thinkers.

To achieve and sustain such a balance over a long period is very difficult. Always in human history the tendency for one or two spheres in collusion to dominate has quickly emerged and some form of *ancien régime* has established itself. Even in the twentieth century, those who worked in the name of the two massive ideologies of right (fascism) and left (communism) have been united in their attempts to bundle things together with one superior master, the state or party. That they only very narrowly failed to return mankind to an undivided world where liberty and real equality of all men would have vanished is well known. The political institutions of modernity are extremely precarious and may well be transient.

If this stark and rough characterization of modernity is correct, it suggests two mysteries already referred to. The state of affairs which first became strongly evident in Holland and England, where liberty, equality (of a sort), and wealth were joined in new ways, is extraordinary. First, it is historically and comparatively unique; no large-scale civilization has ever run for a period of several centuries on these principles. Second, it is extremely difficult to see how such a civilization could have emerged. Normally, the balance tips one way or the other as wealth increases. One sphere, perhaps in collusion with another, comes to dominate and almost necessarily the group comes to dominate the individual. This had always happened in the past, yet, for the first time, it did not happen again. How did this astounding exception occur; what made it not only possible, but happen? This is the question which Maitland sought to answer. Linked to this is the question that has vexed many of the greatest thinkers from Montesquieu to Durkheim; what could possibly hold such a system together? If kinship was restrained, God was kept out of the market, the state inhibited, how or why should people work effectively together? These were the two great unanswered questions by the middle of the nineteenth century.

We can call the two questions about modernity the historical and functional ones. The historical one is basically, when, how and why did the peculiarities of modernity – equality, liberty, individualism, the absence of infrastructural determination, first happen? Once such a civilization had occurred and once it had been shown that it produced wealth and power, it was soon emulated and its spread is less of a problem, though how it happened is very revealing, as we saw in the case of Fukuzawa and Japan. The first instance is particularly baffling and has attracted the thoughts of many great minds from the Enlightenment onwards. Yet the functional question is equally difficult to solve, that is the question of how such a system works. How is it possible to provide a balance which will give people an ability to work effectively together and yet not crush their liberty and individuality? 'Status' had been extremely effective in bringing civilizations up to a high level, but then proved too cramping for 'modernity' to emerge. Yet the conventional wisdom, which was that 'contract' or the division of labour provides the answer, was patently unsatisfactory. Humans only tied together by functional interdependence, as on a conveyor belt, do not have enough incentive for cooperative action outside the specific situation. 'Contract', which is immediate, rational, impersonal, is not a foundation for effective group action. It is temporary and dyadic by definition. Thus the conventional wisdom of nineteenth-century sociology, of the movement from status to contract, from mechanical to organic solidarity, of community to individual, are all unsatisfactory.

The mystery deepens if we rephrase the puzzle in slightly different words as follows. In order for humans to achieve their ends, they need to enter into a social contract with others. This is Thomas Hobbes' main point. To overcome narrow individualistic competition and the war of all against all, it was necessary to forgo some power and allocate it to the governor, Leviathan. More normally, rather than erecting a state, early societies were formed into kinship-based groups, which we term the tribal stage. As state-based systems emerge, they usually build themselves upon these kinship groupings and reorder them through religious (caste) or state hierarchies (Confucian China) which can integrate wider groupings but still maintain their kinship base. What is central to all of this is that these are systems founded upon status, blood birth. What Hobbes envisaged was different, entirely contractual, not based on religion or kinship, but secular and individualistic. Yet Hobbes' system was tied together by one system of loyalties alone, those to the state. The only subordinate groups were corporations licensed by the state.

Thus the large-scale civilizations which first emerged tended to re-inforce the birth-status groupings, caste and kinship, while integrating them into a powerful state. Much of Indian and Chinese history fits broadly within this pattern. A second variant, which we often describe as the *ancien régime*, was somewhat different. There were functionally defined birth statuses – peasants, nobility, bourgeois, clergy – but alongside these there were also many groupings with some contractual mobility. Yet while these groupings were not based on birth, they were explicitly recognized and licensed, as it were, by the state. Thus all meaningful groupings either derived from birth or from delegated power from the state.

In such a social structure, as wealth increases it automatically strengthens the organising institutions of the system. Part of the wealth will flow towards birth-based institutional groupings, whether of kinship or religion, re-inforcing kinship and caste. Part of the wealth will go to strengthen occupational and hierarchical blood divisions, between workers, priests and warriors, for example. Part of the wealth will go towards increasing the power of the state. Each of these institutional orders will cast a jealous eye on the wealth-producers, whether peasants, merchants or craftsmen, and try to siphon off as much as possible of any new surpluses they make.

In such a normal course of events a productive system tends to become over-rigid. All attempts to set up groups other than those based on birth are seen as threats to the kin or the state. Religion often provides the one achievement-based alternative, but by definition is not meant to engage too much in wealth production. Thus the general tendency is for hierarchy, whether based on ritual, class, kinship or political forces, to increase over time. So it is clear that wealth and new technology tends to inflate or feed into the pre-existing structures.

How, then, did something different emerge, which neither fell into the trap of too-powerful birth-based or centralized political systems, nor a too fragmented and individualistic, Hobbesian, world? How could civilizations avoid the Scylla of status and also the Charybdis of contract? The way, obviously, lay through some combination of the best of both; the affective, emotional ties of status, the flexibility and efficiency of contract, forged into something new. This new arrangement must allow a new kind of grouping to emerge which had certain unusual properties.

*

The mystery of how our world came about and, in particular, continues to exist, is made even greater if we investigate the moral, social and psychological costs of the new kind of civilization which has come to dominate the world so recently. The contradictions at its heart were a central concern to all the great Enlightenment thinkers and we need to be reminded of their message.

If, basically, the essence of modernity is an ever-vigilant patrolling of the borders between spheres, one is left with those problems of living in an open society which many, including poets such as Blake and Yeats, or political philosophers such as Popper, have documented. People are often forced to live in a dessicated world of compromises, captured so well by Alexander Pope. They cannot afford to let any particular drive prevail for long. All power tends to corrupt, so power must be muzzled. Kinship loyalties and warmth must be held in check and love can seldom be unreserved. Belief and ritual must be tempered and all ethical judgments are provisional and relativistic. Even the pursuit of wealth has to be moderated and many areas are put 'out of bounds'. All knowledge is provisional; all action is tempered by the knowledge of its hidden cost.

The benefits of this modern world are huge: personal liberty and autonomy, an equality of sorts, and wealth undreamed of for vast numbers of people. The consumer revolution deadens the pain of the loss of integration and meaning and few would go back. But the costs are only just below the surface and when a prophet arises who promises the reintegration of life, the overcoming of alienation and anomie, the togetherness of a purpose, whether a Mao, Hitler or Pol Pot, many are ready to abandon their somewhat dessicated lives of efficiency in order to surrender to the new wholeness. Or they may be attracted to the ecstasies and loss of self of a new Pentecostal religion or New Age faith. For most, however, there are only oases of togetherness, in drink, friendship, sport, music and the institutions of civil society. Much of life is lived in restraint and rational balance.

As well as the costs to the inner core of the modern world, there are the costs incurred as this world spreads outwards, undermining all closed systems through its conspicuous economic success or military might. Local worlds of meaning are drained and a technocratic, managerial, ascetic world partly replaces them. One recompense is the dream of material wealth and leisure. Another is the forms of associationalism in sport, business, religion and elsewhere which partly overcomes the separateness of the lonely crowd. With the fall of communism, the only surviving holistic world system offering an alternative to the open society is Islam.

To many of its critics the modern world is fairly repulsive morally, and psychologically almost intolerable. Yet others believe that it is the worst of all possible systems, except for all the rest, which are even worse. The hedonism, loneliness, lack of purpose, contradictions are unattractive, but the world of communistic, fascistic or other totalitarian systems are even less attractive in the long run, both at the personal level and in terms of what they produce. Liberty, equality and the pursuit of happiness may not encompass all the lofty goals humans can pursue, but there are worse. The modern world that emerged over the long centuries has turned humans into great lords of all things, yet they remain a prey to all, including their own inner self-doubt.

All of this means that humans are not blissfully happy in our modern world. It has a number of the properties of anomie, alienation, loneliness, coldness described by a great many authors. In particular the individual is held in perpetual doubt, as Pope had so elegantly described in his 'Essay on Man'. Every action has a cost as well as a benefit, enthusiasm can be crushed, there are no certainties. This is one of the great attractions of play, art and romantic love, a moment of reintegration and meaning. Usually, one has to settle for a compromise between almost equally balanced loyalties and demands. Yet the balancing of them and the constant contradictions are probably also the cause of the energy of modern civilization. Some kind of fission or explosion occurs again and again. It is those societies where fusion has completely dominated which appear to become inert.

*

So there have been a number of insights provided by the comparative and historical method of the great thinkers who have surveyed the great transformation. First, they have established the central peculiarities which I have discussed briefly above. Second, they have seen that the essential bridge to this new form of civilization was England, though later transferred elsewhere. The third clue lay in relation to the functional question. Something had to be found which would join people together, but the ties must not be based on blood and birth, but must be fluid and be able to balance the allegiances of group and individual, providing the affective warmth of kinship and religious devotion, without being based on kinship and religion.

So by the 1870s the problems had become quite focused. The West was decidedly peculiar in its lack of infrastructure and in its deep contradictions arising out of the separation of spheres. This was noted by outsiders such as Fukuzawa as well. No other civilization in world history had been like this and it was somehow tied to the wealth, productivity and power of the West which now confronted the world. So how had this happened and how did it work? The answer seems to lie in the history of England which, well before 1870, was the dominant imperial power. And within England the answer to the question of how it worked seems to lie in some alternative to the primordial institutions, that is in the various imagined rather than actual communities, not the nation alone, but all the imagined and invented communities of civil society.

The solution or heart of the mystery lay in the hybrid nature of what emerged. The overcoming of the contradictions between status and contract must lie in a new form of association. This new entity must be 'incorporate', that is, have an enduring body, yet it must not be set up by blood (kinship) or by religion, or by the state. It must be answerable to itself. Yet it must be recognized and tolerated by these jealous institutions. Second, it must be recruited and selected on the basis of choice, both of those within the group and those outside. It must be based on achievement rather than ascription, with a right to recruit and expel and a tendency towards recruiting on the grounds of merit and efficiency. Third, it must be able to pursue goals and protect itself from the encroachments of jealous rivals, goals which are rather specific and which are not thrown off course by wider considerations. In other words, it needs to encase a set of individuals and give them a cooperative and protected space where they can pursue the goals of the group.

All civilizations develop temporary, if often weak, versions of this; flower-arranging circles, mutual credit associations, coffee-house cliques. But as soon as any of these gains conspicuous success or begins to accumulate wealth, it tends to be crushed by its rivals. The family resents the time and emotional attraction of groups of this kind; the Church bans Masonic-type institutions; the state crushes any large-scale organization or meeting of potential subversives. Thus nothing much can develop in the interstices between the dominating institutions of kinship, religion and the state.

What is extraordinary and so beautifully described by Maitland is just that development of the myriad sets of such institutions over time in the rather odd civilization of England. The Trust provided just these features, an enduring or embodied entity larger than the individual, recruitment on choice and merit, toleration by the state, religion and kin, providing a sense of mutual sharing and cooperation in pursuit of some goal. Its fruits, as Maitland showed, are to be seen in many fields, in religion, politics, economy, social clubs. One possible side-effect or connection he only touched on is between these new entities and the world of sport and games. He did note their immense importance in sport, as in the Jockey Club or the MCC, but this was only the shell. The extraordinary fact that almost all team games – rugby, football, cricket, hockey, and so on – were invented or developed in England from the later Middle Ages on, is surely not a coincidence.

First, these games need the organization within which they could occur, the bounded areas of space, time and attention that permits a group of people taking time away from the calls of economy, kinship, state and religion, to kick a ball about, or whatever the activity is. This is provided by the 'club' with its rules, pitch, club house, and so on. And then that extraordinary blend of competition and cooperation, self-love and social obligation, which is the quintessence of team games, is encouraged. It is the template for all other kinds of collaborative behaviour. The goal is to win, in sport, war, wealth production, pursuit of merit. The rules are known and involve mutual responsibilities as well as personal gratification. The boundaries of the activities are strictly policed. In theory, during the game itself, the demands of kinship, faith, social status, political power should be excluded, if possible. The game is the thing. The same spirit inspires those who pool their talents and assets to form a trading company, bank, operatic society or a legion of 'Quangos', quasi-autonomous non-governmental organizations, or what is often referred to as 'civil society'.

Once these middling groupings have gained a foothold and been allowed to develop, they soon reach a stage where the inflow of increasing wealth is fed into them. They are like middle-sized plants, filling in densely the space between the high vegetation, the tree-tops of the state and Church, and the single individuals or family on the forest floor. In most civilizations, this middle level has been increasingly cut away, leaving a huge space between the state and the established religion on the one hand, and the clinging bed of short, flattened, lateral links that is the extended family. But once the peculiar associations start to flourish, as Tocqueville noted in America, or Fukuzawa tried to encourage in Japan, they crowd into this middle area, weakening the despotic power of the two extremes, the roof canopy of state and God, the amoral familistic demands of the kinship groupings. Loyalties are multifarious, activities are protected, there are huge advantages to be gained from associating for numerous purposes. A world of clubs, companies, fellowships, sects, and so on, emerge.

This is the safeguard of liberty and equality, as Montesquieu, Tocqueville, Maitland and Fukuzawa all realized, protecting the individual from the tendencies towards political centralization or overpowerful demands of a familistic or religious kind which stress uniformity. Emerging diversity, cooperation with competition, flexibility, constant new forms of organization and innovation are encouraged. This is the secret of the strength and vigour of England, then America, then Japan and now much of the world. It has swept over the world along with English language, law and games, all of which are linked to each other.

For the first time, increasing wealth fed into the middle parts of the system, rather than top and bottom. A prosperous, bourgeois, middle-class world emerged, full of competing small-scale groupings, 'teams' one might say, which tried to outdo each other whether at football, in interpretation of the Christian bible, trade with the Indies, political power. Parties, clubs, associations, these are the organizational secret of modernity. Only they could effectively overcome the two extremes of anomie/contract or holism/status. They made tolerable the separation between different parts of a society and indeed help to maintain it. They constitute the increasing division of the world into small, meaningful, social spaces which cross the boundaries of primordial loyalties. The grounds of recruitment are not status, but contract, but once formed they have some of the warmth of kinship, without the open-ended claims. And because there are many of them, and none has a monopoly, none can become absolutist. Whether competing political parties ever-jostling for power, or religious sects, jostling for salvation, or scientific and artistic associations, competing for truth or beauty, or social clubs, competing for leisure and jollity, or economic associations, competing for wealth, they provide the individual numerous places to develop her or his creativity and energy. The Japanese developed this through a peculiarly flexible sort of kinship system, the English through the Trust. And on these developing institutions were laid the foundations of the first escape into modernity in East and West.

*

One of the characteristics of this world of associations is, of course, that if you are brought up in it and it surrounds you, it becomes invisible. Associationalism is now so 'natural' to the British and Americans that it seems to need no explanation, and it would hardly be such peoples who discovered the power of associations. It tends to be those who have lost or have weakly developed associationalism who first notice its importance. Nowadays it tends to be those, for example, from an East European background who are interested in what will replace communism who praise civil society in the West and stress its centrality.[10] In earlier times it was those outside Europe, like Fukuzawa. Even earlier, it was the French and Scots, living in recently *ancien régime* or clan societies, dominated by status, who were astonished by this peculiar phenomenon.

The new dimension added through Maitland's rejection of Sir Henry Maine's theory of the movement of all progressive societies from status to contract was the historical documenting of the accidental and artificial development of civil society, which for the first time became dominant in a world civilization. Democracy, liberty, equality and wealth all have their roots in this common, largely invisible, bed of associations. Its emergence was an accident, its survival precarious. The infant could easily have been strangled and, if Henry VIII or Hobbes had had their way, the intestinal worms that fed within the body politic would have been poisoned and evacuated. If they had been, the desire to unite in the pursuit of wealth, power, knowledge, would no doubt have been expressed in the multitude of secret societies, Masons, Rosicrucians, Mafia, Triads, Yaku-za, and so on, which infest other bodies politic.

In the majority of historical cases there are the fully accepted, status-based structures and against them the prohibited secret organizations at war with the state. The constant tension saps both parties; the costs of secrecy and the costs of policing are equally great. What is extraordinary in the Anglo-American tradition is that the associations were relatively open. There was little prohibition or interference. The sects, parties, clubs, companies, fellowships, were not driven underground into a world of an 'informal' or 'black' economy, polity or society. They worked with the state and the established church. They paid their taxes, observed the rules of the state, were composed of the most upright citizens who were proud to declare their membership. Hence wealth, power, sociability, knowledge could all be pursued openly. There was little of the friction of surveillance, of intrigue and secrecy. Nor was it difficult to spread successful solutions to practical problems.

As soon as a sect or company or club was set up which appealed to others, the open market in associations encouraged competitors. And the rewards of belonging to such units, whether material or symbolic, did not have to be laundered in any way. The encouragement to honesty, trust and mutual respect, rather than fear, deceit and mutual suspicion is enormous and the advantages of such an open society, whether in the pursuit of truth or wealth or social worth, were decisive. The 'black' alternative systems and double standards which are increasingly the bane of the former Soviet Union, India and many parts of the world, were, on the whole, absent.

Thus at the level of the nation, that same favourable mix of diversity within a common uniformity occurred at a localized level. This encouraged the splitting up of the sources of power, wealth, sociability so that centralization and rigidification became more difficult. As soon as some monopoly began to build up, it was automatically outflanked by smaller, but nimbler, rivals. Even the state itself found itself deprived of many of its lucrative functions by sets of individuals combining in associations which had 'privatized' policing, money making, entertainment, knowledge generation.

As Tocqueville had pointed out, this meant that the almost powerless individual could become strong through associating with other like-minded individuals. Whether through a trades union, a women's institute, a suffragette organization, a slavery abolition society, a disability action group, a minority religion or whatever, a plurality of voices were heard and hitherto disadvantaged groups started to improve their position. Normally, in other countries, protest from such groups, or even a recognition of their common interests, was crushed. Yet the associations gave them power. And this power was at a meaningful level. Marx glumly encouraged the workers of the world to unite, well aware that class solidarity was too nebulous, too factionalized, to be strongly felt. But like-minded individuals could join in communities which could be strongly imagined because they were small enough, directed enough, to make people feel part of a rule-bound, local organization. People could play for and identify with a football club or religious sect. It is more difficult for them to imagine themselves deeply devoted to 'football' or a world religion in the abstract.

In order for the modern world to emerge it was necessary not only to set up a new economic organization, a new political order, or even a set of oppositions and separations between the basic ties and demands of religion, politics, economics and kinship. Somehow the old dichotomies, community and individual, status and contract, rulers and ruled, had to be overcome. Or if one were to put it in Darwinian terms, the selfish gene is not enough. Free competition leads to Hobbes' nasty, brutish and short life. But the other extreme, the complete fusing of the individual in the organic whole is not satisfactory either, leading in extreme cases to the worlds of Stalin, Hitler, Mao and Pol Pot. A tension between competition and cooperation, self-love and social, has both to be maintained and, at the same time, resolved.

When Bernard Mandeville in the early eighteenth century began to speculate on these problems, it was clear that somehow a resolution of the conflict between 'private vice' or self-love, and 'public benefit' or social good, was possible and the 'grumbling hive' worked.[11] Yet neither he nor, to a large extent, even the Enlightenment philosophers could work out how the trick was performed. In the second half of the nineteenth century, Maine, Tönnies, Marx all applied their minds to the same problem, but none came up with a satisfactory answer, for they either thought in terms of binary oppositions (Maine and Tönnies) or tried to return mankind to some primitive, pre-oppositional, situation (Marx). Maitland accepted the disassociations and the disenchantments, the contradictions and the separations. Yet he saw beyond them to new forms of mixture of status and contract, of community and individual, which had until relatively recently never underpinned a civilization. Developing insights of Tocqueville on associations, anticipating recent work on civil society, he saw how humans had invented a system which encouraged the development of numberless small, imagined, communities which still preserved individuality.

These little groupings had bodies, they were emotionally and organizationally more than the sum of the parts, yet they were also artificial bodies. They were not based on birth or inheritance, nor were they merely chartered offshoots of the state. They were autonomous, yet regulated lightly, recognized yet largely ignored, 'nobodies' in Maitland's phrase, yet they filled the teeming middle space of open, democratic societies. This multitude of associations were the bane of all authoritarians, they needed to be 'bundled up' into the state according to those from Hobbes, through Rousseau, to Hitler and Mussolini. If they could not be incorporated into the body politic, they must be exterminated if possible. All alternative groupings to the state, whether these are artificial entities or ethnic ones, must be broken down, destroyed. As the French revolutionaries quoted by Maitland had declared, there must be no other loyalties than to the state. A world of state and citizen alone, with no cross-binding ties between citizens not mediated through the state, was proclaimed.

*

One keen insight into the importance of non-kin-based association-alism is given by Fukuzawa, who saw it from the outside. He had experienced in his childhood a world dominated by the institutional rigidities of hierarchy and the conformities of holistic familism. He had started to escape from this in Japan by moving from his home town into the great cities of Osaka and Tokyo. Yet in neither of these, beyond the glimpses in Ogata's school and elsewhere, could he see how a new institutional order could be constructed. This is what fascinated him on his visits to the West and particularly England where he was intrigued by various types of association.

So when Fukuzawa returned to Japan he tried to build up both the institutions and the arts of associationalism, that 'civil society' which alone could provide the foundational structure for modernity. There were the social and political clubs of the West, so he founded the Kojunsha social club in Tokyo, which survives to this day. It was specifically designed to emulate the London clubs, to foster discussion and a mature approach to politics, a place to talk and create networks of trust and information, share warmth and solidarity. Another kind of association, for the pursuit of knowledge, is the university, an archetype in the West of fellowship and equality. The university had been crucial in the development of western arts and science, yet it had never developed in China and Japan. So Fukuzawa started a high school which later developed into the first private Japanese university, Keio.

Or again there were the exchange banks of the West, without which Japan was losing much of its wealth. So he helped to set up one of the first new-style banks. Likewise he was active in the effort to form a modern police force and founded one of the first daily newspapers. Yet the institutions of association were not enough. He needed to go further, for without the skills to use the institutions they would never work. Practices which had long been taken for granted in the West, the arts of structured conversation, the art of the conference or public meeting, the art of making and listening to speeches (and even of clapping), the art of argument and methods of proof, the art of keeping the accounts of associations in order, all these basic skills had to be learnt for they existed, if at all, only in rudimentary form in Japan before the 1870s.

So Fukuzawa wrote a book on the art of public speaking and built a 'speech hall' in which to practise it. He wrote about the art of argument. He wrote a manual to introduce double-entry book keeping. And in all his writing and public speaking he kept his style simple and accessible so that real communication could take place. Through this and his best-selling descriptions of western institutions, including the numerous techniques of civil society, he helped to undermine the older, rigid order and replace it with a more open, pluralistic and associational one. Thus he showed both an appreciation of the secret of western civilization, the separation of spheres, and a deep understanding of the organizational technology of civil society which makes such a separation possible. He learnt from England, Holland and America the ways in which to open up a society, to build up those countervailing institutions, those 'secondary powers' which Montesquieu and Tocqueville and Maitland realized were essential for the pursuit of liberty, equality and wealth. This is why he is a principal architect of a modern, free, equal and wealthy Japan.

*

If, as Tönnies put it, the opposition is between societies based on contract, reason, the mind, in other words *Gesellschaft* (or what Maitland translated accurately not as 'association', but 'partnership'), as opposed to societies based on emotion, status, blood and place, or *Gemeinschaft* (community) then modern civilizations, in order to work and be tolerable places to live in, have somehow to find a way to fuse the two. This is what 'fellowship' or trust does. It is vaguely related to clubism, to 'matiness' in the Australian sense, but is not gendered. It makes it possible to set up meaningful, enduring, sub-communities within a basically contractual society. These 'communities' are not based on blood and place, but communities of sentiment as well as purely instrumental and practical goals, which make life worth living and complex cooperation possible. Whether a music club, a rowing club, a ballroom dancing club, a gardening club, a political club, a religious fraternity, a business organization, a charity, or a thousand other organizations, the blend of heart and mind, of emotion and reason, of the short-term instrumental and the long-term affections, of self-love and social, can be achieved. It is this invention of associational institutions which explains why most of the major charitable, social, political as well as economic, political and sporting associations were invented in England. The list would include the RSPCA, Salvation Army, Lions clubs, Boy Scouts and Girl Guides, Oxfam, Women's Institutes, Ramblers' Association, and so on almost endlessly.[12] And as Tocqueville had noticed, participation in such self-governing associations are the main bulwarks against dictatorship. The rights of associations are the protection for liberty and all totalitarian aspirants try to curtail them, usually on the pretext of war or the threat of war.

The real mystery is how such anomalous and mixed entities could arise; with too much sentiment to have been achieved by contract alone, with too much choice and reason to be ascribed purely by status. They are logical contradictions, hybrid forms, as Maitland so elegantly described. They are corporate, having bodies, yet not incorporated by the state. They are formally constituted, artificial entities, yet evoking the passionate adherence of their members. Do they have any parallels in the high animals, one wonders, that is associations based on mutual interest and proven capacities independent of birth? Some have lasted up to 700 years in the West, the universities, Inns of Court, religious brotherhoods, guilds and fraternities. Yet the great time of their proliferation was probably the seventeenth to nineteenth centuries when Britain became the richest and most powerful nation in the world. And the whole art of setting up these quasi-groups was exported to America.

This is not to argue that such an associational world had never occurred before or outside the Anglo-American region. This situation of numerous non-kinship, non-state associations is what was characteristic of the small-scale communities of western Europe in the early medieval period. Thousands of semi-contractual, semi-permanent institutions, religious fraternities, guilds, craft mysteries, liberties, vills and manors, feudal associations, universities were present. It was a community of communities. This was, to a certain extent, also the situation in medieval Japan after the collapse of the Chinese-based civilization in the eleventh and twelfth centuries. Numerous semi-contractual associations of a religious and secular kind flourished. Such periods, as in the free cities of southern Germany or Renaissance Italy, are periods of enormous innovation and energy. Yet they usually do not last for long. The parts are knitted up together, the loose confederations and liberties crushed, a few powerful institutions, Leviathan and the papacy, grow and absorb smaller entities until there is a new hierarchical and holistic world. This happened in different ways in *ancien régime* Europe and Tokugawa Japan. They were alike in seeing a move away from contract to status. In only one or two exceptional cases, for example Holland, parts of Scandinavia, England, does one see a move from contract and status to something beyond both of them, namely trust and association.

In continental Europe, with its revived Roman law from the fourteenth century, the new institutions found it difficult to survive and have several times almost been snuffed out in the twentieth century. Likewise it has been difficult for them to take hold in the communist states, which consider all alternatives to the party with deadly hostility. Nor have they always found great favour in caste-based India or, until recently, in much of Latin America. Only in Japan, where the legacy of medieval feudalism was a society already curiously modern in its separations, even if overlaid with the rigidities imposed after the Tokugawa gained dominance in the early seventeenth century, could the Anglo-American system very rapidly take root, even if it was again temporarily repressed in the period up to the Second World War.

These associations fit with a modern world in various ways. First, they tend to fit within a separated sphere. Whereas the traditional spheres tried to be hegemonic, for example kinship dominated religion and the economy, or politics tried to organize the rest, the associations were located within a particular sphere. A religious sect should not interfere much in politics or the market, a gardening club would not pronounce on religion, a sporting club should not tamper with the market. So these associations did not demand a total, but rather a partial, goal-directed, loyalty. On the other hand, they tended to be more than purely utilitarian. They had rules, demanded commitment, excluded as well as included, had a feeling of community, that is to say of belonging. The call to efficiency in pursuit of certain ends, sport, thought, politics, worship, could be heeded. Yet the individual could also have a sense of mutual friendship, fellowship, meaning, social appreciation in Smith's terms. So the whole was more than the sum of the parts.

As far as the relations between these associational groups go, this was flexible, fluid and quite relaxed. There was sometimes games-like competition, as in a college or university boat race. There was sometimes ranking. But on the whole the structure was maintained, as in other acephalous (headless) systems by the tension between the groups. In the same way, the system as a whole worked through structural tensions and contradictions and oppositions, rather than through a merging of top-downwards authority.

Thus, in theory, through the mysterious contradictions of these new mixed forms of association, the individual can expand beyond the isolation of the lonely crowd, to become part of numerous quasi-groups, the fellowship stretching from transitory ones (the pub or communal hot spring) to an enduring group making or doing things together over the years. Even if each woman and man is not part of a continent, in theory each person can visit islands of fellow-ship in a sea of atomistic, contractual, market society. This possibility, and the resolution of the logical contradiction of self-love and social, is the mysterious essence of modernity.

In a trick which is so difficult to understand, a civilization has emerged which has separated off different parts of life, the institutions of power (politics), wealth (economics), knowledge and belief (religion), warmth and procreation (kinship). But the intolerable burden of living in such a world, the enormous inefficiency of a world of isolated, non-trusting, individuals who would be the only locus of contact between the separated spheres, is overcome by a new flexible institution, whose proto-type was the trust. This is something akin to the reciprocal altruism of the biologists, but with humans is much more than that, and develops into an extraordinary mixture of flexibility and commitment, of individual and community, of calculation (reason) and loyalty (emotion). This is what gave Maitland hope that a new world which combined liberty, equality and wealth was both possible and might continue and underlay Fukuzawa's strategies for founding a new Japan.

Notes

Preface to a Study of F.W. Maitland

1 For some of the later work, see Macfarlane, *Marriage and Love* (especially the concluding chapter), *Culture of Capitalism, Savage Wars of Peace, Riddle of the World*.

1. F.W. Maitland and the Making of the Modern World

1 It is republished as the first work in Maitland, *Collected Papers*.
2 The one exception, which I discovered after this book was completed, is the excellent work by David Runciman on *Pluralism and the Personality of the State* (Cambridge, 1997), chapter 5 and pp. 66–70, which provides a detailed account of the legal background to parts of Maitland's work and a discussion of trusts and corporations.
3 Though he is not quite forgotten. On 4 January 2001 he became the first professional historian to have a memorial placed in Poet's Corner in Westminster Abbey and thus became immortal.
4 The rest of this chapter is taken from pp. 277–84 of Macfarlane, *Riddle of the Modern World*. Readers who have recently read the conclusion of that work may wish to skip the rest of this chapter.

2. The Legacy of Sir Henry Maine

1 For a useful introduction to Maine's work, see Feaver, *From Status*; Cocks, *Maine*; and Diamond (ed.), *Victorian Achievement*.
2 Cocks, *Maine*, 13.
3 For the ignoring and implicit criticism, see Cocks, *Maine*, 142–6; for explicit criticism of the fact that Maine 'trusted much to a memory that played him tricks and rarely looked back at a book that he had once read', see Maitland, *Letters*, I, 279.
4 Maine, *Ancient Law*, 185, 258.
5 Maine, *Ancient Law*, 168.
6 Maine, *Ancient Law*, 169.
7 Maine, *Ancient Law*, 170.
8 Maine, *Ancient Law*, 304.
9 Maine, *Ancient Law*, 126.
10 Maine, *Ancient Law*, 227ff.
11 Maine, *Ancient Law*, 280.
12 Maine, *Early History*, 30–1.
13 Maine, *Early History*, 76–7.
14 Maine, *Early History*, 82.
15 Maine, *Early History*, 78.

16 Maine, *Early Law and Custom*, 327.
17 Maine, *Village Communities*, 68.
18 Maine, *Village Communities*, 192.
19 Maine, *Village Communities*, 126.
20 Maine, *Village Communities*, 177.
21 Maine, *Village Communities*, 123.
22 Maine, *Village Communities*, 104.
23 Maine, *Early History*, 82.
24 Maine, *Village Communities*, 112.
25 Maine, *Village Communities*, 141.
26 Maine, *Village Communities*, 76.
27 Maine, *Early Law*, 235.
28 Maine, *Early History*, 102–3.
29 Maine, *Village Communities*, 131.
30 Maine, *Early Law*, 337.
31 Maine, *Early History*, 86–7.
32 Maine, *Village Communities*, 162, 165.
33 Maine, *Early Law*, 325.
34 Maine, *Ancient Law*, 237.
35 Maine, *Ancient Law*, 225.
36 Maine, *Ancient Law*, 225.
37 Maine, *Early Law*, 148.
38 Maine, *Ancient Law*, 295.
39 Maitland, *History*, II, 232–3.
40 Maine, *Village Communities*, 139.
41 Maine, *Village Communities*, 200–1.
42 Maine, *Early Law*, 302ff.
43 Maine, *Village Communities*, 11.
44 Maine, *Village Communities*, 83, 11.
45 Maine, *Village Communities*, 21.
46 Maine, *Early Law*, 167.
47 Maine, *Village Communities*, 147.
48 Maine, *Early Law*, 348.
49 Maine, *Early Law*, 349.
50 Maine, *Early History*, 115.
51 Maine, *Early Law*, 345.
52 Maine, *Early Law*, 149.
53 Maitland, *Collected Papers*, I, 486–7.

3. Life, Work and Methods

1 McFarlane, 'Mount Maitland'.
2 Plucknett, 'Maitland', 184–5.
3 Plucknett, 'Maitland', 191.
4 Quoted in McFarlane, 'Mount Maitland'.
5 Hudson (ed.), *History*, 262–3.
6 For a correction of the myth that it was Vinogradoff who introduced him to these records, see Plucknett, 'Maitland', 186.

7 Maitland, *Pleas of Crown*, vii.
8 Maitland, *Collected Papers*, I, 480–97.
9 Fisher in Maitland, *Constitutional*, vi.
10 Maitland, *Letters*, 80.
11 Maitland, *Letters*, 449.
12 Maitland, *Letters*, 70.
13 Maitland, *Letters*, 343.
14 Maitland, *Letters*, 349.
15 Quoted in McFarlane, 'Mount Maitland'.
16 Maitland, *Letters*, 78.
17 Maitland, *Letters*, 83.
18 Maitland, *Letters*, 87.
19 Maitland, *Letters*, 87.
20 Maitland, *Letters*, 87.
21 Maitland, *Letters*, 109.
22 Maitland, *Letters*, 138.
23 Maitland, *History*, I, vi.
24 Sayles, 'Maitland'.
25 *Letters*, ii, ed. Zutshi, p. 20.
26 *Letters*, ii, ed. Zutshi, no. 174.
27 Maitland, *Selected Essays*, 15.
28 McFarlane, *Mount Maitland*.
29 Quoted in Schuyler, *Maitland*, p. 17.
30 Maitland, *Equity*, v.
31 *Letters*, ii, ed. Zutshi, no. 122.
32 Vinogradoff, 'Maitland', 287; the connection between Maitland's style and music is explicitly or implicitly made by a number of recent writers, see Hudson (ed.), *The History of English Law*, ix and n.3.
33 See Maitland, *Letters*, II, 4.
34 Milsom, 'Review of Elton', 225.
35 Hazeltine, 'Maitland'.
36 Maitland, *Collected Papers*, I, 485–6.
37 Maitland, *Collected Works*, II, 3.
38 Maitland, *Roman Canon Law*, 131.
39 Maitland, *Domesday Book*, 356.
40 Maitland, *Domesday Book*, 520.
41 Maitland, *Letters*, 60.
42 Maitland, *History*, I, 231.
43 Maitland, *Domesday Book*, 9.
44 Maitland, *Collected Papers*, I, 488.
45 Among others Plucknett, 'Maitland', 185; Vinogradoff, 'Maitland', 288; and Paul Hyams in Hudson (ed.), *History of English Law*, 217 comment on the width of his learning and command of continental sources.
46 In Hudson (ed.), *History of English Law*, 13.
47 Maitland, *History*, I, 225.
48 Maitland, *Selected Essays*, 123.
49 Maitland, *History*, I, xxxiv.
50 Maitland, *History*, II, 210; I, 225; Maitland, *History*, I, civ; Maitland, *Forms*, 43.

51 Maitland, *History*, II, 10–11; Maitland, *Constitutional*, 20.
52 Maitland, *Constitutional*, 6–7.
53 Maitland, *Constitutional*, 7.
54 Maitland, *Constitutional*, 154.
55 Maitland, *Constitutional*, 9.
56 Maitland, *History*, I, 79.
57 Maitland, *History*, I, 88.
58 Maitland, *History*, I, 93–4.
59 See Maitland, *History*, I, 104–7.
60 Maitland, *Collected Papers*, II, 418.
61 Maitland, *Collected Papers*, II, 418.
62 Maitland, *Selected Essays*, 98.
63 Maitland, *Constitutional*, 1–2.
64 Maitland, *Constitutional*, 5.
65 Maitland, *Constitutional*, 122.
66 Maitland, *Constitutional*, 44.
67 Maitland, *Constitutional*, 148.
68 Maitland, *Constitutional*, 148.
69 Maitland, *Constitutional*, 151.
70 Maitland, *Domesday Book*, 282.
71 Maitland, *Constitutional*, 151.
72 Maitland, *History*, I, xxix.
73 Maitland, *History*, I, xxx.
74 Maitland, *History*, I, xxxi.
75 Maitland, *History*, II, 255.
76 Maitland, *History*, II, 403.
77 Maitland, *Domesday Book*, 345.
78 Maitland, *Domesday Book*, 345–6; for another similar long attack, see Maitland, *Collected Papers*, III, 294–9.
79 Maitland, *Collected Papers*, I, 470.

4. Power and Property

1 Maitland, *History*, I, 67.
2 Maitland, *Constitutional*, 152, 153.
3 Maitland, *History*, I, 237.
4 Maitland, *Domesday Book*, 258
5 Maitland, *History*, I, 68.
6 Maitland, *History*, I, 230.
7 Maitland, *Constitutional*, 143–4.
8 Maitland, *Constitutional*, 143.
9 Maitland, *History*, I, 235.
10 Maitland, *Constitutional*, 163–4; allodial property is held in absolute ownership.
11 Maitland, *History*, II, 265.
12 Maitland, *Constitutional*, 164.
13 Maitland, *Constitutional*, 161.
14 Maitland, *Constitutional*, 161.

15 Maitland, *History*, I, 303.
16 Maitland, *Constitutional*, 162.
17 Maitland, *Constitutional*, 32.
18 Maitland, *Constitutional*, 162.
19 Maitland, *Constitutional*, 162.
20 Maitland, *Constitutional*, 163.
21 Maitland, *Constitutional*, 162.
22 Maitland, *Constitutional*, 162–3.
23 Maitland, *Constitutional*, 163.
24 Maitland, *History*, I, 252–3.
25 Maitland, *History*, I, 253.
26 Maitland, *History*, I, 172; for instance, the centralized justice of *novel disseisin* and the assize of *mort d'ancestor* in the twelfth century, Maitland, *History*, I, 146–8.
27 Maitland, *History*, I, 84.
28 Maitland, *Constitutional*, 38.
29 Bloch, *Feudal*, I, 138.
30 Maitland, *Feudalism*, i, 142.
31 Bloch, *Feudal*, II, 443.
32 Maitland, *History*, II, 240–1.
33 Maitland, *History*, II, 269ff, 296–7.
34 Maitland, *History*, II, 241.
35 Maitland, *History*, II, 242.
36 Maitland, *History*, II, 243.
37 Maitland, *History*, II, 243.
38 Maitland, *History*, II, 386–7.
39 Maitland, *Domesday Book*, 349.
40 For example, see Radcliffe-Brown, *Kinship*, 15 and more generally Fox, *Kinship*, ch. 6.
41 Marx, *Capital*, III, 616.
42 Maitland, *History*, II, 308.
43 Maitland, *History*, II, 27.
44 Simpson, *Land Law*, 51.
45 Maitland, *History*, II, 309, 313.
46 Blackstone, *Commentaries*, II, 116–18, described some of the devices for doing so.
47 Chamberlayne, *Present State*, 337.
48 Macfarlane, *Individualism*, 83.
49 Maitland, *History*, II, 12–13, 446; I, 647.
50 Maitland, *History*, I, 344.
51 Maitland, *History*, II, 312.
52 Maitland, *History*, II, 260.
53 Maitland, *History*, II, 286.
54 Maitland, *History*, II, 286
55 Maitland, *History*, II, 19.
56 Maitland, *Constitutional*, 29.
57 Maitland, *History*, I, 343–4.
58 Maitland, *History*, I, 344.
59 For criticism and my replies, see Macfarlane, *Culture*, 192–7.

60   Maitland, *History*, II, 248.
61   Maitland, *History*, II, 250–1.
62   Maitland, *History*, II, 251.
63   Maitland, *History*, II, 251–2.
64   Maitland, *History*, II, 252.
65   Maitland, *History*, II, 255.

5. Social Relations

1   Maitland, *Constitutional*, 51.
2   Maitland, *Collected Papers*, II, 313.
3   Maitland, *History*, I, 534, 564.
4   Maitland, *History*, I, 616.
5   Maitland, *History*, I, 620–1.
6   Maitland, *History*, I, 623.
7   Maitland, *History*, I, 629.
8   Maitland, *History*, I, 630.
9   Maitland, *History*, I, 688.
10   Maitland, *Collected Papers*, II, 360.
11   Maitland, *Collected Papers*, II, 360.
12   For another documented discussion along the same lines, see Maitland, *Township*, 25.
13   Maitland, *Domesday Book*, 340–1.
14   Maitland, *Domesday Book*, 346.
15   Maitland, *Domesday Book*, 346, and ibid., n. 1.
16   Maitland, *Domesday Book*, 348.
17   Maitland, *Domesday Book*, 348.
18   Maitland, *Domesday Book*, 349.
19   Maitland, *Domesday Book*, 353.
20   Maitland, *Collected Papers*, II, 362.
21   Maitland, *Constitutional*, 79.
22   Maitland, *Constitutional*, 79–80.
23   Maitland, *Constitutional*, 171.
24   In Maitland, *History*, I, xlvii.
25   Maitland, *History*, I, 224; and ibid., II, 402.
26   Maitland, *History*, I, 225.
27   Maitland, *History*, II, 396–7.
28   Maitland, *History*, I, 407.
29   Maitland, *History*, I, 407.
30   Maitland, *History*, I, 408.
31   Maitland, *History*, I, 408.
32   Maitland, *History*, I, 408.
33   Maitland, *History*, I, 409, 411.
34   Maitland, *History*, II, 446.
35   Maitland, *History*, I, 411.
36   Maitland, *History*, I, 412.
37   Maitland, *Letters*, no. 86.
38   Maitland, *History*, I, 415.

39   Maitland, History, I, 416.
40   Maitland, *History*, I, 416–17.
41   Maitland, *History*, I, 417.
42   Maitland, *History*, I, 418.
43   Maitland, *History*, I, 419.
44   Maitland, *History*, I, 419.
45   Maitland, *History*, I, 428.
46   Maitland, *History*, I, 429.
47   Maitland, *History*, I, 430.
48   Maitland, *History*, I, 431.
49   Maitland, *History*, I, 432.
50   Maitland, *History*, I, 432.
51   Rogers, *Six Centuries*, 34.
52   Rogers, *Six Centuries*, 44.
53   Sugarman, 'Law', 40.
54   Maitland, *History*, II, 437.
55   Maitland, *History*, II, 438.
56   Maitland, *History*, II, 439.
57   Maitland, *History*, II, 440.
58   Maitland, *History*, II, 441.
59   Maitland, *History*, II, 403.
60   Maitland, *History*, II, 432.
61   Maitland, *History*, I, 262.
62   Maitland, *History*, II, 406.
63   Maitland, *History*, II, 437.
64   Maitland, *History*, II, 437.
65   Maitland, *History*, II, 411.
66   Maitland, *History*, II, 433.
67   Maitland, *History*, II, 433.
68   Maitland, *History*, I, 482.
69   Maitland, *History*, I, 485.

6. The Divergence of Legal Systems

1   Maitland, *History*, I, 515–16.
2   Maitland, *History*, I, 512.
3   Maitland, *Constitutional*, 100, 198–9.
4   Maitland, *History*, I, 344.
5   For example, Vinogradoff, *Roman Law*, Stein and Shand, *Legal Values*.
6   Maitland, *History*, I, xxxvi.
7   Maitland, *History*, I, 188.
8   Maitland, *History*, II, 185.
9   Maitland, *History*, II, 361.
10   Maitland, *History*, I, 344.
11   Maitland, *History*, I, 266.
12   Maitland, *Collected Papers*, II, 30–1.
13   Maitland, *Collected Papers*, II, 484–5.
14   Maitland, *Collected Papers*, II, 495–6.

15 Maitland, *History*, I, 13–14.
16 Maitland, *History*, I, 24.
17 Maitland, *Collected Papers*, II, 439–40.
18 Maitland, *Selected Essays*, 100; for a similar description, see also Maitland, *Collected Papers*, II, 428–9.
19 Maitland, *History*, I, 20–1.
20 Maitland, *History*, I, 24.
21 Maitland, *History*, I, 184.
22 Maitland, *Collected Papers*, I, 483.
23 Maitland, *History*, I, 688.
24 Maitland, *History*, I, 146.
25 Maitland, *History*, II, 445.
26 Maitland, *History*, II, 257–8.
27 Maitland, *Collected Papers*, II, 441.
28 Maitland, *Collected Papers*, II, 441.
29 Maitland, *Collected Papers*, II, 443.
30 Maitland, *Collected Papers*, II, 444.
31 Maitland, *Collected Papers*, II, 444.
32 Maitland, *Collected Papers*, II, 444–5.
33 Maitland, *Selected Essays*, 105.
34 Maitland, *Collected Papers*, II, 434.
35 Maitland, *Collected Papers*, II, 438.
36 Maitland, *Collected Papers*, II, 438.
37 Maitland, *Collected Papers*, II, 439.
38 Maitland, *Selected Essays*, ch. vii.
39 Elton, *Maitland*, 79–88 summarizes some of the arguments.

7. Fellowship and Trust

1 Fukuyama, *Trust*, has recently endorsed this general view.
2 For some of the background to his work, and particularly the relations with German jurisprudence and the work of Gierke, see Runciman, *Pluralism*, in particular chs 3–5.
3 Maitland, *History*, I, 486.
4 Maitland, *History*, I, 488.
5 Maitland, *Township*, 18.
6 Maitland, *Township*, 18.
7 Maitland, *Political Thought*, xxviii.
8 Maitland, *Political Thought*, xxx.
9 Maitland, *Political Thought*, xxx.
10 Maitland, *History*, I, 490.
11 Maitland, *Collected Papers*, III, 310.
12 Maitland, *Political Theories*, xxxi.
13 Maitland, *Collected Papers*, III, 310.
14 Maitland, *Collected Papers*, III, 311.
15 Quoted in Fisher, *Life*, 124–5.
16 Maitland, *Collected Papers*, II, 403.
17 Maitland, *Equity*, 6.

18 Maitland, *Equity*, 32.
19 Fisher, *Life*, 134.
20 Fisher, *Life*, 134.
21 *Letters*, ed. Fifoot, no. 364; see also the letter of 15 November to the same.
22 Maitland, *Collected Papers*, III, 272.
23 Fisher, *Life*, 147.
24 Maitland's hints were largely concealed. Thus even the normally perceptive John Burrow in his treatment of Maitland's work on 'the spirit of association' and the nature of the Trust can suggest that Maitland treated the subject as roughly equivalent to 'clubbability', the 'ethics of returning library books' (Burrow, 'Village Community', 280).
25 Maitland, *Equity*, 23; Otto Gierke, part of whose work Maitland translated (in *Political Theories*) was one of the very greatest of modern legal theorists.
26 Maitland, *Collected Papers*, III, 323.
27 Maitland, *Collected Papers*, III, 273.
28 Maitland, *Collected Papers*, III, 323.
29 Maitland, *Equity*, 23.
30 Maitland, *Collected Papers*, III, 322.
31 Maitland, *Collected Papers*, III, 277.
32 Maitland, *Collected Papers*, II, 404.
33 Maitland, *Collected Papers*, III, 283.
34 Maitland, *Collected Papers*, II, 407–8.
35 Maitland, *Collected Papers*, III, 335.
36 Maitland, *Collected Papers*, III, 335–6.
37 Maitland, *Collected Papers*, III, 337; for another version of this story, see Maitland, *Equity*, 26–7.
38 Maitland, *Collected Papers*, II, 492.
39 The story is well told in Maitland, *Equity*, 1–6.
40 Maitland, *Collected Papers*, III, 354.
41 Maitland, *Collected Papers*, III, 354.
42 Maitland, *Collected Papers*, II, 493.
43 Maitland, *Collected Papers*, III, 279.
44 Maitland, *Political Thought*, xxix.
45 Maitland, *Political Thought*, xxxi.
46 Maitland, *Collected Papers*, III, 365.
47 Maitland, *Collected Papers*, III, 368.
48 Maitland, *Collected Papers*, III, 367.
49 Maitland, *Collected Papers*, III, 317.
50 Maitland, *Political Theories*, xxxiv.
51 Maitland, *Political Theories*, xxiii.
52 Maitland, *Collected Papers*, III, 383.
53 Maitland, *Collected Papers*, III, 322.
54 Maitland, *Equity*, 23.
55 Maitland, *Collected Papers*, III, 272–3.
56 Maitland, *Collected Papers*, III, 275.
57 Maitland, *Equity*, 31.
58 Maitland, *Equity*, 29.

59   Maitland, *Equity*, 47–8.
60   Maitland, *Equity*, 29–30.
61   Maitland, *Equity*, 31.
62   Maitland, *Equity*, 33.
63   Maitland, *Collected Papers*, III, 325.
64   Maitland, *Equity*, 23.
65   Maitland, *Equity*, 23–4.
66   Maitland, *Collected Papers*, III, 315.
67   Maitland, *Collected Papers*, III, 283.
68   Maitland, *Political Thought*, xxxiii.
69   For an excellent and detailed account of how the Inns acted without incorporation and the various advantages of not being incorporated, see Baker, 'Inns of Court'. A number of the more general arguments in this chapter are also given depth by Professor Baker's analysis.
70   Maitland, *Collected Papers*, III, 317.
71   Maitland, *Collected Papers*, III, 370–1.
72   Maitland, *Collected Papers*, III, 387.
73   For example, Maitland, *Collected Papers*, III, 400.
74   Maitland, *Collected Papers*, III, 376.
75   Maitland, *Collected Papers*, III, 312–13.
76   Maitland, *Collected Papers*, III, 400.
77   Maitland, *Collected Papers*, III, 397.
78   Maitland, *Political Theories*, xxxvi.
79   Maitland, *Political Theories*, xxxvi.
80   Maitland, *Political Theories*, xxxvi–vii.
81   Maitland, *Collected Papers*, III, 402.
82   Maitland, *Collected Papers*, III, 403.
83   Maitland, *Political Theories*, xxv.
84   Maitland, *Collected Papers*, III, 403.
85   Maitland, *Political Theories*, xxxvi, note 3.
86   Maitland, *Collected Papers*, III, 363.
87   Maitland, *Collected Papers*, III, 364.
88   Maitland, *Collected Papers*, II, 366.
89   Maitland, *Political Theories*, xxix.
90   Maitland, *Collected Papers*, III, 369.
91   Maitland, *Political Theory*, xxix.
92   Maitland, *Collected Papers*, III, 389–92.
93   Maitland, *Collected Papers*, III, 372.
94   Maitland, *Collected Papers*, III, 374.
95   Maitland, *Collected Papers*, III, 390.
96   For example Mancur Olson in various works, including in Wilson and Skinner (eds.), *Market and State*, 109–12.
97   Maitland, *Collected Papers*, III, 322.
98   Maitland, *Collected Papers*, III, 394.
99   Maitland, *Political Thought*, xxxiii.
100 Maitland, *Collected Papers*, III, 378.
101 Maitland, *Collected Papers*, III, 376.
102 Maitland, *Collected Papers*, III, 385.
103 Maitland, *Collected Papers*, III, 377.

104 Maitland, *Collected Papers*, III, 388.
105 Maitland, *Collected Papers*, III, 278–9.
106 Maitland, *Collected Papers*, III, 356.
107 Maitland, *Collected Papers*, III, 283.
108 Maitland, *Collected Papers*, III, 279.
109 Maitland, *Political Theories*, xxv.
110 For the necessity of trust in economic development, see Fukuyama, *Trust*; for science, Shapin, *Social History*.
111 Maitland, *Collected Papers*, III, 402.
112 Maitland, *Equity*, 44.
113 Maitland, *Collected Papers*, III, 352.

8. Maitland and Durkheim

1 Parkin, *Durkheim*, 59.
2 Quoted in Lukes, *Durkheim*, 139.
3 Durkheim, *Division*, 16–17.
4 Durkheim, *Division*, 22, note.
5 Durkheim, *Division*, 169.
6 The quote is in Lukes, *Durkheim*, 197.
7 Lukes, *Durkheim*, 217.
8 Quoted in Nisbet, *Durkheim*, 11.
9 Durkheim, *Division*, 203–4.
10 Durkheim, *Division*, 123.
11 Quoted in Nisbet, *Sociology*, 78.
12 Durkheim, *Division*, 214.
13 Durkheim, *Division*, 174.
14 Durkheim, *Division*, 175.
15 Durkheim, *Division*, 181.
16 Lukes, *Durkheim*, 148, quoting Durkheim.
17 Durkheim, *Division*, 406.
18 Durkheim, *Division*, 377.
19 Parkin, *Durkheim*, 65.
20 Durkheim, *Division*, 56.
21 Durkheim, *Division*, 78.
22 Durkheim, *Division*, 29, quoted in Parkin, *Durkheim*, 27.
23 See, for example, Lukes, *Durkheim*, 159.
24 Nisbet, *Durkheim*, 69.
25 Quoted in Nisbet, *Durkheim*, 72.
26 Durkheim, *Professional*, 61.
27 Durkheim, *Division*, 28.
28 Quoted in Lukes, *Durkheim*, 325.
29 Durkheim, *Professional Ethics* quoted in Nisbet, *Durkheim*, 73.
30 Durkheim, *Suicide*, quoted in Nisbet, *Durkheim*, 68–9.
31 Durkheim, *Suicide*, quoted in Nisbet, *Durkheim*, 66.
32 Durkheim, *Division*, 10.
33 Durkheim, *Division*, 30–1.
34 Parkin, *Durkheim*, 77–9.

35 See Durkheim, *Division*, 9, 11, and *Professional Ethics*, 33.
36 Durkheim, *Division*, 5; Durkheim's emphasis.
37 Both quotations from Nisbet, *Sociology*, 135.
38 Durkheim, *Professional*, 35.
39 Durkheim, *Professional*, 31.
40 Parkin, *Durkheim*, 77.
41 Durkheim, *Suicide*, quoted in Nisbet, *Durkheim*, 67.
42 Durkheim, *Division*, 27.
43 Nisbet, *Durkheim*, 69.
44 Durkheim, *Professional*, 103.
45 Parkin, *Durkheim*, 78.
46 Quoted in Nisbet, *Sociology*, 148.
47 Durkheim, *Professional*, 65.
48 Parkin, *Durkheim*, 75.
49 Durkheim quoted in Lukes, *Durkheim*, 285.
50 Durkheim, *Division*, 19, n. 24.
51 For example, Parkin, *Durkheim*, 76.
52 It has been pointed out to me, rightly, that neither Maitland nor I have mentioned class solidarity and class consciousness. Some there has been, but, as Marx famously lamented, not enough to make it relevant to this argument.

9. Maitland Assessed

1 That is scutage, *Quia Emptores* and the writ of trespass, all technical matters.
2 Bell, *Maitland*, 30.
3 Bell, *Maitland*, 2.
4 Bell, *Maitland*, 68.
5 He argues that Maitland's disparaging view of the law book *Fleta* is too strong, that his theory that Domesday Book was a 'geld' book is wrong, and that Maitland has ignored the plaint by bill.
6 Milsom, in Maitland, *History*, I, lxxiii.
7 Milsom, 'F.W. Maitland', 281.
8 Elton, *Maitland*, 45.
9 Elton, *Maitland*, 47.
10 Elton, *Maitland*, 46.
11 Elton, *Maitland*, 48.
12 Vinogradoff, 'Maitland', 288–9.
13 Hexter, *Historians*, 156.
14 Collingwood, *Idea*, 127.
15 Hay, *Annalists*, 169.
16 Bloch, *Feudal Society*, I, xxi.
17 Maitland, *Selected Essays*, xxix.
18 Sayles, 'Maitland'.
19 Burrow, *Liberal Descent*, 131.
20 McFarlane, 'Mount Maitland'.
21 Maitland, *History*, I, lxxiii.

22 See the essays in Hudson (ed.), *History of English Law*.
23 In Hudson (ed.), *History of English Law*, 19.
24 Holt, 'Foreword', v.
25 Wormald, *Making*, xi, 17.
26 Wormald, *Making*, x.
27 Wormald, *Making*, xi.
28 Wormald, *Making*, 19.
29 Campbell, *Anglo-Saxons*, 27–8.
30 *Select Pleas*, xi–xii.
31 For one overview, see Macfarlane, *Guide*.
32 www-earlscolne.socanth.cam.ac.uk
33 See Macfarlane, *Family Life* and *Diary*.
34 Macfarlane *Resources*; Macfarlane 'Law and Custom in Japan'; Macfarlane, '"Japan" in an English Mirror'.
35 www-earlscolne.socanth.cam.ac.uk
36 Bloch, *Feudal*, I, 181.
37 Bloch, *Feudal*, I, 184.
38 Bloch, *Feudal*, II, 370.
39 Bloch, *Feudal*, I, 184.
40 Bloch, *French*, 127, 128.
41 Bloch, *Feudal*, II, 370.
42 Bloch, *Feudal*, I, 128.
43 Bloch, *Feudal*, I, 274.
44 Bloch, *Feudal*, II, 425–6.
45 Bloch, *Feudal*, II, 430, 371.
46 Bloch, *Feudal*, II, 331.
47 Bloch, *Feudal*, II, 331.
48 Bloch, *Feudal*, II, 331.
49 Bloch, *Land*, 58–9.
50 Bloch, *Land*, 61–2.
51 Bloch, *Feudal*, I, 271.
52 Bloch, *Feudal*, I, 272.
53 Bloch, *Feudal* I, 248.
54 Bloch, *Land*, 60–1.
55 Bloch, *Land*, 66.
56 Schuyler, *Maitland*, p. 20.

Preface to a Study of Yukichi Fukuzawa

1 Blacker, *Fukuzawa*, 27.
2 The others chosen were Montesquieu, Adam Smith, de Tocqueville and F.W. Maitland. The first three are described in Macfarlane, *Riddle*.
3 The only book in the English language is Blacker, *Fukuzawa*, which is extremely good but deals only with certain aspects of his work and particularly in relation to his place in the Japanese Enlightenment.

10. Yukichi Fukuzawa and the Making of the Modern World

1   Taken from *Riddle*, pp. 269–76. Those who have read *Riddle* recently may wish to to skip the rest of this chapter.

11. Early Experience and Character

1   Morse, *Day*, ii, 205; Edward Morse was one of the most acute and intelligent of the foreign visitors to Japan during the Meiji period.
2   Griffis, *Mikado*, ii, 660.
3   Griffis, *Mikado*, ii, 661.
4   Griffis, *Mikado*, ii, 660.
5   Chamberlain, *Things*, 365.
6   Chamberlain, *Things*, 366–7.
7   Bacon, *Japanese Girls*, 307.
8   Hirakawa Sukehiro in Jansen (ed.), *Cambridge*, v, 460–1.
9   Kodansha, *Illustrated Encyclopedia*, 429.
10   Blacker, *Fukuzawa*, esp. ch.4 on 'The New Learning'.
11   Beasley, *Japan*, esp. chs. 4 and 5.
12   Sukehiro in Jansen (ed.), *History of Japan*, ch. 7.
13   See for example Bowring, *Ogai*.
14   Braisted (trans.), *Meiroku Zasshi*.
15   Quoted in Blacker, *Fukuzawa*, 13.
16   Quoted in Craig, 'Fukuzawa', 148.
17   Blacker, *Fukuzawa*.
18   Fukuzawa, *Autobiography*, 303.
19   Fukuzawa, *Autobiography*, 1.
20   Fukuzawa, *Autobiography*, 12.
21   Fukuzawa, *Autobiography*, 303.
22   Fukuzawa, *Autobiography*, 44.
23   Fukuzawa, *Autobiography*, 5–6.
24   Nishikawa, 'Fukuzawa', 3.
25   Fukuzawa, *Autobiography*, 296.
26   Fukuzawa, *Autobiography*, 296.
27   Fukuzawa, *Autobiography*, 3.
28   Fukuzawa, *Autobiography*, 2.
29   Fukuzawa, *Autobiography*, 14.
30   Fukuzawa, *Autobiography*, 15.
31   Fukuzawa, *Autobiography*, 180.
32   Fukuzawa, *Autobiography*, 4.
33   Fukuzawa, *Civilization*, 185.
34   Fukuzawa, *Civilization*, 185.
35   *Koshôgumi* were daimyo attendants, consisting especially of boys who had not yet come of age; *nakakosho* 'often acted as grooms and stablemen, though their studies were not necessarily fixed'; *tomokoshô* 'often acted as close attendants on the daimyo, walking behind him carrying his sword', etc.; *koyakunin* were 'low ranking samurai with

various light duties such as guarding the gate'; *ashigaru* were the 'lowest rank of samurai, sometimes hardly considered to have samurai status', Fukuzawa, *Kyûhanjô*, 309.
36 Fukuzawa, *Kyûhanjô*, 309.
37 Fukuzawa, *Kyûhanjô*, 310.
38 Fukuzawa, *Kyûhanjô*, 311; the use of the terms *kyunin* for upper samurai, and *kachi* for lower samurai, we are told is 'unusual, and may have been peculiar to the Nakatsu clan'.
39 Fukuzawa, *Kyûhanjô*, 310.
40 Fukuzawa, *Kyûhanjô*, 311.
41 Fukuzawa, *Kyûhanjô*, 317.
42 Fukuzawa, *Kyûhanjô*, 310–11.
43 Fukuzawa, *Kyûhanjô*, 318.
44 Fukuzawa, *Kyûhanjô*, 318.
45 Fukuzawa, *Kyûhanjô*, 318.
46 Fukuzawa, *Kyûhanjô*, 312–13; a *koku* is a measure of rice, the average annual consumption of one person.
47 Fukuzawa, *Kyûhanjô*, 314.
48 Fukuzawa, *Kyûhanjô*, 313.
49 Fukuzawa, *Kyûhanjô*, 320.
50 Fukuzawa, *Kyûhanjô*, 313.
51 Fukuzawa, *Kyûhanjô*, 317; a *furoshiki* is a cloth for wrapping books or other objects.
52 Fukuzawa, *Autobiography*, 331.
53 Fukuzawa, *Autobiography*, 261.
54 Fukuzawa, *Autobiography*, 329.
55 The arrangements were very complicated and only partly described in Fukuzawa, *Autobiography*, 42. I am grateful to Professor Nishikawa for advice on this point.
56 Fukuzawa, *Civilization*, 156.
57 Fukuzawa, *Autobiography*, 49.
58 Fukuzawa, *Speeches*, 74.
59 Blacker, *Fukuzawa*, 71.
60 Fukuzawa, *Autobiography*, 179.
61 Fukuzawa, *Civilization*, 136.
62 Fukuzawa, *Civilization*, 136.
63 Fukuzawa, *Autobiography*, 6.
64 Fukuzawa, *Civilization*, 39.
65 Fukuzawa, *Civilization*, 155.
66 Fukuzawa, *Autobiography*, 179.
67 Fukuzawa, *Autobiography*, 180.
68 Fukuzawa, *Civilization*, 168.
69 Fukuzawa, *Autobiography*, 18.
70 Fukuzawa, *Autobiography*, 9.
71 Fukuzawa, *Autobiography*, 9.
72 Fukuzawa, *Autobiography*, 35.
73 Fukuzawa, *Autobiography*, 10.
74 Fukuzawa, *Learning*, 75.
75 Fukuzawa, *Autobiography*, 16–17.

76   Fukuzawa, *Autobiography*, 17.
77   Fukuzawa, *Learning*, 94.
78   Fukuzawa, *Civilization*, 111–12.
79   Fukuzawa, *Civilization*, 149.
80   Fukuzawa, *Autobiography*, 336.
81   Chamberlain, *Things*, 408.
82   Fukuzawa, *Learning*, 98.
83   Fukuzawa, *Autobiography*, 85.
84   Fukuzawa, *Learning*, 93.
85   Fukuzawa, *Learning*, 93.
86   Fukuzawa, *Learning*, 93.
87   Quoted in Craig, 'Fukuzawa', 134.
88   Fukuzawa, *Autobiography*, 290.
89   Fukuzawa, *Autobiography*, 325.
90   Fukuzawa, *Autobiography*, 19.
91   Fukuzawa, *Autobiography*, 19.
92   Fukuzawa, *Autobiography*, 324.
93   Fukuzawa, *Autobiography*, 286.
94   Fukuzawa, *Autobiography*, 325.
95   Fukuzawa, *Autobiography*, 79.
96   Fukuzawa, *Autobiography*, 309.
97   Fukuzawa, *Autobiography*, 315.
98   Fukuzawa, *Autobiography*, 309.
99   Fukuzawa, *Autobiography*, 321.
100   Fukuzawa, *Autobiography*, 315.
101   Fukuzawa, *Autobiography*, 284.
102   Fukuzawa, *Autobiography*, 286.
103   Fukuzawa, *Autobiography*, 209.
104   Fukuzawa, *Autobiography*, 314.
105   Fukuzawa, *Autobiography*, 11.
106   Fukuzawa, *Autobiography*, 287.
107   Fukuzawa, *Autobiography*, 265.
108   Fukuzawa, *Autobiography*, 292.
109   Fukuzawa, *Autobiography*, 296.
110   Fukuzawa, *Autobiography*, 271.
111   Fukuzawa, *Autobiography*, 295.
112   Fukuzawa, *Autobiography*, 52.
113   Fukuzawa, *Autobiography*, 326.
114   Fukuzawa, *Autobiography*, 328.
115   Fukuzawa, *Women*, 85.
116   Fukuzawa, *Women*, 200.
117   Fukuzawa, *Women*, 134.

12. Travels and Comparisons

1   Fukuzawa, *Autobiography*, 20.
2   Fukuzawa, *Autobiography*, 19.
3   Fukuzawa, *Autobiography*, 21.

4 Fukuzawa, *Autobiography*, 21.
5 Fukuzawa, *Autobiography*, 22.
6 Fukuzawa, *Autobiography*, 25.
7 Fukuzawa, *Autobiography*, 25–6.
8 Fukuzawa, *Autobiography*, 84.
9 Fukuzawa, *Autobiography*, 88.
10 Fukuzawa, *Autobiography*, 88.
11 Fukuzawa, *Autobiography*, 89.
12 Fukuzawa, *Autobiography*, 91.
13 Fukuzawa, *Autobiography*, 216.
14 Quoted in Kato, *Japanese Literature*, III, 81.
15 Fukuzawa, *Autobiography*, 92.
16 Fukuzawa, *Autobiography*, 98.
17 Fukuzawa, *Autobiography*, 98.
18 Fukuzawa, *Autobiography*, 101.
19 Fukuzawa, *Collected Works*, 34.
20 Fukuzawa, *Autobiography*, 104.
21 Fukuzawa, *Autobiography*, 115–16.
22 Fukuzawa, *Autobiography*, 113.
23 Fukuzawa, *Autobiography*, 116.
24 Fukuzawa, *Autobiography*, 116.
25 Fukuzawa, *Autobiography*, 114.
26 Fukuzawa, *Autobiography*, 116.
27 Fukuzawa, *Autobiography*, 120.
28 Fukuzawa, *Autobiography*, 116.
29 Nishikawa, 'Fukuzawa', 5.
30 Fukuzawa, *Autobiography*, 124.
31 Fukuzawa, *Autobiography*, 125.
32 Fukuzawa, *Autobiography*, 131.
33 Fukuzawa, *Autobiography*, 132.
34 Fukuzawa, *Collected Works*, 37.
35 Fukuzawa, *Autobiography*, 154.
36 Fukuzawa, *Autobiography*, 115.
37 Fukuzawa, *Autobiography*, 133.
38 Fukuzawa, *Collected Works*, 38.
39 Fukuzawa, *Autobiography*, 134.
40 Fukuzawa, *Autobiography*, 131.
41 Blacker, *Fukuzawa*, 6–7; for a fuller account see Blacker, 'First Japanese Mission'.
42 Fukuzawa, *Collected Works*, 40.
43 Fukuzawa, *Autobiography*, 129.
44 Fukuzawa, *Autobiography*, 134.
45 Fukuzawa, *Autobiography*, 134–5.
46 Fukuzawa, *Autobiography*, 133; the work is more normally given the translated title of 'Conditions in the West'.
47 Blacker, *Fukuzawa*, 7.
48 Fukuzawa, *Autobiography*, 333.
49 Fukuzawa, *Kyûhanjô*, 327.
50 Fukuzawa, *Women*, 80.

51 Fukuzawa, *Civilization*, 67.
52 Fukuzawa, *Autobiography*, 276.
53 Fukuzawa, *Civilization*, 172.
54 Fukuzawa, *Collected Works*, 30.
55 Fukuzawa, *Civilization*, 1–2.
56 Fukuzawa, *Collected Works*, 62.
57 Fukuzawa, *Civilization*, 99.
58 Fukuzawa, *Women*, 148.
59 Fukuzawa, *Women*, 148.
60 Fukuzawa, *Civilization*, 44.
61 Fukuzawa, *Learning*, 99.
62 Fukuzawa, *Learning*, 99.
63 Fukuzawa, *Women*, 96.
64 Fukuzawa, *Learning*, 95.
65 Fukuzawa, *Kyûhanjô*, 308.
66 Fukuzawa, *Civilization*, 3.
67 Fukuzawa, *Civilization*, 3.

13. The Making of a New Japan

1 Fukuzawa, *Autobiography*, 199–200.
2 Fukuzawa, *Collected Works*, 44.
3 Quoted in Blacker, *Fukuzawa*, 27.
4 Blacker, *Fukuzawa*, 28.
5 Blacker, *Fukuzawa*, 28.
6 Fukuzawa, *Autobiography*, 182.
7 Fukuzawa, *Autobiography*, 183.
8 Fukuzawa, *Autobiography*, 183.
9 Fukuzawa, *Autobiography*, 185.
10 Fukuzawa, *Autobiography*, 273.
11 From the preface, quoted in Nishikawa, 'Fukuzawa', 6.
12 *Kodansha Encyclopedia*, s.v. *Seiyō Jijō*, 54.
13 *Kodansha Encyclopedia*, s.v. *Seiyō Jijō*, 54.
14 Fukuzawa, *Collected Works*, 41.
15 Fukuzawa, *Collected Works*, 41.
16 Fukuzawa, *Autobiography*, 334.
17 Fukuzawa, *Collected Works*, 90.
18 Fukuzawa, *Autobiography*, 282–3.
19 Fukuzawa, *Autobiography*, 219.
20 Blacker, *Fukuzawa*, 11.
21 Fukuzawa, *Autobiography*, 335.
22 Blacker, *Fukuzawa*, 27.
23 Fukuzawa, *Collected Works*, 80.
24 Fukuzawa, *Collected Works*, 80–1.
25 Fukuzawa, *Collected Works*, 81.
26 Fukuzawa, *Collected Works*, 81.
27 Fukuzawa, *Collected Works*, 82.
28 Nishikawa, 'Fukuzawa', 8.

29 Fukuzawa, *Autobiography*, 246.
30 Fukuzawa, *Collected Works*, 38.
31 Fukuzawa, *Collected Works*, 38.
32 Fukuzawa, *Speeches*, 21.
33 Fukuzawa, *Collected Works*, 87.
34 Fukuzawa, *Civilization*, 91.
35 Fukuzawa, 'Kyûhanjô', 323–4.
36 Fukuzawa, 'Kyûhanjô', 324.
37 Fukuzawa, 'Kyûhanjô', 325.
38 Fukuzawa, *Civilization*, 160.
39 Fukuzawa, *Civilization*, 189.
40 Fukuzawa, *Civilization*, 189.
41 Fukuzawa, *Women*, 79.
42 Fukuzawa, *Autobiography*, 214.
43 Fukuzawa, *Autobiography*, 246–7.
44 Fukuzawa, *Civilization*, 189.
45 Fukuzawa, *Civilization*, 193.
46 Fukuzawa, *Civilization*, 195.
47 Fukuzawa, *Autobiography*, 214–15.
48 Fukuzawa, *Autobiography*, 334.
49 Blacker, *Fukuzawa*, 93.
50 Fukuzawa, *Civilization*, 2.
51 Fukuzawa, *Civilization*, 192.
52 Fukuzawa, *Autobiography*, 110.
53 Fukuzawa, *Learning*, 30.
54 Fukuzawa, *Civilization*, 18.
55 Fukuzawa, *Civilization*, 37.
56 Fukuzawa, *Civilization*, 17.
57 Blacker, *Fukuzawa*, 30.
58 Blacker, *Fukuzawa*, 30.
59 Blacker, *Fukuzawa*, 32.
60 Blacker, *Fukuzawa*, 129.
61 Blacker, *Fukuzawa*, 130.
62 Blacker, *Fukuzawa*, 130.
63 Blacker, *Fukuzawa*, 131.
64 Nishikawa, 'Fukuzawa', 13.
65 Blacker, *Fukuzawa*, 132.
66 Blacker, *Fukuzawa*, 134.
67 Fukuzawa, *Women*, 50.
68 Blacker, *Fukuzawa*, 135.
69 Blacker, *Fukuzawa*, 137.
70 Craig, 'Fukuzawa', 126.
71 Quoted in Craig, 'Fukuzawa', 126.
72 Quoted in Craig, 'Fukuzawa', 128–9, emphasis added by Craig.
73 Craig, 129.
74 Craig, 147.
75 Craig, 135.
76 Yasukawa, 'Fukuzawa Yukichi', 21–2. See also pp. 29–36 for further evidence of his nationalist ideas.

77 Quoted in Craig, 'Fukuzawa', 136; cf. the same passage in *Autobiography*, 335.
78 Craig, 'Fukuzawa', 136.
79 Fukuzawa, *Learning*, 60.
80 Fukuzawa, *Learning*, 60.
81 Fukuzawa, *Autobiography*, 333.
82 Fukuzawa, *Autobiography*, 335.

14. The Essence of the Modern World

1 Fukuzawa, *Collected Works*, 4.
2 Fukuzawa, *Collected Works*, 5.
3 Fukuzawa, *Collected Works*, 6.
4 Fukuzawa, *Autobiography*, 217.
5 Fukuzawa, *Collected Works*, 6.
6 Fukuzawa, *Collected Works*, 2.
7 Nishikawa, 'Fukuzawa', 8.
8 Fukuzawa, *Autobiography*, 146.
9 Fukuzawa, *Collected Works*, 10.
10 Fukuzawa, *Collected Works*, 36.
11 Fukuzawa, *Collected Works*, 37.
12 I owe this example to the kindness of Toshiko Nakamura.
13 See William and Robert Chambers (publisher), *Political Economy for Use in Schools, and for Private Instruction* (Edinburgh, 1852), 53–4, actually written by John Hill Burton.
14 From Craig, 'Fukuzawa', 106, and note 10.
15 Fukuzawa, *Collected Works*, 51.
16 Fukuzawa, *Women*, 170.
17 Nishikawa, 'Fukuzawa', 9.
18 Fukuzawa, *Women*, 171.
19 Fukuzawa, *Women*, 172.
20 Fukuzawa, *Women*, 171.
21 Fukuzawa, *Civilization*, 53.
22 Fukuzawa, *Civilization*, 52–3.
23 Fukuzawa, *Civilization*, 52–3.
24 Fukuzawa, *Civilization*, 15.
25 Blacker, *Fukuzawa*, 146, note 15.
26 Nishikawa, 'Fukuzawa', 17, note 26.
27 Blacker, *Fukuzawa*, 146, note 15.
28 Fukuzawa, *Civilization*, 14.
29 Blacker, *Fukuzawa*, 98–9.
30 Blacker, *Fukuzawa*, 112.
31 Blacker, *Fukuzawa*, 92–3.
32 Craig, 'Fukuzawa', 124.
33 Craig, 'Fukuzawa, 137.
34 Fukuzawa, *Civilization*, 147.
35 Fukuzawa, *Civilization*, 135.
36 Fukuzawa, *Civilization*, 125.

37 Fukuzawa, *Civilization*, 135.
38 Fukuzawa, *Civilization*, 125.
39 Fukuzawa, *Civilization*, 160.
40 Fukuzawa, *Civilization*, 135.
41 Fukuzawa, *Civilization*, 135.
42 Blacker, *Fukuzawa*, 110.
43 Blacker, *Fukuzawa*, 108.
44 Fukuzawa, *Learning*, 70.
45 Fukuzawa, *Civilization*, 155.
46 Fukuzawa, *Civilization*, 138.
47 Fukuzawa, *Civilization*, 21–2.
48 Fukuzawa, *Civilization*, 22.
49 Fukuzawa, *Civilization*, 22.
50 Polanyi, *Great Transformation*.
51 See Macfarlane, *Individualism*, ch. 2, for a summary of their views.
52 Fukuzawa, *Autobiography*, 262.
53 Fukuzawa, *Autobiography*, 263.
54 Fukuzawa, *Autobiography*, 281.
55 Fukuzawa, *Autobiography*, 285.
56 Fukuzawa, *Autobiography*, 190.
57 Fukuzawa, *Autobiography*, 190.
58 As Koestler, *Lotus*, 221, for instance, noted.
59 Fukuzawa, *Autobiography*, 190.
60 Fukuzawa, *Autobiography*, 191.
61 Fukuzawa, *Civilization*, 123.
62 Fukuzawa, *Civilization*, 122.
63 Fukuzawa, *Civilization*, 145.
64 Blacker, *Fukuzawa*, 49; cf. 87.

15. Liberty, Equality and Human Relations

1 Fukuzawa, *Civilization*, 65.
 2 Fukuzawa, *Civilization*, 160.
 3 Fukuzawa, *Civilization*, 161.
 4 Fukuzawa, *Civilization*, 153.
 5 Fukuzawa, *Civilization*, 153.
 6 Fukuzawa, *Civilization*, 153.
 7 Fukuzawa, *Civilization*, 73.
 8 Fukuzawa, *Learning*, 3.
 9 Fukuzawa, *Women*, 101.
10 Fukuzawa, *Learning*, 50.
11 Fukuzawa, *Civilization*, 155.
12 Fukuzawa, *Civilization*, 160–1.
13 Fukuzawa, *Civilization*, 161.
14 Fukuzawa, *Women*, 81–2.
15 Fukuzawa, *Women*, 30.
16 Fukuzawa, *Autobiography*, 245.
17 Fukuzawa, *Autobiography*, 193.

18 Blacker, *Fukuzawa*, 101.
19 Fukuzawa, *Learning*, 10.
20 Fukuzawa, *Learning*, 1.
21 Fukuzawa, *Learning*, 10.
22 Fukuzawa, *Learning*, 10.
23 Fukuzawa, *Civilization*, 161.
24 Fukuzawa, *Speeches*, 72.
25 Fukuzawa, *Speeches*, 72.
26 Fukuzawa, *Women*, x.
27 Fukuzawa, *Women*, 117.
28 Fukuzawa, *Autobiography*, 114.
29 Fukuzawa, *Women*, 177; the reference to bathing together was obviously an allusion to the widespread custom of men and women bathing in the same public bath or hot spring in Japan.
30 Fukuzawa, *Women*, 35.
31 Fukuzawa, *Civilization*, 116.
32 Fukuzawa, *Autobiography*, 304.
33 Fukuzawa, *Women*, 14.
34 Fukuzawa, *Women*, 39.
35 Fukuzawa, *Women*, 61.
36 Fukuzawa, *Women*, 60.
37 Fukuzawa, *Women*, 9.
38 Fukuzawa, *Women*, 11.
39 Fukuzawa, *Women*, 11.
40 Fukuzawa, *Women*, 18.
41 Fukuzawa, *Women*, 157.
42 Fukuzawa, *Women*, 199–200.
43 Fukuzawa, *Women*, 57.
44 Fukuzawa, *Women*, 218.
45 Fukuzawa, *Women*, 53–4.
46 Fukuzawa, *Women*, 51.
47 Fukuzawa, *Women*, 10.
48 Fukuzawa, *Women*, 12.
49 Fukuzawa, *Women*, 26.
50 Fukuzawa, *Women*, 75.
51 Fukuzawa, *Women*, 39.
52 Fukuzawa, *Learning*, 52.
53 Fukuzawa, *Learning*, 52.
54 Fukuzawa, *Women*, 211.
55 Fukuzawa, *Learning*, 52.
56 Fukuzawa, *Learning*, 69.
57 Fukuzawa, *Women*, 128.
58 Fukuzawa, *Women*, 103.
59 Fukuzawa, *Women*, 118.
60 Fukuzawa, *Women*, 128–9.
61 Fukuzawa, *Women*, 129.
62 Fukuzawa, *Women*, 226.
63 Fukuzawa, *Women*, 226.
64 Fukuzawa, *Women*, 226.

65 Fukuzawa, *Women*, 227.
66 Fukuzawa, *Women*, 129.
67 Fukuzawa, *Women*, 130.
68 Fukuzawa, *Women*, 48.
69 Fukuzawa, *Women*, 48–9.
70 Fukuzawa, *Women*, 120.
71 Fukuzawa, *Women*, 120.
72 Fukuzawa, *Women*, 120.
73 Fukuzawa, *Women*, 229.
74 Fukuzawa, *Women*, 123.
75 Fukuzawa, *Women*, 229.
76 Fukuzawa, *Women*, 188.
77 Fukuzawa, *Women*, 230.
78 Fukuzawa, *Women*, 230.
79 Fukuzawa, *Women*, 139.
80 Fukuzawa, *Women*, 19.
81 Fukuzawa, *Women*, 124.
82 Fukuzawa, *Women*, 124.
83 Fukuzawa, *Women*, 139.
84 Fukuzawa, *Women*, 128.
85 Fukuzawa, *Women*, 179–80.
86 Fukuzawa, *Women*, 181.
87 Fukuzawa, *Women*, 239–40.
88 Fukuzawa, *Women*, 33.
89 Fukuzawa, *Women*, 48.
90 Nakamura, 'Fukuzawa'.
91 Fukuzawa, *Learning*, 70–1.
92 Fukuzawa, *Learning*, 71.
93 Fukuzawa, *Civilization*, 182; Fukuzawa was speaking of the early 1870s.
94 Fukuzawa, *Women*, 195.
95 Fukuzawa, *Autobiography*, 300.
96 Fukuzawa, *Autobiography*, 299.
97 Blacker, *Fukuzawa*, 157–8.
98 Fukuzawa, *Women*, xiv.
99 Craig, 'Fukuzawa', 103, n. 7.
100 In particular Toshiko Nakamura, 'Fukuzawa Yukichi's Ideas on Family in Civilization', *The Hokkaido Law Review*, vol. XLIV, nos. 3, 4, 6 (1993) and a number of conversations I have had with Professor Nakamura where she has explained her ideas to me.
101 Macfarlane, *Marriage*.

16. The Making of the Modern World

1 Macfarlane, *Savage* and *Riddle*.
2 Macfarlane, *Riddle*.
3 Tocqueville, *Ancien*, 6–7.
4 See Fukuyama, *End of History*, 50.
5 Wrigley, *People, Continuity*.

6 Rostow, *Stages*.
7 For a strong expression of such a view by a distinguished historian, see William McNeill in Hall and Jarvie, *Gellner*, 571–2.
8 See the introductions to Macfarlane, *Individualism*, and *Culture*.
9 Campbell, *Anglo-Saxon*, xxix, 261, 267, 259.
10 See for example the work of E. Gellner, particularly *Conditions of Liberty* and, for a more critical assessment, from an East European perspective, Hann and Dunn, *Civil Society*.
11 Mandeville, *Fable*.
12 See Veliz, 'A World Invented in England' in *New World*.

Bibliography

The bibliography includes all works referred to in the text, except for those by the two main authors – Fukuzawa and Maitland. Their works are listed at the front of the work. All books are published in London, unless otherwise indicated.
The following abbreviations have been used.

ed.	edited or editor
edn	edition
eds.	editors
Jnl.	Journal
n.d.	no date
tr.	translated by
Univ.	University

Beasley, W.G., *Japan Encounters the Barbarians: Japanese Travellers in America and Europe*, New Haven, 1995
Bell, H.E., *Maitland. A Critical Examination and Assessment*, 1965
Blacker, Carmen, 'The First Japanese Mission to England', *History Today*, vii (Dec. 1957).
Blacker, Carmen, *The Japanese Enlightenment, A Study of the Writings of Fukuzawa Yukichi*, Cambridge, 1969.
Blackstone, William, *Commentaries on the Laws of England*, 18th edn, 1829.
Bloch, Marc, *Feudal Society*, 2nd edn, 1962, tr. L.A. Manyon.
Bloch, Marc, *Land and Work in Medieval Europe*, 1967, tr. J.E. Anderson.
Bloch, Marc, *French Rural History: An Essay on its Basic Characteristics*, 1966, tr. J. Sondheimer.
Bolingbroke, Viscount, *The Philosophical Works of the Late Right Honorable Henry St John, Lord Viscount Bolingbroke*, 5 vols, London, 1754 (pub. David Mallet).
Bowring, Richard, *Mori Ōgai and the Modernization of Japanese Culture*, Cambridge, 1979.
Braisted, William R. (trans.), *Meiroku Zasshi, Journal of the Japanese Enlightenment*, Tokyo, 1976.
Burrow, J.W., '"The Village Community" and the uses of History in Late Nineteenth Century England', in Neil McKendrick (ed.), *Historical Perspectives: Studies in English Thought*, 1974.
Burrow, J.W., *A Liberal Descent; Victorian Historians on the English Past*, Cambridge, 1987.
Campbell, James, *The Anglo-Saxon State*, 2000.
Campbell, R.H. and Skinner, A.S., *Adam Smith*, 1982.
Chamberlain, Basil Hall, *Japanese Things, Being Notes on Various Subjects Connected with Japan* (1904), Tokyo, 1990.
Chamberlayne, E., *The Present State of England*, 19th impression, 1700.

Cocks, Raymond J.C., *Sir Henry Maine: A Study in Victorian Jurisprudence*, Cambridge, 1988.

Collingwood, R.G., *The Idea of History*, Oxford, 1961.

Craig, Albert M., 'Fukuzawa Yukichi: The Philosophical Foundations of Meiji Nationalism', in Robert E. Ward (ed.), *Political Development in Modern Japan*, New Jersey, 1968.

Diamond, Alan (ed.), *The Victorian Achievement of Sir Henry Maine*, Cambridge, 1991

Durkheim, Emile, *The Division of Labour in Society* (1893), Free Press edn, New York, 1964, trans. George Simpson.

Durkheim, Emile, *Professional Ethics and Civic Morals*, 1957, tr. Corneila Brookfield.

Elton, Geoffrey, *F.W. Maitland*, 1985.

Feaver, George A., *From Status to Contract: A Biography of Sir Henry Maine, 1822–88*, 1969.

Fisher, H.A.L., *Frederick William Maitland*, Cambridge, 1910.

Fox, Robin, *Kinship and Marriage*, Penguin, 1967.

Fukuyama, Francis, *The End of History and the Last Man*, 1992.

Ganshoff, F.L., *Feudalism*, tr. Philip Grierson, 3rd edn, 1964.

Gellner, Ernest, *Conditions of Liberty; Civil Society and its Rivals*, 1996.

Griffis, W.E., *The Mikado's Empire*, 2 vols, New York, 1903.

Hall, John and Jarvie, Ian (eds.), *The Social Philosophy of Ernest Gellner*, Amsterdam, 1996.

Hann, Christopher and Dunn, Elizabeth (eds.), *Civil Society, Challenging Western Models*, 1996.

Hay Denys, *Annalists and Historians, Western Historiography from the Eighth to the Eighteenth Centuries*, 1977.

Hazeltine, H.D., 'Maitland, Frederic William', in *Encyclopedia of the Social Sciences*, 1st edn, vol. X, New York, 1935.

Hexter, J.H., *On Historians, Re-appraisals of Some of the Makers of Modern History*, 1979.

Holt, J.C., 'Foreword' to F.W. Maitland, *Domesday Book and Beyond*, new edn, Cambridge, 1987.

Hudson, John, (ed.), *The History of English Law; Centenary Essays on 'Pollock and Maitland'*, Oxford, 1996.

Hume, David, *Essays, Literary, Moral and Political*, n.d. *c.* 1870; Ward, Lock & Tyler reprint of 2 vols. octavo edn.

Jansen, Marius B. (ed.), *Cambridge History of Japan; the Nineteenth Century*, vol. V, Cambridge, 1989.

Kames, Lord, *Sketches of the History of Man*, Basel (Basle), 1796.

Kato, Shuichi, *A History of Japanese Literature, Vol. 3, The Modern Years*, tr. Don Sanderson, Tokyo, 1979.

Kodansha Encyclopedia of Japan, Tokyo, 1983.

Kodansha, *Japan. An Illustrated Encyclopedia*, Tokyo, 1993.

Koestler, Arthur, *The Lotus & the Robot*, 1960

Lukes, Steven, *Emile Durkheim; His Life and Work*, 1973.

Lux, Kenneth, *Adam Smith's Mistake*, 1990.

Macfarlane, Alan, *The Family Life of Ralph Josselin; An Essay in Historical Anthropology*, Cambridge, 1970.

Macfarlane, Alan (ed.), *The Diary of Ralph Josselin*, Oxford, 1976.

Macfarlane, Alan, *Reconstructing Historical Communities*, Cambridge, 1977.

Macfarlane, Alan, *The Origins of English Individualism*, Oxford, 1978.

Macfarlane, Alan, *A Guide to English Historical Records*, Cambridge, 1983.

Macfarlane, Alan, *Marriage and Love in England 1300–1840*, Oxford, 1986

Macfarlane, Alan, *The Culture of Capitalism*, Oxford, 1987.

Macfarlane, Alan, *The Savage Wars of Peace: England, Japan and the Malthusian Trap*, Oxford, 1997

Macfarlane, Alan, *The Riddle of the Modern World; Liberty, Wealth and Equality*, 2000.

McFarlane, K.B., 'Mount Maitland' in *New Statesman*, 4 June 1965.

Maine, Sir Henry S., *Ancient Law* (1861), 13th edn, 1890.

Maine, Sir Henry S., *Village-Communities in the East and West* (1871), 3rd edn, 1876.

Maine, Sir Henry S., *Lectures on the Early History of Institutions*, 1875.

Maine, Sir Henry S., *Dissertations on Early Law and Custom* (1883), new impression 1901.

Mandeville, Bernard, *The Fable of the Bees*, ed. Philip Harth, Penguin, 1970.

Marx, Karl, *Capital*, vol. III, Lawrence and Wishart edn, 1954.

Milsom, S.F.C. 'A Supremely Good Historian', review of G.R. Elton, *F.W. Maitland* in *Times Literary Supplement*, 28 February 1986.

Milsom, S.F.C., 'F.W. Maitland', *Proceedings of the British Academy*, LXVI (1980).

Nakamura, Toshiko, 'Fukuzawa Yukichi's Ideas on Family in Civilization', parts 1–3, *Hokkaido Law Review*, vol. XLIV, nos. 3, 4, 6 (1993).

Nisbet, Robert A., *Emile Durkheim*, New Jersey, 1965, with selected essays by others.

Nisbet, Robert A., *The Sociology of Emile Durkheim*, 1975.

Nishikawa, Shunsaku, 'Yukichi Fukuzawa (1835–1901)', in *Prospects*, vol. XXI, no. 2, UNESCO, 1991, reprinted in *Fukuzawa Yukichi nenkan*, vol. 20, December 1993.

Parkin, Frank, *Durkheim*, Oxford, 1992.

Phillipson, Nicholas, *Hume* (1989).

Plucknett, T.F.T., 'Maitland's View of Law and History', *Law Quarterly Review*, vol. 67 (1951).

Polanyi, Karl, *The Great Transformation*, Boston, 1957.

Popper, Karl, *The Open Society and Its Enemies*, 1966.

Radcliffe-Brown, A.R. and Forde, Daryll (eds.), *African Systems of Kinship and Marriage*, Oxford, 1950.

Ross, Ian Simpson, *The Life of Adam Smith*, Oxford, 1995.

Rostow, Walt W., *The Stages of Economic Growth*, Cambridge, 1962.

Runciman, David, *Pluralism and the Personality of the State*, Cambridge, 1997.

Sayles, G.O., 'Frederic William Maitland' in *International Encyclopedia of the Social Sciences*, 2nd edn., 1968.

Schuyler, Robert Livingstone, *Frederic William Maitland. Historian*, 1960.

Shapin, Steven, *A Social History of Truth*, Chicago, 1994.

Simpson, A.W.B., *An Introduction to the History of the Land Law*, Oxford, 1973.

Skinner, Andrew S. and Wilson, Thomas (eds.), *Essays on Adam Smith*, Oxford, 1975.

Smith, Adam, *The Theory of Moral Sentiments* (1759), George Bell, 1907.

Stein, Peter and Shand, John, *Legal Values in Western Society*, Edinburgh, 1974.

Sugiyama, Chuhei, 'Fukuzawa Yukichi', *Enlightenment and Beyond; Political Economy Comes to Japan*, eds. Chuhei Sugiyama and Hiroshi Mizuta, Tokyo, 1988.

Surgarman, David, 'In the Spirit of Weber; Law, Modernity and "The Peculiarities of the English"', *Institute for Legal Studies*, Working Paper, Series 2 (Univ. of Wisconsin-Madison Law School).

Stubbs, William, *The Constitutional History of England*, Oxford, 1974–8.

Thorold Rogers, J.E., *Six Centuries of Work and Wages*, 12th edn, 1917.

Tocqueville, Alexis de, *L'Ancien Régime* (1856), tr. by M.W. Patterson, Oxford, 1956.

Veliz, Claudio, *The New World of the Gothic Fox: Culture and Economy in English and Spanish America*, California Univ. Press, 1991.

Vinogradoff, Paul, 'Frederic William Maitland', *English Historical Review*, vol. xxii, April 1907.

Vinogradoff, Paul, *Roman Law in Medieval Europe*, Oxford, 1929.

Weber, Max, *The Protestant Ethic and the Spirit of Capitalism*, 1930, tr. Talcott Parsons.

Wormald, Patrick, *The Making of English Law: King Alfred to the Twelfth Century*, vol. I, Oxford, 1999.

Wrigley, E.A. *Peoples, Cities and Wealth: the Transformation of Traditional Society*, Oxford, 1992.

Yasukawa, Jyunosuke, 'Fukuzawa Yukichi', in *Ten Great Educators of Modern Japan*, ed. Benjamin C. Duke, Tokyo, 1989.

Index

as protection against lords and
church   79
unified   12, 78
monasteries, rights in land   56
money, Fukuzawa's fear of   222–3
Mongol invasions   144
monopoly   103, 266
Montesquieu, Baron de   4, 6, 10,
75, 150, 210
compared with Durkheim   119
compared with Maitland   34,
134
German origins of liberty and
equality   7, 42
on historical progress   142–4
need for balancing institutions
114
theory of material wealth   11–12,
150
morality
Fukuzawa's theory of   243–4
of modern civilizations   259–61
private   223
Morgan, Lewis   15, 109
Morse, Edward, on Fukuzawa   151
Murata, General   192
mutual assurance   102, 103

Nagasaki, Japan   175–6
Nakamura, Professor Toshiko, on
Fukuzawa   241–5
Nakatsu clan, Japan   154, 175,
184, 200
naming system, Japan   162
national rights, Fukuzawa's view
of   196
natural law
Fukuzawa's disillusionment
with   206–7
progress as   216
navy, English   12
nobility   11, 63, 130
of blood   9, 13, 63, 131
distinction of English   67–8,
131–2
privileges of   64, 65, 132
nonconformist religion, role of
trusts in   101–2
Norman Conquest   63, 74, 135

free trade in land   55
and land tenure   40
strength of monarchy   39
as unifying factor   78–9
Normans   39, 41, 76
novel disseisin, statute of   79

O-Jun (mother of Fukuzawa)   154,
155–6, 166, 229
Obligations, law of   94
Ogai, Mori   152
Ogata, Koan, tutor to
Fukuzawa   176, 177, 210
Okudaira Clan of Nakatsu   154
open field system   22, 60–1
open society   218–19, 260
role of associations in   265–6
Opium Wars (1839–42)   201
order, social, as central to
Durkheim   108–10
organizations, anti-state   106, 265
Osaka, Japan   155
Oxford University   80, 105

Paris, jurisprudence of parliament
of   75, 79
parish registers, for Earls
Colne   127
Parliament   10, 131
nature of debate in   198–9
role in development of trusts   91
parliamentary system   6, 50, 131,
251
parliaments, as intermediary
bodies   84
partnership
Gesellschaft   85, 93, 109, 269
in Roman law   85, 93
patriarchal rights (*patria
potestas*)   68, 128
patriarchy   17, 83
in Japan   162
peace, and stagnation   147, 186
peasantry   11
Pel, C.M.H., Dutch author   210
Perry, Commodore, arrives in Japan
(1854)   175
personality, fictive   84–5
Philip II, King of Spain   81